MIKE PENTELOW & PETER ARKELL

FREEDOM PASS
LONDON

26 SPECIAL DAYS OUT IN & AROUND THE CAPITAL

UPDATED BY NEIL & HELEN MATTHEWS

Bradt Guides Ltd, UK
Globe Pequot Press Inc, USA

Second edition published September 2024
First published 2014
Bradt Travel Guides Ltd
31a High Street, Chesham, Buckinghamshire, HP5 1BW, England
www.bradtguides.com
Print edition published in the USA by The Globe Pequot Press Inc,
PO Box 480, Guilford, Connecticut 06437-0480

Text copyright © Peter Arkell, 2024
Maps copyright © Bradt Travel Guides Ltd, 2024; contains Ordnance Survey data © Crown copyright and database right, 2024
Photographs copyright © Individual photographers (see below), 2024
Project Managers: Anna Moores & Samantha Cook
Editor: Samantha Cook
Cover research: Pepi Bluck, Perfect Picture

ISBN: 9781804692271

British Library Cataloguing in Publication Data
A catalogue record for this book is available from the British Library

Photographs © individual photographers credited beside images & also from picture libraries credited as follows: Alamy.com (A); Dreamstime.com (DT); Shutterstock.com (S); Superstock.com (SS)

Front cover Top: Tower Bridge (Alessandro Saffo/4Corners); below: Springtime in the Isabella Plantation, Richmond Park (Eden Breitz/A)
Back cover Camden Lock, on the Regent's Canal (BBA Photography/S)
Title page The view from Parliament Hill on Hampstead Heath (Laura Stubbs/S)

Maps David McCutcheon FBCart.S FRGS, assisted by Daniella Levin & Pearl Geo Solutions

Typeset and designed by Ian Spick, Bradt Travel Guides

Production managed by Gutenberg Press; printed in Malta
Digital conversion by www.dataworks.co.in

Paper used for this product comes from sustainably managed forests, and recycled and controlled sources.

FOREWORD

Celebrating 50 years of the Freedom Pass
By Peter Walker

Just over 50 years ago, on 23 September 1973, I organised the launch of the Freedom Pass on Lower Road, Bermondsey. At the time I was the Head of the Leader's Office at the Greater London Council (GLC). I worked for Sir Reg Goodwin who had just become Leader of the GLC.

Sir Reg launched the Freedom Pass, which allowed London's pensioners to travel free of charge on the capital's buses. Subsequently the scheme was extended to cover free travel for the over-60s and some people with disabilities, on trains, tubes and buses within Greater London.

At the time, the scheme was seen as a revolutionary initiative, allowing those who were retired to travel across the capital for shopping, leisure or to visit friends and relatives without worrying about the cost.

Just over 50 years later, 1.4 million Londoners aged over 60 are able to travel without charge on public transport. On reflection I am amazed that the Freedom Pass survived the tumultuous events of the last half-century. When drafting policies which laid the plans for the Freedom Pass, I did not think then, as a 26-year-old, that I would live to see the benefit of the scheme as I do now.

*Peter Walker worked as a policy adviser on economics for the Labour Party, nationally and in London, and later as Deputy Director of Amnesty International, where he produced **The Secret Policeman's Ball** with John Cleese. A longer version of this foreword appeared on the website of Age UK London (⊗ ageuk.org.uk/ London), a charity which campaigns for specific change to improve the lives of older Londoners.*

AUTHOR & PHOTOGRAPHER

Mike Pentelow was editor of *Landworker* (the newspaper of rural workers) for ten years and editor of *Fitzrovia News* (London's oldest community newspaper, to which he contributed for some 40 years), giving him a feel for both town and country. An author and journalist for 50 years, his books include *Characters of Fitzrovia*, *Norfolk Red* and *A Pub Crawl Through History*. Mike was a keen rambler, having walked the entire length of the River Thames and many other waterways. He was a member of The Ramblers, the Woodland Trust, the Campaign for Real Ale, the Inn Sign Society, Camden History Society, Socialist History Society, St Marylebone Society, Society of Authors, the National Union of Journalists and the Mecca Bingo Club. Mike died in April 2020, an early victim of Covid-19.

Peter Arkell has been a photographer since 1970, covering news, social issues, the environment and sport. He supplied all of the photos for the previous edition of this book and some of the photos for this new edition. He co-wrote *Unfinished Business, The Miners' Strike for Jobs, 1984–5* and took the photographs for *A Pub Crawl Through History*, about commoners who have had pubs named after them. A keen rambler (with Mike and others) he has walked the Thames Path, the South West Coast Path, the Isle of Wight Coastal Path and Peddars Way/Norfolk Coast Path. He has lived in London for more than 45 years and currently produces photo features and writes reviews for *Real Democracy Movement*.

UPDATERS

Neil and Helen Matthews are authors of Bradt's *Slow Travel: The Chilterns & the Thames Valley* and *Heritage Weekends: 52 breaks exploring Britain's past*. They both studied in London, and have spent much of their lives working in, and exploring, the capital.

KEY TO SYMBOLS

▥ Main road		⊞	Historic/important building
▭ Other road		🏰	Castle/fortification
⋈ Railway		⚱	Museum
⋅⋅►⋅⋅ Route of walk		🎭	Theatre
⋅⋅⋅⋅⋅⋅ Footpath/track		👤	Statue/monument
☛ Start/resume point		†	Church/cathedral
✋ Drop-out point (text only)		🍺	Pub
🚏 Bus stop		🍺	CAMRA-recommended pub (text only)
🅿 Car park			Built-up area
🚆 Train station			Lake/river
⊖ Underground station			Park/gardens
𝒊 Information			Woods
• Point of interest			

See *How to use this book*, page xiii for more information.

FEEDBACK REQUEST

At Bradt Guides we're aware that guidebooks start to go out of date on the day they're published – and that you, our readers, are out there in the field doing research of your own. So why not tell us about your experiences? Contact us on ☏ 01753 893444 or e info@bradtguides.com. We will forward emails to the author, who may post updates on the Bradt website at ⊘ bradtguides.com/updates. Alternatively, you can add a review of the book to Amazon, or share your adventures with us on Facebook, X (formerly Twitter) or Instagram (@BradtGuides).

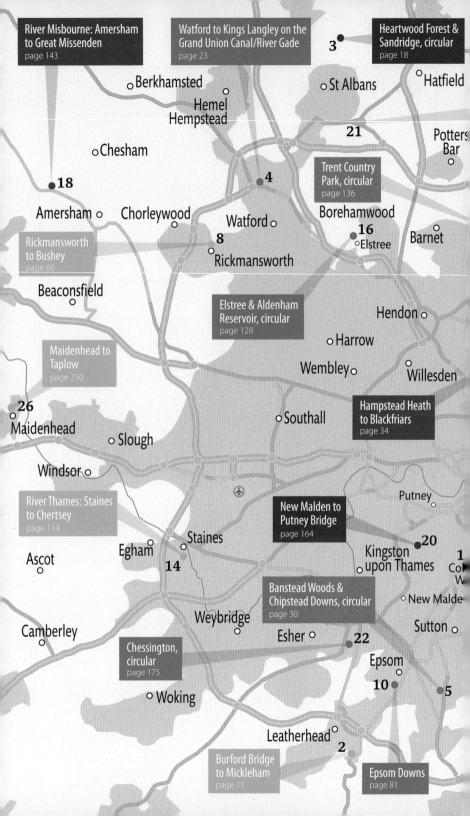

River Misbourne: Amersham to Great Missenden
page 143

Watford to Kings Langley on the Grand Union Canal/River Gade
page 23

Heartwood Forest & Sandridge, circular
page 18

3

Berkhamsted

St Albans Hatfield

Hemel Hempstead

21

Chesham

Potters Bar

18

Trent Country Park, circular
page 136

Amersham Chorleywood

Watford

Borehamwood

4

8

16

Rickmansworth

Elstree Barnet

Rickmansworth to Bushey
page 66

Beaconsfield

Elstree & Aldenham Reservoir, circular
page 128

Hendon

Harrow

Maidenhead to Taplow
page 230

Wembley

Willesden

26

Southall

Hampstead Heath to Blackfriars
page 34

Maidenhead

Slough

Windsor

River Thames: Staines to Chertsey
page 114

Putney

New Malden to Putney Bridge
page 164

20

Ascot

Egham Staines

Kingston upon Thames

1

Co
W

14

New Malde

Banstead Woods & Chipstead Downs, circular
page 30

Camberley

Weybridge

Sutton

Esher

22

Chessington, circular
page 175

Epsom

10

5

Woking

Leatherhead

2

Burford Bridge to Mickleham
page 11

Epsom Downs
page 81

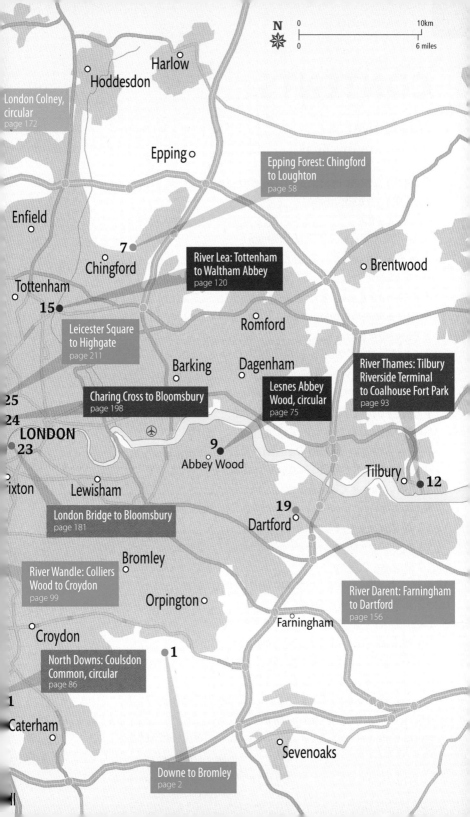

N

0 — 10km
0 — 6 miles

Harlow

Hoddesdon

London Colney, circular
page 172

Epping

Epping Forest: Chingford to Loughton
page 58

Enfield

7

Chingford

Brentwood

River Lea: Tottenham to Waltham Abbey
page 120

Tottenham

15

Romford

Leicester Square to Highgate
page 211

Barking

Dagenham

River Thames: Tilbury Riverside Terminal to Coalhouse Fort Park
page 93

Charing Cross to Bloomsbury
page 198

Lesnes Abbey Wood, circular
page 75

25

24

LONDON

23

9

Abbey Wood

Tilbury

12

ixton

Lewisham

London Bridge to Bloomsbury
page 181

19

Dartford

Bromley

River Wandle: Colliers Wood to Croydon
page 99

Orpington

River Darent: Farningham to Dartford
page 156

Farningham

Croydon

1

North Downs: Coulsdon Common, circular
page 86

1

Caterham

Sevenoaks

Downe to Bromley
page 2

CONTENTS

INTRODUCTION

Since its introduction in 1973, the Freedom Pass has been a travel boon for Greater London's senior citizens and citizens with disabilities, helping them to explore the full breadth of the capital and its environs. Detailing 26 special days out, involving walks of between two and eleven miles, this is the only book on the market that aims to help Freedom Pass holders make the most of their free travel. And of course you can still use this book if you don't qualify for a Freedom Pass – the walks are for everyone.

Many of the walks will appeal if you're a city dweller and you want to discover the countryside around London: from Heartwood Forest near St Albans in the north to Box Hill near Dorking in the south; from East Tilbury and Farningham in the east to Chertsey and Great Missenden in the west. Many offer excellent opportunities for foraging: brambles, crab apples, chestnuts and haws (page xii). Other walks in the heart of the capital will be attractive if you live in the suburbs and would like to get to know central London better.

In and around London, town meets countryside in so many places: in Green Belt terrain, in suburbs which resemble villages, along urban rivers and in commons, parks, woodlands and nature reserves. While enjoying opportunities for tranquil reflection, you can see or hear numerous species in or on the water, in the woods and grasslands and in the air – not least the capital's rose-ringed parakeets which have become a common sight and sound in recent years.

Along the way you'll bump into some of history's most influential people, from Charles Darwin and William Penn to Karl Marx; famous writers such as Roald Dahl, Charles Dickens and Mary Wollstonecraft; and inspiring women including Elizabeth I, Lady Ottoline Morrell and Edith Cavell. And you'll encounter great eccentrics, such as the Dorking man buried head downwards at his own request, and the politician who became friends with a man who had shot him in a duel.

So what are you waiting for? Get your walking boots on – it's time to discover the diversity, beauty, history and eccentricity of Greater London.

THE FREEDOM PASS You can qualify for a Freedom Pass if your sole or principal residence is in London and if:

1. You are aged 66 or above (an Older Person's Freedom Pass); or
2. You have a statutory disability such as total or partial loss of sight, or profound or severe hearing loss (a Disabled Person's Freedom Pass). Some London boroughs issue discretionary Freedom Passes to people with disabilities who do not meet the statutory eligibility criteria.

SAM TANNO/S

LUSCOMBE PHOTOS/S

PETER FLEMING/S

ABDUL SHAKOOR/DT

1 Missenden Abbey as seen across the River Misbourne (page 152). **2** Signpost in Aldenham's 100 Aker Wood (page 132). **3** Route 8 takes in a scenic stretch of the Ebury Way (page 71). **4** The River Wandle in Morden Hall Park (page 104).

For more details and to apply, visit ⊘ tfl.gov.uk and search 'Freedom Pass'. The Freedom Pass enables free travel across London:

- **On bus, tram, Tube, Docklands Light Railway (DLR), London Overground and the Elizabeth Line** – from 09.00 Mon–Fri and any time at weekends and on bank holidays. (NB this applies to the Older Person's

RECIPE: HAWTHORN BERRY KETCHUP

Hawthorn (*Crataegus* species) is a familiar friend in the world of herbal medicine. Renowned for heart health, the tree's autumnal red berries also lend themselves brilliantly to a delicious ketchup. It is perfect as a spread on sandwiches, a dip for chips, or as a unique complement to grilled vegetables. Simple, comforting, and medicinal – exactly how nature intended.

Ingredients
- 500g fresh hawthorn berries
- 120ml apple cider vinegar
- 120ml water
- 60g honey
- a pinch each of cardamom, cinnamon & nutmeg
- a dash of sea salt & black pepper
- 60ml red grape juice

Method
1. Gently remove berries from stalks, and wash in cold water.
2. Combine berries, vinegar and water in a saucepan and bring to the boil.
3. Reduce heat and leave to simmer until the berries' skins start to break – about 30 minutes.
4 Cool the mixture and use the back of a spoon to push it through a sieve to discard the pips. You want to extract as much pulp as possible.
5. Return the liquid to the pan, add honey, and stir in your spices with a little salt and pepper. Simmer gently until thick – about five minutes.
6 Add some red grape juice bit by bit, aiming for your ideal ketchup consistency. You may also wish to add a little more salt and pepper for extra flavour.
7. Pour into a sterilised bottle, keep refrigerated, and use within two months.
8. You can also freeze small portions to benefit from this medicinal food throughout the year.

Kristine De Block, BSc Hons
Medical Herbalist
For more inspiring herbal wisdom, visit ⊘ thecraftyherbalist.org.uk

Freedom Pass; holders of the Disabled Person's Freedom Pass can use it at any time.)

- **With National Rail** – travel in Standard Class on most local rail services within the Freedom Pass boundaries (from 09.30 Mon–Fri and at any time at weekends and on bank holidays).
- This does not include East Midlands, Grand Central and Hull Trains services, the Gatwick Express, the Heathrow Express, LNER and Southeastern high-speed services to and from St Pancras International

The Pass also entitles you to discounts on selected river bus services, river tours and the Emirates Air Line.

Freedom Pass holders can also travel on local buses across England during off-peak times (09.30–23.00 Mon–Fri and at any time at weekends and on bank holidays).

A map showing the Freedom Pass area is available online at ⊘ londoncouncils. gov.uk/services/freedom-pass/how-use-your-freedom-pass.

NB Some walks in this book are at the edge of the Freedom Pass area or just beyond. So the total cost of every stage of your journey may not be covered. We have indicated where that is the case.

- In those cases, you may need to pay for a short additional journey from the Freedom Pass zone to the walk start point, or to return from the end point.
- If you are travelling beyond the Freedom Pass zone on a National Rail service, you can buy an extension ticket **before you travel**, to cover the difference (show your Freedom Pass with your photograph at the ticket office when buying extension tickets). You may be able to get a discount on this, using a railcard such as a Senior Citizen's Railcard or Disabled Person's Railcard.
- Selected walks also include transport options which do not accept the Freedom Pass. We have indicated where that is the case.

HOW TO USE THIS BOOK

Each route begins with an **information panel**, detailing the length of the walk and approximate walking times (excluding stops), which Ordnance Survey map to take, a list of places to pause for refreshment and details of how to get to the starting point by public transport. Some walks are circular, others go point to point, with return by public transport: 🚌 bus, 🚃 train and ⊖ tube. We have given what3words references /// for the start and end points.

Detailed **route directions** guide you through each walk. Please bear in mind that things inevitably go out of date: signposts change, path junctions appear and disappear. If you find any directions that don't work as well as they should, please let us know (page v). The symbol ☛ indicates where the directions start or resume. Note that in addition to the detailed OS or street maps that we recommend for each route, you might choose to use an app such as komoot or Outdooractive.

Each **point of interest** has a number, both within the text and on the route map(s). Opening times are, of course, subject to change, so we recommend that you check in advance of your visit. Where there is an **entrance fee**, we have used a price code to indicate the cost per head: **£** = up to £10; **££** = £10–£20; **£££** = £20+. The symbol 🥮 indicates that a **senior citizen's discount** is available. We have also indicated where an attraction is owned or managed by the National Trust or English Heritage; if you are a member, you may be entitled to free entry.

If you only want to do part of a walk, we've suggested **drop-out points** (✋), adding information on how to get to stations or bus stops for your journey home. Hard economic times and a pandemic have led to the closure of several of the many **pubs** featured in the first edition of this book, but plenty remain. The symbol 🍺 shows that the pub is featured in the 2023 *Good Beer Guide*. We have included other refreshment options, such as cafés, worth considering if you wish to **take a break**.

USEFUL RESOURCES
Online Google Maps is helpful, especially for investigating public transport options. We used the **komoot** app to stay on track while researching these walks.

Books
A–Z Master Atlas of Greater London (Geographers' A–Z Map Co). This A4 hardback covers the area of almost all the walks in this book. It's probably most useful when planning your trips. The same publishers also produce the pocket-sized *London A–Z Street Atlas*. The main mapping extends beyond central London from Heathrow Airport to Chingford.

The Good Beer Guide (CAMRA Books). If you're willing to extend – or divert – a walk for a good pub, this is an invaluable reference point.

Fruit Every Day! Hugh Fearnley-Whittingstall (Bloomsbury). For enthusiastic foragers, with plenty of ideas and recipes.

1 A NATURAL SELECTION AT DOWNE

A REMARKABLY RURAL KENTISH LANDSCAPE MUCH WALKED BY THE GREAT VICTORIAN EVOLUTIONARY THINKER

On this ramble you're in very good company. Charles Darwin (1809–82) lived here for 40 years, at Down House, and, though often unwell, frequently made it a rule to walk three times a day. It was here that he wrote his world-changing thesis *On the Origin of Species by Means of Natural Selection*, the sensational publication which in 1859 provoked mass book-burning by Creationists and changed the view of how life on this planet evolved. Indeed this walk within the London Borough of Bromley is a 'natural selection' for those keen to find out more about the man, to view the hallowed study where he carried out his research, and to wander the grounds of his house.

The route starts with an opportunity for a visit to Down House, passing through rolling farmland, and takes in Darwin's church (where there is a memorial to him), and a woodland which he used as a 'living laboratory' to observe wildlife development. Elsewhere on the walk, you'll find the 300-year-old tavern in which music-hall star 'Little Tich' was born, and a church that is more than a thousand years old, and have the chance to feed the animals at a farm and come back with armfuls of blackberries.

↑ Charles Darwin's 'Orchis Bank', Downe. (DP Landscapes/A)

WHERE: Kent: Downe to Bromley
STATS: Just over 5 miles/1½ –2hrs; easy–moderate: easy on the flat with two steep climbs of 400 strides each
START POINT/GETTING THERE: Down House /// trader.keen.admiral 🚃 To Bromley South station from London Victoria (16–26mins; 8–10 an hour). Turn right out of the station to Bus Stop Y for 🚌 146 to Downe Church (20mins; 1 an hour). From the bus stop, cross to Luxted Rd & follow the signs to Down House. (If you do not want to pay to visit the house, turn right into West Hill before reaching Down House. A path on the left will take you to the footpath beyond the gate from the gardens & the start of the walk.)
FINISH: Bromley South station /// comet.double.lasts
DROP-OUT POINT: After 3 miles
MAP: OS Explorer map 147
TAKING A BREAK: Blacksmith's Arms, Christmas Tree Farm, George & Dragon, Queen's Head

1. DOWN HOUSE (Luxted Rd, Downe, Bromley BR6 7JT 🖉 01689 859119; English Heritage ◔ Apr–Oct daily; Nov–Mar varying days **££** 🍴) Down House was Darwin's home for the last 40 years of his life. In its extensive garden, Darwin conducted experiments with worms, insects and plants. He even devised a system of giving IQ tests to some of the million worms in the garden which involved them pulling down triangles of paper.

He thought through a lot of his ideas while walking. The sand walk in his garden he nicknamed his 'Thinking Path' for that very reason. To measure how far he had walked he kicked a flintstone to one side after each circuit, although his children sometimes mischievously removed them or added to them to mess up his calculations. On one of these strolls he was so struck by one particular notion that he stopped dead in his tracks, frozen in thought. He was so still that two young squirrels ran up his back. The discovery that gave him the greatest pleasure was that the local cowslips were of two kinds and so not self-pollinating.

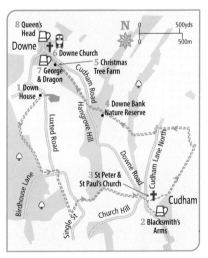

Darwin became a pigeon fancier to observe the effects of selective breeding (and joined one club that met in a gin palace). But when it came to human selective breeding, as espoused by those

PETER ARKELL

VICKY JIRAYU/S

1 & **2** Charles Darwin's Down House.

of his followers who supported eugenics, he distanced himself. He believed the instinct to care for the weak and helpless was to humanity's evolutionary advantage, and that nobody should be prevented from reproducing. Darwin and his wife (and cousin) Emma were both grandchildren of Josiah Wedgwood; ironically, Darwin's experiments led him to doubt the wisdom of inbreeding.

In the house you can see the billiard room, which he had converted from a dining room. When he wanted a game he summoned his butler, Joseph Parslow, with a bell pull. In the evenings Darwin would often lie on the chaise longue in the drawing room, listening to Emma playing the piano with 'vigour and spirit, but not passion', according to their daughter Henrietta. The Darwins had ten children, three of whom died young. Signs of their presence include a specially made slide which enabled them to come downstairs with extra speed.

A 250-year-old mulberry tree grows in the garden. Also surviving from Darwin's time is the weed garden, where he tested his ideas, and a laboratory where he observed honey bees.

☞ To start the walk, go past the greenhouses in the back garden, and out through a kissing gate into a field. Bear left (in the direction of a yellow arrow) through the field, over a stile into woods. At a crossing of paths, take the left one (signposted to 'Birdhouse Lane'). Continue along the woodland path (with a golf course on the right) and pick up signs for 'Cudham Circular Walk'.

When the track reaches a lane, turn left (into Birdhouse Lane) then right at the road junction, then right at Luxted Farm into a track (signed 'Cudham Circular Walk'). Climb over a stile to follow a path between a hedge and a fence (signed 'Cudham Circular Walk' and 'Berry Green Circular Walk').

Continue by the side of a field, and over a stile at the far side. Then immediately turn left over another stile almost hidden between a holly bush and a telegraph pole. This takes you between house garden fences on to a road (Single Street), which you cross and then go straight ahead between a fence and a hedge into a Woodland Trust woodland. Follow the track ahead around the woods and then through them, eventually going down steps.

Emerge via a kissing gate into a strikingly beautiful valley which teems with butterflies in summer.

Go straight ahead, along a path down a field in the valley and up again (a climb which continues for 400 strides and gets steeper as you ascend). Go through a kissing gate at the other side, up a woodland path on to a lane. Turn left (Church Hill), then immediately right at a junction, and up to another crossroads. Turn right at this crossroads (Cudham Lane South) and after about two or three minutes you will come to the junction with New Barn Lane where on the left is:

2. BLACKSMITH'S ARMS (Cudham Lane South, Cudham, Bromley TN14 7QB ⊘ theblacksmithsarmscudham.com) Little Tich the music-hall star was born Harry Relph in this pub on 21 July 1867 (as confirmed by a blue plaque outside). He was the 16th child of Richard Relph who ran the pub from 1865 to 1878 and his height – only four feet six inches – made him a star for nearly 50 years, from the age of 12 until a few months before his death in 1928. Music-hall posters have pride of place in the bar, along with his celebrated boots, known at the time as 'slapshoes': boots that stuck out 28 inches from his toes (of which he had six on each foot). These he wore for his most popular act, his comic 'Big Boot Dance'.

His stage name came from an ironic reference to the obese 'Tichborne' claimant (a famous legal case) which he abbreviated to 'Tich' – hence the adjective 'titchy'. Originally a farmhouse built in 1628, the building became an inn in 1730, and now has an extensive beer garden and serves hot food as well as real ales (including Sharp's Doom Bar, Adnams and Hogs Back).

✋ To end the walk here you can get the R5 or R10 bus to Orpington railway station (no Sun service). The R10, on the same side as the pub, takes 40 minutes, and the R5, on the other side, 20 minutes, to the station. Take whichever comes first, as it's the same bus doing a circular route, alternating direction (and its route number) every hour. There is no designated stop so you have to hail the bus; sit outside the pub to make sure you don't miss it.

☞ To continue the walk, turn right, retrace your steps (about 350) to the crossroads, then turn right into Church Approach, at the top of which is:

3. ST PETER & ST PAUL'S CHURCH (Church Approach, Cudham, Bromley TN14 7QF) Two yew trees in the churchyard here have girths of over 30 feet, which indicates they are more than a thousand years old. The church itself has been restored over the centuries: a street signpost refers to it as 11th century but the earliest records date back to AD953. The oldest of its ten bells in the tower was cast in 1490.

☞ Go out through the other side of the churchyard and turn left, round the edge of playing fields. This is a good place to have a picnic on one of the benches under the shade of copper beech trees.

Continue out of the playing field through a kissing gate on the left, over the lane and through another kissing gate and through a paddock. Go through another kissing gate into a field, then through a woodland path to a lane. Turn left into the lane and, after about 100 steps, turn right into a field (signposted

'Downe 1¼m'). Go through the field to another, to a hedge where you turn left and follow it on your left as directed by a yellow arrow sign. Cross over a stile (signposted 'Cudham Circular Short Walk') to a short grass track up to a lane. Turn left and then, after about 100 steps, turn right at another signpost (also 'Downe 1¼m') into a short track into a lane, then into a track ahead through woodland.

Where the path splits, take the right fork between posts (with 'No Horse Riding' and 'Cudham Circular Short Walk' signs). Follow the path downhill then up again. There now follows a steep climb of about 400 strides. Near the top on the left is:

4. DOWNE BANK NATURE RESERVE (Hang Grove Hill, Downe,
Bromley BR6 7LH) This chalk grassland site is where Darwin studied the local flora and fauna – a living laboratory in which he developed his theory of evolution and natural selection. In particular he studied the special relationship between orchids and their insect pollinators, which is why he called it Orchis Bank (although it was officially Rough Pell). Nine species of wild orchid still grow here along with many other plants.

Downe Bank forms part of Hangrove Wood, where Darwin observed what he described as 'the quiet but dreadful war going on in the peaceful and smiling fields'. You can explore it by turning left off the path which you have been following, and along the 'permissive footpath' which soon turns right uphill (just before a gate), then right at the top and back to the main path. Several unusual plants such as stinking hellebore, squinancywort and adder's tongue fern thrive in this area. In the spring it is smothered with primroses and cowslips, and in the summer with orchids. Butterflies abound (including a few of the rare white-letter hairstreak). Rare and endangered species here include dormice, slow-worms and Roman snails.

☛ After returning to the main footpath continue up the steps to the top of the hill, then turn left into a track (signposted 'Downe ⅓m'). This takes you into a lane (Cudham Road) where you turn right, and after just 20 yards take the

COURAGEOUS TASTINGS
Some of Darwin's research was distinctly brave. He ate the caterpillars of the sphinx moth and found them 'very palatable' (according to *Why Not Eat Insects?* by Vincent M Holt, publ. Pryor Publications 2007). He also consumed an owl, as president of the Glutton Club at Cambridge University, opining afterwards the taste was 'indescribable'.

path (on the left between a fence and a hedge parallel with the road) in the same direction along the side of a horse field. When the path rejoins the lane, follow it a few yards and on the left is:

5. CHRISTMAS TREE FARM (Cudham Rd, Downe, Bromley BR6 7LF ⌂ xmastreefarm.co.uk ☉ daily, hours vary; kitchen & tearoom daily except Mon £) At this 'children's petting farm' you can feed various extremely friendly farm animals including pigs, donkeys, cows, sheep, alpacas, rabbits, ducks, chickens, geese and goats. It has an adjoining tea garden.

☛ Continue along Cudham Road to:

6. DOWNE CHURCH (25 High St, Downe, Bromley BR6 7US) Charles Darwin was an active member of the congregation at Downe Church (St Mary's) for 40 years. A memorial sundial is dedicated to him on the outside of the church tower and there's a flat granite tomb between the main gate to the churchyard and the front door of the church. The building itself dates from 1291.

Despite his active support for this church, Darwin was attacked from its pulpit during the height of the controversy over his theory of evolution, seen by many to contradict the Church's view of creation. This so upset a fellow member of the congregation, his friend and fellow naturalist Sir John Lubbock (who became the first Lord Avebury) that he stopped attending services here.

Darwin was a long-standing friend of the parish priest, Rev. John Brodie Innes. During the evolution controversy Innes defended Darwin to bishops, declaring: 'I never saw a word in his writings which was an attack on religion. He follows his own course as a naturalist and leaves Moses to take care of himself.'

Although his faith later dwindled, Darwin remained an active parishioner, supervised the finances of the church and its school, ran its Coal and Clothing Fund for the needy, and started its Friendly Club for those suffering financial hardship (and was its treasurer for over 30 years). His wife Emma is buried near the fence bordering High Elms Road. She also helped the local poor and needy, by giving them bread and homemade gin cordial which was 'a heady concoction of wine laced with laudanum, sugar, peppermint and bitters'.

Four of their children, Mary Eleanor (who died in 1842 after just two weeks), Charles Waring (1856–58), Elizabeth (1847–1926) and Henrietta (1843–1927), are buried in the same grave near the main door to the church. And Darwin's butler of 36 years, Joseph Parslow, is buried with his wife Eliza in the northern part of the churchyard.

Inside the church are some impressive early 17th-century brasses, depicting Jacob Verzelin of Venice and his wife Elizabeth from Antwerp.

HELEN MATTHEWS

PETER ARKELL

PETER ARKELL

PETER ARKELL

1 Downe Church. **2** The Charles Darwin mural. **3** Harry Relph's boots on display in the Blacksmith's Arms.
4 One of the ancient yew trees at the church of St Peter & St Paul, Cudham.

☞ Continue along Cudham Road to a choice of two pubs, either side of the bus stop where you started:

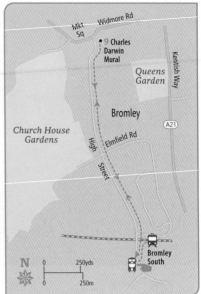

7. GEORGE & DRAGON (26 High St, Downe, Bromley BR6 7UT ☝ georgeanddragondowne.com)
A real log fire blazes in this beamed 15th-century coaching inn. It is family-friendly (with a play area and garden), has a dartboard and serves hot meals and real ale (including Harvey's, Sussex Best Bitter, Fuller's London Pride and Timothy Taylor's Landlord).

8. QUEEN'S HEAD 🍺 (25 High St, Downe, Bromley BR6 7US

☝ queensheaddowne.com) This 16th-century pub has three fireplaces, plus hot and cold food. It serves Harvey's Sussex Best Bitter and three changing beers, often Bexley, Northdown and Westerham.

☞ After refreshing yourself, get the 146 bus back to Bromley South station. When you get off at the station, walk up the High Street in the same direction as the bus for about five minutes until it forks and becomes Market Square. Take the right fork where you will find:

9. CHARLES DARWIN MURAL (20–25 Market Square, Bromley BR1 1NA) A huge mural depicts Darwin under a tree in his garden at Down House with the various branches representing evolution. It was painted by Kentish artist Bruce Williams.

☞ Retrace your steps down the High Street to Bromley South station.

2 ON THE BOX

One of the best-known features of the North Downs, Box Hill is a Sunday afternoon favourite with Londoners escaping from the city. The only snag is that on the best summer days everyone seems to be escaping at the same time, and the car parks are brimming to capacity. But for walkers, it's a satisfying summit to reach, and you soon lose the crowds. Box Hill takes its name from box trees, which are among the numerous tree species in the locality, in addition to yew, beech, pine, sallow, willow, oak and hazel.

This has long been civilised countryside, with opulent houses looking out over the Surrey Hills and towards the distant South Downs. It is the location of a famous scene in Jane Austen's novel *Emma*. On this route through downland cloaked with woods, a river valley, rolling farmland and a park, you encounter the former residences of the pioneer of birth control, the inventor of television and a very eccentric major, among others, as well as the resting place of an early aviator.

You may well spot deer among ancient trees and butterflies (including rarities such as the silver-spotted skipper) as well as orchids on the grassy downland slopes. Bats find sanctuary in the Old Fort (which was built in the 1890s when a French invasion was feared).

↑ The view from Box Hill. (Yujie Chen/DT)

WHERE: Surrey: Burford Bridge to Mickleham
STATS: 5 miles/2–2½hrs; moderate; includes a steep climb
START POINT/GETTING THERE: Burford Bridge /// prove.baked.magma 🚆 From London Waterloo to Chessington South (34mins; 2 an hour) or Surbiton (23–28mins; 8 an hour) 🚌 465 to Burford Bridge calls at Chessington South and Surbiton stations (2 an hour, 1 an hour on Sun). From Chessington South turn right out of the station, then right at the junction to Bus Stop D on the right (28mins). From Surbiton turn left at end of the station approach road into Victoria Rd to Bus Stop NP on the left (40mins).
FINISH: Running Horses bus stop, Mickleham /// souk.pulse.taker
DROP-OUT POINT: After 3 miles
MAP: OS Explorer map 146
TAKING A BREAK: National Trust café, Salomon's Memorial & Viewpoint, Burford Bridge Hotel, Denbies Wine Estate, Stepping Stones, Running Horses

👉 Go up the chalk path right next to the Burford Bridge bus stop, between woods and open fields up Box Hill. Be warned: this is a steep climb. At the top of the fields bear right to a footpath through more woods. As you get near the summit this takes you to:

1. MAJOR PETER LABELLIERE'S GRAVESTONE

The eccentric Dorking resident buried here in 1800 at the age of 75 was placed head downwards because he believed 'as the world is turned upside down on judgment day only he would be the correct way up'. After correctly predicting the precise date of his death, he asked for the youngest son and daughter of his landlady to dance on his coffin as he wanted it to be an occasion of rejoicing rather than sorrow. The girl just sat on it while the boy danced with abandon. A major of the marines, Labelliere was very generous to the poor, often giving away his own coat or shoes to those who needed them more. The grave marks the spot of his favourite view – until he lost an eye after falling into the dense undergrowth there.

👉 Continue up the path to the top and then turn left. On the right is:

2. PLAQUE FOR JOHN LOGIE BAIRD'S HOUSE (SWISS COTTAGE)

The inventor of television, John Logie Baird (1888–1946), lived here from 1929 to 1932; note, though, that the house is on private ground and not visible from here. His experiments had a knack of backfiring; he was evicted from a previous residence for causing an explosion, and on another occasion he accidentally cut off most of Glasgow's power supply. In 1924 he produced his first television transmitter from a tea chest, a hat box and a

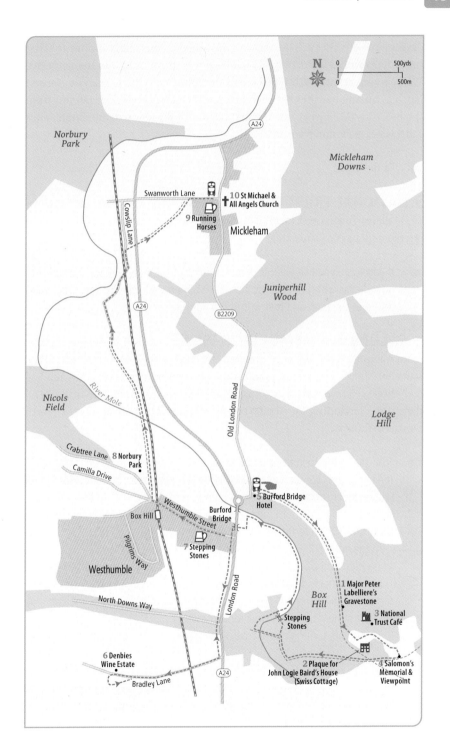

darning needle. By 1928 he had demonstrated colour television for the first time, but it would be many years before it was introduced into living rooms. While living at Swiss Cottage he had to organise events to televise himself (such as boxing matches between his staff) because of a lack of interest from the BBC. In 1932 he became the first person in Britain to demonstrate 'ultra short wave' television transmission.

☞ To the left is:

3. NATIONAL TRUST CAFÉ (Zig Zag Rd, Tadworth KT20 7LB ⊙ 10.00–16.00 daily) You can get local maps and information and take a break in the refreshment bar or picnic area.

☞ If you wish, you can walk on past the front of the café to reach the Old Fort, intended as a bastion against the French but now a haven for bats. Otherwise, return to the path and follow it to the right for:

4. SALOMON'S MEMORIAL & VIEWPOINT This derives its name from Leopold Salomon, who donated the land to the National Trust. Stone seats here make a tempting **picnic stop**: you can munch your sandwich 634 feet above sea level with a wide-ranging view encompassing 25 miles in all directions, including Devil's Dyke and Chanctonbury Ring on the South Downs in Sussex.

☞ Take the footpath in front of the viewpoint, to the right downhill. At the first fork bear left, continuing downhill through yew trees on an earthen path with wooden steps. Ignore a small path to the left and stick to the main path, which bends to the right. Just after this bend you will get a great view of the River Mole down to the left.
   At the next fork you can *either* go left and cross the river by stepping stones *or* go right and cross the river by a wooden footbridge a few yards away.
   On the other side of the river turn right and follow the bank for a short distance until you reach the A24 road by Burford Bridge. Here you can stop for refreshments, end the walk, or continue.
   To stop off, turn right and cross the bridge to:

5. BURFORD BRIDGE HOTEL (Box Hill RH5 6BX ✆ 020 7660 0684) Two distinguished guests to have stayed at this 16th-century inn were Horatio Nelson and John Keats, when it was called the Fox & Hounds. It has oak beams and a beer garden.

👋 Opposite the hotel there is a bus stop where the 465 bus goes back to Chessington South and Surbiton railway stations.

👉 To continue the walk, go through the subway under the A24, with a bright mural of a country scene, and then turn left (signposted 'North Downs Way'). Follow the A24 for ten minutes or so until on the right you reach:

6. DENBIES WINE ESTATE (London Rd, Dorking RH5 6AA ⌀ denbies.co.uk ⊙ subject to seasonal variation) Denbies is the UK's largest single estate vineyard, covering 265 acres and producing 400,000 bottles a year. Its reputation has spiralled and it has picked up a good number of awards in recent years. There is an art gallery exhibition space, a shop and two **restaurants** in addition to a farm shop and opportunities for tours and tastings.

👉 Retrace your steps along the A24 until you come to Westhumble Street on the left and turn into it. A short distance away on the left is the:

7. STEPPING STONES (Westhumble St, Westhumble RH5 6BS ⌀ steppingstonesdorking.co.uk) Food is the main attraction here, but you can pop in just for a beer or glass of wine, and it's dog-friendly.

👉 Continue along Westhumble Street a few minutes to Box Hill and Westhumble railway station (it is just outside the Freedom Pass zone). Before you reach the station, on the wall of Cleveland Court note the blue plaques to Sir James Hopwood Jeans, an astronomer and physicist, and his second wife Susi, an organist and scholar. Past the station, cross a bridge and go down the footpath to the right, alongside the rail track through:

8. NORBURY PARK (⌀ surreywildlifetrust.org/visit) A working landscape with three farms and a functioning sawmill, Norbury Park is designated a Site of Special Scientific Interest for its wide range of plants and animals. These include all three British woodpeckers, deer, badgers, foxes and several butterfly species.

Marie Stopes (1880–1958), the pioneer of birth control, lived in a manor in these grounds for the last 20 years of her life.

👉 As you follow the path through the park you rejoin and cross the River Mole over a wooden footbridge (near a railway bridge). Continue ahead through a kissing gate into an arable field, bearing left away from the rail track, through another kissing gate into a lane alongside a farm with pigs and other animals. Keep to the main lane, which turns right, then left, after which

DR JON/S

PETER ARKELL

ALEXEY FEDORENKO/S

PETER ARKELL

1 Vines at Denbies Wine Estate. **2** The grave of eccentric Dorking resident Major Peter Labelliere.
3 St Michael & All Angels Church, Mickleham. **4** Stepping stones over the River Mole.

you will see the River Mole again (about 50 feet below on the left). Continue under a railway bridge and then (just before the lane bends right) take a small signed 'Public Footpath' on the right, up to the main road. Cross over it and go through a gate on the other side. This takes you through more woods and a meadow (sheep grazing on the right and football pitches on the left). When you come to a track (with a pony paddock on the right), turn first left, then right into Swanworth Lane. At the end you come to the main road and on the right is the:

9. RUNNING HORSES (Old London Rd, Mickleham RH5 6DU

therunninghorses.co.uk) A 16th-century traditional country inn with timbered beams and a real log fire, the Running Horses, judged as best in the UK in the 2023 National Pub & Bar Awards, used to be a coaching house which stabled horses who were exercising on nearby gallops for the Derby. A picture of the 1828 Derby, which was a dead heat, is on the pub sign. The two horses were Cadland (4–1) and The Colonel (7–2 favourite). In those days they did not share the prize money so a run-off between the two took place, with Cadland winning by just a neck.

Real ales include Fuller's London Pride, Brakspear and Ringwood.

☞ Opposite the pub is:

10. ST MICHAEL & ALL ANGELS CHURCH (Old London Rd,

Mickleham RH5 6EB) A plaque by the entrance to the church proclaims that the community was recorded in the Domesday Book. Of Saxon foundation, the church has some notable connections. One is buried in the churchyard: Graham Gilmour (1885–1912), an early aviator who died after his plane crashed, which is depicted on his gravestone. He asked there be 'no moaning or mourning at his funeral, and that everyone should be merry and bright' (*The Times*, 19 February 1912). Hundreds of villagers gathered at this unusual funeral when 'the little corner of the churchyard blazed with every conceivable hue – glorious red tulips, pink carnations, yellow daffodils, violets and crimson roses'.

Married in the church in 1793 were Fanny Burney (1752–1840), the novelist known for her wit and satirical caricatures, and General Alexandre d'Arblay, a royalist who had fled the French Revolution. They moved to France in 1802, but when the general refused to fight against England he was interned until 1812, when the couple returned to England.

☞ Outside the pub you can get the 465 bus back to the railway stations.

3 IN WOODLAND WE TRUST

A FEEL-GOOD TALE OF TREES TRANSFORMING A LANDSCAPE INTO A WILDLIFE HAVEN NEAR ST ALBANS

Definitely a walk deserving binoculars as well as a camera, this shows you the fruits of an ambitious plan started in 2008, and completed in 2019, to turn bare land into England's largest new native woodland of 600,000 trees. Volunteers, particularly children, have helped the Woodland Trust plant saplings in new land around the existing ancient woodlands every October.

Wildlife has been encouraged by the creation of new hedges to provide habitats; these supplement the long-established ones of hazel, field maple, blackthorn and hawthorn. Thousands of young saplings of ash, oak and hornbeam have been planted on areas of rough grassland, where cherry trees, wild raspberries and poppies flourish. Around the new plantations are three blocks of ancient woodland that display superb examples of oak and hornbeam, and in spring there are impressive carpets of bluebells and wood anemones. It is in these areas that you may see buzzards circling above the woods hunting for food. The meadow by Well Wood is where to look for red kites (easily identified by their forked tails), yellowhammers, linnets and buzzards. The walk we describe here goes

↑ Around the new plantations, find wildlife-rich ancient woodland. (Caroline Eastwood/A)

round the wood rather than through it, but you can plot alternative routes through the wood using leaflets from 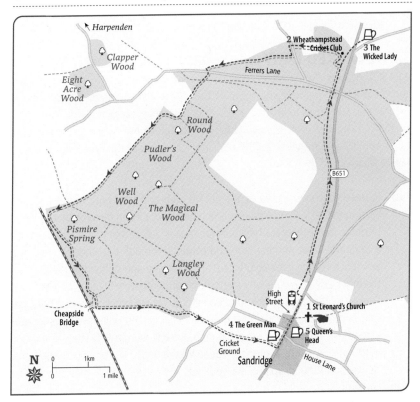 woodlandtrust.org.uk/heartwood.

WHERE: Hertfordshire: Heartwood Forest & Sandridge, circular
STATS: 5 miles/2hrs; easy
START POINT/GETTING THERE: St Leonard's Church, Sandridge /// libraries.evenly.
blocks 🚆 London Overground from Euston (45mins; 3 an hour) to Watford Junction station (note: Freedom Pass valid for this but not for faster mainline trains). Next to the station, go to Bus Stop 5 & get 🚌 321 (40mins; 2 an hour) or 725 (32mins; 1 an hour) to St Peter St, St Albans. At St Peter St, go to Bus Stop 13 for 🚌 304 or 357 to St Leonard's Church (11mins; 4–5 an hour, 1 an hour/90mins on Sun).
DROP-OUT POINTS: Throughout: the walk is never far from a road well served by buses
MAP: OS Explorer map 182. Maps showing footpaths & areas of public access in the forest are available from pubs & shops in the village, or can be downloaded from woodlandtrust.org.uk/heartwood
TAKING A BREAK: Wicked Lady, Green Man, Queen's Head

1. ST LEONARD'S CHURCH (Church End, Sandridge AL4 9DL) The
kernel of the building was consecrated in 1119, but part of the arch is thought to
date back to AD946. It is named after the patron saint of prisoners and pregnant
women. The font may date from Norman times, while a stone screen was added
to the wall between the nave and the chancel in the late 14th century.

☞ Turn right out of the church along the main road, past the next bus stop. Just
after passing a large care home, a sign for 'Public Bridleway 32 Sandridge.
Nomansland Common ½ mile' points to a path running parallel to the road.
Continue along this path, with tree planting to the left and the hedge to the
right, until you reach Ferrers Lane. Cross Ferrers Lane and on your left is:

2. WHEATHAMPSTEAD CRICKET CLUB (Nomansland,
Wheathampstead AL4 8EL) One of the oldest cricket clubs in Hertfordshire
(established in 1824). Cricket is played on the common on Saturday and Sunday
throughout the season, with occasional mid-week and evening fixtures.

☞ Continue past the cricket club, and a sign 'Wheathampstead, Pre-Roman
Riverside Village', to find on your right:

3. THE WICKED LADY (Nomansland, cnr Dyke Lane, Wheathampstead
AL4 8EL ⏣ thewickedladypub.co.uk) This contemporary gastropub with a beer
garden and open log fires sits opposite the village cricket pitch, with a stop for
the 304 and 620 buses to St Albans. The pub takes its name from Lady Katherine
Ferrers, a 17th-century heiress and highwaywoman whose deeds were the subject
of a popular 1945 movie – *The Wicked Lady* – starring Margaret Lockwood and
James Mason.

☞ Retrace your steps towards the cricket club and turn right along the lane
leading to the pavilion – there is a sign nearby depicting the Wheathampstead
Heritage Trail. Follow the lane past the cricket club and continue as it becomes
a footpath. Cross another lane and continue through the wooded area until
you reach Ferrers Lane again. Cross Ferrers Lane and follow the footpath on
the other side. At a gate with steps, turn right and you will reach a Heartwood
Forest sign at the entrance to Round Wood. Do not enter the wood here, but
follow the bridleway to the right and then left. You will have a panoramic
view of the countryside to your right. Continue along the bridleway through
wild-flower meadows, passing Round Wood, Pudler's Wood and Well Wood,
as well as Pismire Spring, on your left. When you reach the railway line,
turn left.

HELEN MATTHEWS

CHRIS BARBER71/S

PETER ARKELL

1 Wildflower meadows near Round Wood. **2** Listen carefully for the insect-like call of the grasshopper warbler. **3** Volunteers have helped the Woodland Trust to plant saplings in 170 acres of land.

Just before you reach a lane with a railway bridge (Cheapside Bridge) to the right, you will see a kissing gate on the left. Follow this path into the newly planted area towards Langley Wood and then take the path to your right. Near the end of Langley Wood, go through a kissing gate on the right. Turn left along the Hertfordshire Way. When you reach Sandridgebury Lane, turn left and then take the footpath on the right, signposted 'Public Footpath 11 Sandridge Village'. Pass the cricket ground on the right and continue through the car park, past the village hall, to the High Street. Turn left and after a short distance you will come to:

4.THE GREEN MAN (🍺 31 High St, Sandridge AL4 9DD ∂ greenmansandridge.co.uk) This pub has a heated rear patio and a garden with a small aviary. Dogs are welcome in the conservatory. It serves Greene King Abbot, Sharp's Atlantic and Tring Side Pocket for a Toad as well as hot food at lunchtimes and (Thu–Sat evenings) pizza.

☛ Continue up the High Street, past the Village Store (which stocks tasty Cornish pasties) back to St Leonard's Church and the bus stop back, on the corner of Church End. Right next to the bus stop is a great place to wait for the bus. This is the:

5. QUEEN'S HEAD (7 Church End, Sandridge AL4 9DL 🄵 thequeensheadsandridge) This traditional timbered pub has a real fire, real ale (including Sharp's Doom Bar, Fuller's London Pride and Young's bitter), a dartboard and a beer garden.

4 A GRAND CANAL & A GREAT ROAD

WATFORD'S WATERWAY WANDER, WITH A CURIOUS ROYAL CONNECTION

'Danger: Crocodiles', says an improbable sign, designed to deter swimmers on this fascinating river/canal walk (the River Gade is part of the Grand Union Canal for much of the route). The walk takes in a burial place with royal connections as well as a *Star Wars* film location; you might also spot (as we did) anglers cooking their own freshly caught fish over a campfire – chub and pike can be caught on the waterway. The meal could feature locally picked blackberries to follow.

Despite the walking route passing under the M25, one day we observed foxes on the snowy hillside and narrowboat dwellers warming by a log fire in the icy conditions, all near the motorway. On the water you should spot ducks, moorhens and swans; in the woods you might glimpse deer.

WHERE: Hertfordshire: Watford to Kings Langley on the Grand Union Canal/River Gade
STATS: 7½ miles/2½–3hrs; easy
START POINT/GETTING THERE: Watford tube station (Metropolitan Line) /// echo. down.phones ⊖ To Watford station; turn right out of the station
FINISH: Saracen's Head, Kings Langley /// glare.splash.reds
DROP-OUT POINT: After 4 miles
MAPS: OS Explorer maps 172 & 182
TAKING A BREAK: Cassiobury Park Tea Pavilion, King's Head, Rose & Crown, Saracen's Head

↑ The Grand Union Canal passing through Cassiobury Park. (Apostolis Giontzis/S)

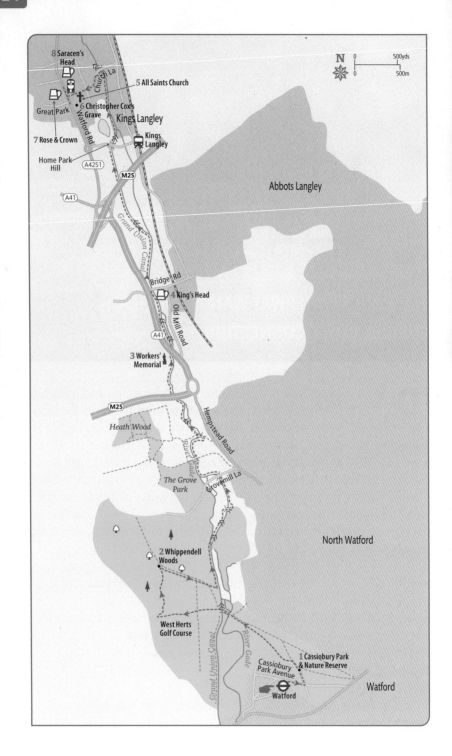

N
0   500yds
0   500m

8 Saracen's Head

Church La

5 All Saints Church

6 Christopher Cox's Grave

Great Park

Kings Langley

7 Rose & Crown

Watford Rd

Kings Langley

Home Park Hill

A4251

M25

A41

Grand Union Canal

Abbots Langley

Bridge Rd

4 King's Head

Old Mill Road

A41

3 Workers' Memorial

M25

Heath Wood

Hempstead Road

River Gade

The Grove Park

Grovemill La

North Watford

Whippendell Woods

West Herts Golf Course

Grand Union Canal

River Gade

Cassiobury Park Avenue

1 Cassiobury Park & Nature Reserve

Watford

Watford

☞ After turning right into Cassiobury Park Avenue, take the first left into Shepherds Road, which takes you into:

1.CASSIOBURY PARK & NATURE RESERVE (⊘ watford.gov.uk/cassioburypark) Watford's major open space has the usual playing fields you might expect, but also includes a much-valued woodland nature reserve of alder, willow, lime and oak trees. It is a rich habitat for all sorts of species: 46 types of bird, including red kites and kingfishers, muntjac deer, butterflies, over 300 species of moth, five species of bat, great crested newts and dragonflies. The park, once part of the lands of the earls of Essex, was voted one of the UK's ten favourite parks in 2022. Its features, all worth pausing to admire, include a restored bandstand, an 'owl tree' with animal artwork carvings on the trunk, and a miniature railway. Fortify yourself for the journey at the **Tea Pavilion** (◷ 09.00–16.00 daily), whose menu includes in-season produce from a farm in nearby Radlett. The café welcomes children and dogs, but there is also a quiet room for adults and (seated, well-behaved) children. Top tip: buy a tub of chocolate brownie trimmings for later in the journey.

☞ Inside the park, go ahead past the tennis courts, turn left round them and follow the path as it bends right diagonally through the park to a crossing of paths; you turn left here. This takes you through a tree-lined avenue down past a playground on the left. You then cross the 1920s 'Rustic Bridge' over the River Gade with willow trees and watercress on its bank, and then another (labelled as Bridge 167) over the Grand Union Canal by a lock (Ironbridge Lock).

Ahead is Public Footpath 31, which takes you through West Herts Golf Course. You cross a fairway, go through some woodland, cross another fairway (watch out for flying golf balls) and turn right for an information board welcoming you to:

2. WHIPPENDELL WOODS (⊘ cassioburypark.info/whippendell-wood) This long-established woodland of oak, beech, silver birch, ash, hazel, holly, hawthorn and wild cherry has been a Site of Special Scientific Interest (SSSI) since 1954. Over 60% is classified as ancient woodland, meaning that parts have been here for at least 400 years. Whippendell has connections with Hollywood and professional football. Many scenes from the *Star Wars* films were shot here, including exterior shots of Naboo for *The Phantom Menace*, as well as TV episodes of *Silent Witness* and *Holby City*. Watford football players were instructed by legendary manager Graham Taylor (later the England manager) to run through the woods as part of their training regime. Spectacular expanses of bluebells appear in spring, usually around late April and early May.

☞ After entering the woods, walk ahead up Northern Drive and, at the junction of paths (Rond Point), turn right along Main Avenue. Follow the signs to Cassiobury Park to return to the towpath. Then turn left and, after about eight minutes, you will reach the lock-keeper's cottage by Cassiobury Locks with its slightly worse-for-wear warning notice: 'Danger: Crocodiles. No Swimming'. Just past the locks, cross a wooden bridge to the other side of the canal and follow the towpath there. Then go under Bridge 165 and Bridge 164 (Grove Bridge). At the next bridge (No 163) cross the canal to the other side (signposted 'Public Footpath 50a') and continue along the towpath (also signposted 'The Grove Trails'). This takes you past some meadows and under the M25 exit road to Watford.

Just before the next bridge, which takes the A41 over the canal, there is a wall on the left in which there is a:

3. WORKERS' MEMORIAL The stone commemorates the deaths
of two workers who were killed when constructing the nearby Gade Valley Trunk Sewer in 1970: G Christopher (died on 1 January) and Charles Curran (7 June).

☞ Continue under the bridge, past the Hunton Bridge Locks to Hunton Bridge itself (Bridge 162). Here is an opportunity to have a drink and/or to drop out. To do either, do not scramble up the steep, muddy bank before the bridge, but go under it to the steps up to the road on the other side. Cross over the canal and on the right is the:

4. KING'S HEAD (Bridge Rd, Hunton Bridge WD4 8RE ✆ 01923 262307)
This traditional pub with timber beams serves a good Sunday roast dinner and real ales including Abbot.

✋ If you would like to finish the walk here, retrace your steps over the bridge and continue to the main road. Turn left for the Langleybury Church bus stop and take the 508 bus (2 an hour) to Watford.

☞ Otherwise return to the canal and continue along the towpath, past North Grove Lock, and under the M25 (Bridge 160), then under Bridge 159, past another lock (Home Park, No 70). As you continue there is a lake on the left.

When you reach Bridge 158, take the road off it to the left (Water Lane). This soon becomes Church Lane which you follow ahead, until you come on the left to:

PETER. FLEMING/S

NEIL MATTHEWS

PETER ARKELL

HELEN MATTHEWS

1 Footbridge over the canal at Hunton. **2** The Tomb of Edmund de Langley, All Saints Church, Kings Langley. **3** The 'owl' tree at Cassiobury Park. **4** An amusing warning sign by a lock-keeper's cottage.

5. ALL SAINTS CHURCH (Church Lane, Kings Langley WD4 8JT) A medieval church with parts dating back to the 13th century, All Saints has a significant royal connection to a crucial figure in the dynastic struggles that led to the Wars of the Roses.

The tomb of Edmund de Langley (1341–1402), son of Edward III, uncle of Richard II and Henry IV and great-grandfather of Edward IV and Richard III, is in the Langley Chapel. Edmund shares the tomb with his first wife Isabel, daughter of Pedro of Castile. Edmund was 'of Langley' because he was born and brought up here. He retired to Langley at the end of his life after the murder of Richard II and the accession of Edmund's nephew Henry Bolingbroke (Henry IV). There is some debate among historians about the tomb, with one theory being that Richard II originally ordered the tomb for himself and his wife, before she predeceased him and Edmund got the use of the tomb. Whatever the truth, the tomb itself is most impressive in alabaster and Purbeck marble, and the set of shields along the side is politically and historically interesting. A later monarch, Queen Victoria, looks down on the tomb from a stained-glass window.

☛ Continue up Church Lane, then turn left into Watford Road, and at a short distance on the left is the main entrance to the churchyard, just inside which is a war memorial. Just to the left of the memorial is:

6. CHRISTOPHER COX'S GRAVE A local farm worker (1889–1959), Cox received the Victoria Cross for exceptional bravery in World War I. While serving as a stretcher bearer during the Battle of the Somme in July 1916, he was shot in the leg but was soon back on the front after the bullet was removed. During several days near Achiet-le-Grand in March 1917, he carried around 20 wounded men from where they fell back to the dressing stations under a horrendous barrage of sustained machine-gun and artillery fire, and dressed a further 40 to 60 as they lay wounded in shell holes. Six weeks later he was wounded twice in the foot during the Battle of Arras and was invalided out of the army. He was offered a commission and a house, but refused both out of respect for his fallen comrades. He returned to Kings Langley and showed bravery again as a member of the Home Guard during World War II, entering the bombed-out Griffin pub in an attempt to rescue the publican, who was found dead. Cox worked for 32 years as a maintenance labourer at the nearby Ovaltine factory, until falling off its roof in 1954, which meant he spent the last five years of his life in and out of hospital. His grave is inscribed: 'In loving memory of a devoted husband and father, Christopher A Cox VC, Beds & Herts Regiment, 1914–18, died 28 April, 1959. Until we meet.' A memorial to Cox was also unveiled outside Achiet-le-Grand in 2007.

☞ Return to the junction of Watford Road and Church Lane where there is a choice of pubs. On the junction on the left is the:

7. ROSE & CROWN (High St, Kings Langley WD4 9HT
🖋 roseandcrownkingslangley.co.uk) A Premium Country Pub, part of the Mitchells & Butlers chain, the Rose & Crown offers a selection of craft beers and ales and a substantial food menu.

☞ A little further on the right is the:

8. SARACEN'S HEAD (47 High St, Kings Langley WD4 9HU
🖋 saracensheadkingslangley.co.uk) This 16th-century coaching inn with a real log fire is one of the best pubs we have visited. Friendly, cosy and timber-beamed, it serves food (including a Sunday roast) and a range of real ales.

☞ Between the two pubs, on the same side as the Saracen's Head, is the Langley Hill bus stop where you can get the 508 bus (2 an hour Mon–Sat, 1 an hour Sun) or the 501 (Sun only, 1 an hour) for a 13-minute journey to Watford Junction station. At Watford Junction you can use your Freedom Pass on the London Overground for the 45-minute journey to Euston (3 an hour) or the faster mainline trains for a small supplement.

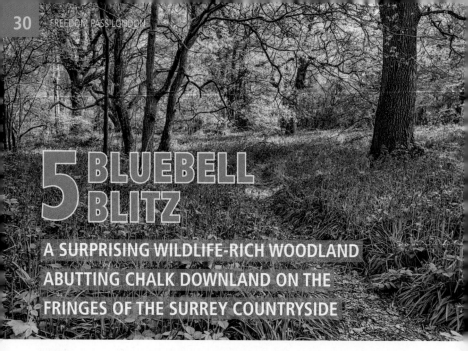

5 BLUEBELL BLITZ

A SURPRISING WILDLIFE-RICH WOODLAND ABUTTING CHALK DOWNLAND ON THE FRINGES OF THE SURREY COUNTRYSIDE

We saw deer, pheasants and a fox and heard a great spotted woodpecker on this stroll through ancient woodland and a pleasantly open patch of chalk downland that makes a memorable escape from London's southern fringes. Time it if you can to coincide with the carpets of bluebells in Banstead Woods, usually at their peak in late April. It is part of a nature reserve next to Chipstead Downs Site of Special Scientific Interest, and depending on when you are here you might encounter red rhododendrons, forget-me-nots or cowslips.

Trees in Banstead Woods include sessile oaks (which are rare in Surrey), goat willow, sweet chestnut, ash, yew, birch, hazel and maple. There are some very rare arable weeds such as ground pine, cut-leaved germander and mat-grass fescue. The downland grass is grazed by goats and sheep to keep down invasive scrub and to encourage wild flowers, and is a habitat for a wide range of insects, including grizzled skipper, brown argus and chalkhill blue butterflies.

WHERE: Surrey: Banstead Woods & Chipstead Downs, circular
STATS: 3 miles; 1–1½ hrs; easy
START POINT/GETTING THERE: Chipstead railway station /// visit.award.plan
🚆 To Chipstead railway station from London Victoria (40mins, change East Croydon; 1–2 an hour), London Bridge (37–44mins, direct or change Norwood Junction; 1–2 an hour) or East Croydon (20mins; 3 an hour, 2 an hour Sun). Take the exit from Platform 1 of the station.
MAP: OS Explorer map 146
TAKING A BREAK: Rambler's Rest

↑ Visit in late spring for a proliferation of bluebells across this ancient woodland. (atomov/S)

☞ Walk down Chipstead Station Parade, turn left at the bottom (into Outwood Lane). Then take first right (into Lower Park Road), and go a few yards round the corner to a car park on the left. Go through a kissing gate next to a sign for 'Banstead Woods and Chipstead Downs Local Nature Reserve'. Continue past a small circular picnic area with information boards, into:

1.BANSTEAD WOODS
This is ancient woodland, and in the 13th century it was fenced off as a deer park and hunting lodge for royalty. Between 1500 and 1850, compass oaks in the wood were used for shipbuilding, with branches bent and staked at 45-, 90- and 135-degree angles. In 1881 the land was bought by Francis Baring (founder of Barings Bank) who built a mansion in the middle. This mansion was turned into an emergency military hospital in 1939, and the woods housed a prisoner-of-war camp. From 1946 until 1998 the mansion housed the Queen Elizabeth Ho spital for Children, and after that the woods were made a public open space (about three-quarters of a mile square) by the local authority.

☞ Several footpaths are signposted from the top of the car park, including one to Perrotts Farm (1½ miles) and the Banstead Woods Nature Trail. Near the start of the trail is a fine chainsaw sculpture of a lion – a depiction of Aslan from CS Lewis's Narnia stories, part of a Narnia-themed nature trail. Elsewhere in the woods you can find the wardrobe entrance to Narnia and Lucy Pevensie waiting by a lamp post.

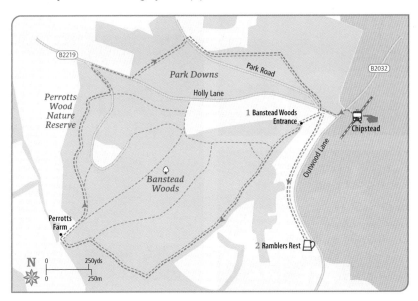

ASDF_1/DT

AGAMI PHOTO AGENCY/DT

PAOP/DT

PAOP/DT

PETER ARKELL

HELEN MATTHEWS

1 &. **3** Look out for grizzled skipper and chalkhill blue during the warmer months. **2** The paths through the woods are beautiful whatever the season. **4** & **5** Follow the Narnia-themed nature trail at Banstead Woods. **6** Cowslips flower between April and May.

TWO BANSTEAD CHARACTERS

A rich eccentric, Henry 'Dog' Smith (1549–1628) was a City of London Alderman who, according to local legend, dressed as a tramp and walked round the area with his dog. The manner in which the locals treated him in this guise would determine the amounts of money he gave for the relief of the poor. Banstead still benefits from this.

The naval hero Matthew Buckle (1718–84) may have been the inspiration for the *Hornblower* novels. He joined the navy at the age of 13 and rose to become a vice admiral. He lived in Nork House (the building is no longer there) in Nork Park, which was part of the estate owned by his family.

We chose to skirt the perimeter of the woods in a clockwise direction, starting in the northeast corner and ending in the northwest corner. When you reach Perrotts Farm, keep left at the fork to skirt the edge of the wood and emerge in Elizabeth Drive.

Turn right into Holly Lane, walk a few yards to 'Permissive Ride' and 'Public Footpath' signs on the left which you follow to Park Downs. After turning right and going through the downs you reach Park Road. Cross over the road into the woods opposite, then turn right following the line of the road. This will take you back to the car park where you started.

Turn left, then first right into Outwood Lane. You can walk on a grass track parallel to the road. After about ten minutes you come to:

2. RAMBLER'S REST (Outwood Lane, Coulsdon, Croydon CR5 3NP ⌀ theramblersrest.co.uk) An old farmhouse, this is now an excellent traditional pub which serves hot food (⊙ noon–18.00 daily) as well as real ale (including Sharp's Doom Bar, Broadside and guest beers), wine and cocktails. In good weather you can enjoy the large beer garden. Dogs and children are welcome.

☞ Retrace your steps along Outwood Lane and right into Chipstead Station Parade back to the station.

6 FLEET OF FOOT

FROM NORTH LONDON'S HIGH GROUND TO THE HEART OF THE CAPITAL, WITH AN EXPLORATION OF ONE OF THE CITY'S LESSER-KNOWN RIVERS

Not many people notice the River Fleet as it makes its way through north London to the Thames as it is underground most of the way, yet it was once the capital's second largest navigable river. Londoners didn't treat it very kindly and it became so heavily polluted that it was turned into a sewer in 1766.

Following its route from Hampstead Heath to Blackfriars Bridge, however, has something for everyone: beyond the countrified heights of the Heath you pass the houses of some famous artists, writers and politicians, look over central London from Primrose Hill, and wander through an unexpected nature reserve in the inner city. Beyond the Gothic spikiness of St Pancras Station the mood changes as you head through Bloomsbury, past the British Museum, stopping off maybe for a drink at one of the few London pubs to survive the Great Fire of 1666, and entering Lincoln's Inn Fields, with its two remarkable museums (both free to enter): Sir John Soane's Museum and the Hunterian Museum within the Royal College of Surgeons (not for the faint of stomach).

↑ The view from Primrose Hill across London. (Rechitan Sorin/DT)

WHERE: London: Hampstead Heath to Blackfriars
STATS: 9 miles; 3½–4hrs; easy
START POINT/GETTING THERE: Hampstead tube station (Northern Line, Edgware Branch) /// shift.lazy.once ⊖ To Hampstead station; turn left out of the station
FINISH: Blackfriars tube station (Circle & District Lines) /// neat.chins.levels
DROP-OUT POINTS: Numerous potential drop-out points; there is always a tube station nearby. If you would like to tackle this long walk over two days, we have suggested a break point in Camden High Street (4 miles into the walk).
MAP: Any A–Z
TAKING A BREAK: The Flask, The Roebuck, The Engineer, Camley Street Natural Park, The Ship, The Seven Stars, Ye Olde Cheshire Cheese, The Blackfriar

☞ Take the first left into Flask Walk (which gets its name from flasks used to collect water from the nearby well, which was fed by the River Fleet). Here on the right is:

1. THE FLASK (14 Flask Walk, cnr Back Lane, NW3 1HE ⊘ theflaskhampstead.co.uk) A great Grade II-listed Victorian pub with two bars and a real fire, the Flask was built in 1874 on the site of the Thatched House, where water from local springs had been sold by the flask. The interior includes paintings by the appropriately named Belgian artist Jan van Beers. Hot food every day, and Young's beer is served.

☞ Follow Flask Walk ahead (past the Wells and Campden Baths and Wash Houses of 1888) to the end. Go straight ahead into Well Walk (which gets its name from the Fleet-fed well). On the corner of Well Walk to your left is Burgh House (⊘ burghhouse.org.uk), a Grade I-listed museum relating to the house's residents and the history of the area. A short distance along Well Walk on the right, a plaque marks the house where Marie Stopes, the social reformer and pioneer of the family-planning movement, lived (1909–16). Also along Well Walk is the Chalybeate Well, which the Hon Susanna Noel and her son, the 3rd Earl of Gainsborough, gave to the poor of Hampstead in 1698, along with six acres of land. At the end of Well Walk, cross over East Heath Road and go straight ahead into:

2. HAMPSTEAD HEATH Like Epping Forest, there was a struggle in the 19th century to prevent this common land from being built over by the lord of the manor (page 64). The villain of the piece in Hampstead was Sir Thomas Maryon Wilson, who tried to put through parliamentary bills to enclose it, and felled a lot of trees to make way for a sand-extraction business. The local people fought the enclosure bill, forming the Heath Protection Committee, which successfully defeated the bill to prevent further building. The sand pits are now lovely hollows that adorn the landscape and these 800 acres of rural land (the highest in London) are safe for people to enjoy. You can swim in its ponds and observe the wildlife, which includes kingfishers, muntjac deer, foxes, parakeets, bats, rabbits, squirrels, frogs and jackdaws.

☞ Follow the main track ahead, and keep following it downhill to the very bottom, to a stream going under the track. This is the:

3. RIVER FLEET The somewhat beleaguered river has its main source underground nearby to the left, with another in Highgate Ponds. The name 'Fleet'

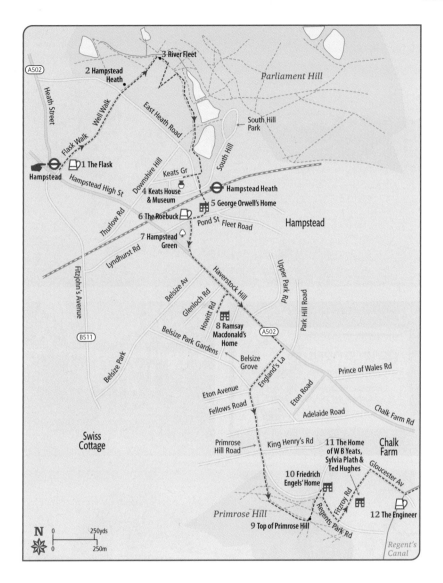

comes from an Anglo-Saxon word meaning tidal inlet capable of floating boats, and in its better days the river had five bridges and a harbour. Things gradually turned sour, though, and by the 13th century it had become so polluted that it was known as 'the stinking river'.

☛ Turn right and follow the path by the stream. When the path forks you can bear right and go to the top of the hill. From here you have a great view down to the Thames where the River Fleet ends up. After that go back

BEATAALDRIDGE/DT

PETER ARKELL

PHOTOCRITICAL/S

ALEX_MASTRO/S

1 Spring on Hampstead Heath. **2** Plaque on George Orwell's house. **3** Flask Walk, Hampstead (The Flask is on the left). **4** Keats House and Museum.

down to the left and rejoin the path along the Fleet (obscured by bushes). This will take you to three ponds in a row on the left and a 'Hampstead Mixed Bathing Pool' noticeboard. These are all headwaters fed by the River Fleet. Follow the edge of them and, when you come to the end of the last pond, you will see where the river goes off underground through a grill (as the path departs from the pond, look to the right bank and you will see it about 30 yards away). The river from here on was covered up and turned into a sewer, as mentioned, in 1766. To continue the walk, do not cross the walkway between the ponds – continue on the original path, and follow it to a stretch of green parallel to South End Road. Just before the end there is a path to the right which takes you a few yards to the road, where directly opposite is Keats Grove. Go up it and a short distance on the left is:

4. KEATS HOUSE & MUSEUM (10 Keats Grove, NW3 2RR
⏀ cityoflondon.gov.uk/keats ◷ Apr–Oct noon–17.00 Tue–Sun; Nov–Mar 11.00–13.00 & 14.00–17.00 Wed–Fri & Sun **£** 🪙 Free to Art Pass holders, reduction for National Trust members) The poet John Keats (1795–1821) lived in this house from 1818 to 1820, and it is the setting that inspired some of his most memorable poetry. Here he wrote *Ode to a Nightingale*, and fell in love with Fanny Brawne, the girl next door. It was from this house that he travelled to Rome, where he died of tuberculosis aged just 25. The son of an ostler, Keats was an anti-militarist, like his friend Shelley. When Keats contracted tuberculosis, Shelley invited him to Italy in the hope that the climate would benefit him, but he died in Rome within a few months of arriving. Exhibits include Keats' notebook from his medical training, his death mask and the engagement ring he gave to Fanny.

☛ Return to South End Road and turn right, going downhill, passing Hampstead Heath station (London Overground) on the left. Continue to the corner of Pond Street to the site of:

5. GEORGE ORWELL'S HOME (1 South End Rd, NW3 2PT) The
author (1903–50) lived and worked here from 1934 to 1935, when it was called Booklover's Corner. Just above head height is a plaque to him; the small bust of Orwell which used to accompany it has been stolen. This is where he wrote the 1936 novel *Keep the Aspidistra Flying*. During World War II he worked for the Ministry of Information at Senate House, Malet Street, in Bloomsbury (page 50), which he used as a model for the Ministry of Truth in his 1949 novel *Nineteen Eighty-Four*. Another plaque marking an Orwell residence is not far away in Parliament Hill (page 225).

☞ Turn right into Pond Street, going uphill, with the Royal Free Hospital on the left. Just past it on the right is:

6. THE ROEBUCK (15 Pond St, NW3 2PN ⌀ roebuckhampstead.com) This comfortable pub has a real fire and a garden, and serves hot food every day along with Young's real ales.

☞ Opposite the pub and to the right of the Royal Free Hospital is a footway off Pond Street. This footway has no name sign at this end, but is in fact Hampstead Green. This takes you up to (on the right):

7. HAMPSTEAD GREEN (Pond St, NW3 2PP) This green area is protected to encourage wild flowers, such as daffodils, cowslips, primroses and bluebells. The juice of the latter, an information board tells us, used to be turned into starch by Elizabethans to 'stiffen their ruffles', and later was useful as gum for bookbinding. In addition to the oak, sycamore and poplar trees, logs are stacked to encourage woodlice, spiders and beetles. Special boxes are also provided to shelter birds.

Next to the green is the Victorian Gothic building of St Stephen's Church (⌀ ststephenstrust.co.uk), a restored Grade I-listed building now used as a venue for public and social events.

☞ At the top of Hampstead Green, turn left into Haverstock Hill, and then right into Howitt Road (opposite Belsize Park tube station). A few doors along on the left is a plaque (more easily spotted from the other side of the road) marking:

8. RAMSAY MACDONALD'S HOME (9 Howitt Rd, NW3 4LT) James Ramsay MacDonald (1866–1937), the first Labour Prime Minister, lived here from 1916 to 1925. The illegitimate son of a ploughman, he lived in the deepest poverty after first moving to London. From 1923 to 1924 he was Prime Minister for the first time and again from 1929 to 1931 (on both occasions without a House of Commons majority). Then from 1931 to 1935 he led the National Coalition government which tarnished his reputation with socialists, who believed he betrayed their cause. He also lived in Lincoln's Inn Fields (page 51).

☞ Continue down Haverstock Hill until reaching England's Lane on the right and turn into it. An interesting mixture of shops here includes a traditional butcher and the Chamomile Café. Then turn left into Primrose Hill Road. Just past St Mary-the-Virgin and St Paul's Primary School on the right, turn right into the green area of Primrose Hill itself. Take the path to the left and go uphill, over a crossing of paths ahead, and left at another crossing of paths a few yards further on, to:

9. THE TOP OF PRIMROSE HILL From here you get a great view of

London to the Thames in the distance. A panel identifies the visible landmarks, including Guy's Hospital, which is close to the end of the walk at Blackfriars. On a low wall in front of the viewing area is a quotation from William Blake (1757–1827): 'I have conversed with the spiritual sun. I saw him on Primrose Hill.' Behind the wall a plaque set into the ground is dedicated to Iolo Morganwg (1747–1826), a stonemason, poet, antiquarian, political radical and anti-slavery campaigner. His original name was Edward Williams, but his romantic vision of Wales and Welshness led him, among other things, to form the Gorsedd – a community of Welsh bards – in a ceremony here on 21 June 1792.

☞ Turn left from the top, going downhill to the corner where Primrose Hill Road heads into Regent's Park Road. Turn left into Regent's Park Road and cross the road to:

10. FRIEDRICH ENGELS' HOME (122 Regents Park Rd, NW1 8XL)

Engels (1820–95) lived here from 1870 to 1894 where he was often visited by his comrade and collaborator, Karl Marx. They jointly wrote *The Communist Manifesto* in 1848. Engels on his own wrote the book *Conditions of the Working Class in England* in 1844 and donated the royalties to Marx. Another of Engels' major works was *Origin of the Family, Private Property and the State* in 1884. After the death of Marx in 1883, Engels edited and translated his friend's writings, producing the second and third volumes of *Das Kapital* in 1885 and 1894.

☞ Go back along Regent's Park Road, past the junction with Primrose Hill Road, until you almost reach a zebra crossing then turn left into Fitzroy Road. Four doors past Fitzroy Yard on the right is:

11. THE HOME OF WB YEATS, SYLVIA PLATH & TED HUGHES (23 Fitzroy Rd, NW1 8TP) A plaque confirms that WB Yeats (1865–

1939), the Irish poet and playwright, lived here from 1867 to 1872. In later years, as a youth interested in mysticism, he joined the Hermetic Order of the Golden Dawn, which held magic rituals and believed sex was a source of power. A strong Irish nationalist, he became a senator of the Irish Free State from 1922 to 1928, and received the Nobel Prize for Literature in 1923.

Sylvia Plath (1932–63), the poet and novelist, took her own life by gassing herself on the top floor here, where she had lived since 1962, and inadvertently almost gassed her neighbour downstairs at the same time. Like Yeats, Sylvia and her husband, the poet and writer Ted Hughes (1930–98), had an interest in the occult and evoking spirits. She thought the fact that Yeats had lived here was a good omen…

☛ Continue along Fitzroy Road to the end, then turn right into Gloucester Avenue where on the right, on the corner of Princess Road, is:

12. THE ENGINEER (65 Gloucester Av, NW1 8JH ⊘ theengineerprimrosehill. co.uk) A cosy pub with a restaurant, the Engineer serves hot food every day and has a garden. As well as real ales (such as Sharp's Doom Bar and Saddleback) it serves cocktails and wine.

☛ Directly opposite the pub on the Gloucester Avenue side is a path running down to the Regent's Canal. When you reach the canal turn left (signposted 'Camden Lock' and 'King's Cross 1½ miles') and follow the towpath on the left bank. Almost immediately go under a railway bridge. A bit further along, you pass a crenellated brick building, the Pirate Castle (a boating and outdoor activities charity ⊘ thepiratecastle.org). Continue under Bridge 20a (Oval Road), past the huge Camden Lock Market, and over a footbridge across the canal and continue along the right bank. You will soon reach Bridge 24 (Chalk Farm Road).

✋ To finish here, turn right and continue into Camden High Street (where Camden Town tube station is a short distance away on the left).

☛ Alternatively, to continue the walk, turn left to cross the bridge over the canal to the other side and continue along the towpath on the left bank. You will pass Hawley Wharf, and plenty of food stalls in the Waterside Halls buildings (⊘ camdenmarket.com). Keep following the towpath until you reach Bridge 31 (Camley Street). Come off the canal here into Camley Street and turn right. Continue past Granary Street on the right; just after the road bends under a railway bridge, on the left is St Pancras Cruising Club. Next door to it is:

13. CAMLEY STREET NATURAL PARK (12 Camley St, NW1 0PW ⊘ wildlondon.org.uk/nature-reserves ⊙ Apr–Sep 10.00–17.00 daily; Oct & Nov 10.00–16.00 daily) Created from an old coal yard in 1984, this is now a quiet refuge from the city and surrounding railway tracks. It features key habitats including grassland, woodland and wetland, and has an amazing range of wildlife and plants including the Daubenton's bat, holly blue butterfly, reed warblers,

1 Camden Lock. **2** Street food at Camden Market. **3** Camley Street Natural Park.

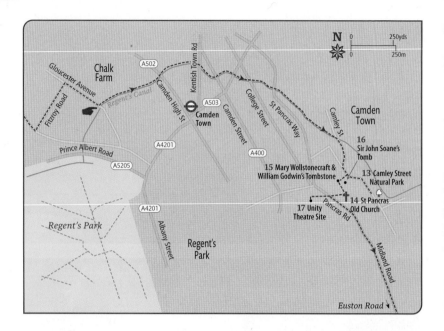

kingfishers, geese and mallards, along with reed bunting, snake's head fritillary and rare earthstar fungi. Pond dipping and educational activities are available for children, along with trainee schemes in conservation skills and numerous family events throughout the year. This makes a pleasant comfort stop, with a **café** and toilets.

☛ After visiting the natural park, retrace your steps under the railway bridge and turn left after a few yards through a gateway into St Pancras Gardens and:

14. ST PANCRAS OLD CHURCH (Pancras Rd, NW1 1UL) One of the earliest Christian churches in Europe, St Pancras Old Church dates back to AD314, but was ruined in the 13th century, rebuilt in the 14th century, and half abandoned in the mid-19th century. During the Civil War it was taken over by Oliver Cromwell's troops as a barracks and stables.

The River Fleet behind the church is shown in an 1827 picture on the railings in front of the church. *A Tale of Two Cities* by Charles Dickens, published in 1859, has body-snatcher Jerry Cruncher stealing corpses from the churchyard.

Among the literary figures associated with St Pancras Old Church is Thomas Hardy (1840–1928) the novelist, who worked for the Midland Railway Line. The company built the railway track over part of the church's graveyard in the 1860s, and Hardy was responsible for removing the bodies and dismantling the tombstones. Some headstones were placed around an ash tree, which became known as the Hardy Tree, spreading in and around the stones. Unfortunately, in late 2022, the tree collapsed due to a combination of a long-term fungal infection and strong winds. The headstones remain.

The Beatles were photographed in and around the churchyard (including next to the tomb of Sir John Soane; see below) on 28 July 1968. The pictures were eventually used in 1973 on the sleeves of two compilation albums – *1962–1966* (Red Album) and *1967–1970* (Blue Album).

☛ About 20 yards ahead as you enter the churchyard from Camley Street you will see a four-sided tombstone about four feet tall which is:

15. MARY WOLLSTONECRAFT & WILLIAM GODWIN'S TOMBSTONE Mary Wollstonecraft (1759–97), the feminist author of *A Vindication of the Rights of Woman*, and her anarchist husband William Godwin (1756–1836), who wrote *Political Justice*, were both married and buried in St Pancras Old Church. Godwin lived in nearby Chalton Street and, when he married Mary, they moved nearby to 29 The Polygon (on the corner of Chalton Street, Werrington Street and Polygon Road), which is now occupied by a block of modernist flats called Oakshott Court. A plaque to Mary is on the Werrington Street corner of the square. Mary's daughter, also called Mary (1797–1851), married poet Percy Bysshe Shelley (1792–1822) and plighted her troth to him over her mother's grave here. William's second wife, yet another Mary, was also buried here.

☛ Also in the churchyard to the left of this tombstone (between the church and the rail track) is:

16. SIR JOHN SOANE'S TOMB The tomb of Sir John Soane (whose astonishing museum is featured later in this walk) is said to have been the inspiration for Giles Gilbert Scott's K2 telephone box (which can still be seen on our streets).

☛ Leave the churchyard in front of the church and turn right into Pancras Road, and a few yards on the left is Goldington Crescent. Follow this to the second turning on the left which is Chalton Street, and on the left is:

17. UNITY THEATRE SITE (Unity Mews, 150 Chalton St, just off Goldington Crescent, NW1 1NP ⊘ unitytheatre.org.uk) A plaque proclaims: 'Unity Theatre run by the people for the people, 1936–75'. Unity Theatre began

as a theatre club to avoid the censorship of the Lord Chamberlain in order to put on left-wing plays as part of the Workers' Theatre Movement. It started in a hall in nearby Britannia Street on 5 January 1936 but moved to this site the following year. Although an amateur group, it attracted many professional actors who would appear for free, including Paul Robeson who turned down several West End roles to perform here in 1938. Many famous playwrights used it to stage the premieres of their plays, including Sean O'Casey, Jean-Paul Sartre, Maxim Gorky and Bertolt Brecht. Music-hall shows were also staged. It burned down on 8 November 1975. The Unity Theatre Trust preserves the theatre's ethos through its charitable work fostering, promoting and increasing the interest of the public in the art of drama and in the related arts.

☛ Retrace your steps to St Pancras Gardens and Old Church through Goldington Square Gardens, passing aluminium sculptures that represent clouds and double as play equipment. Local schoolchildren chose the designs. Continue down Pancras Road, ahead into Midland Road past St Pancras station on the left, and the British Library on the right, to Euston Road. Turn right, then first left into Mabledon Place, right at Mabel's Tavern into Flaxman Terrace, right into Dukes Road and immediately left into Woburn Walk, through to Upper Woburn Place.

So far the walk has roughly followed the course of the River Fleet. From here the underground river actually goes east to King's Cross Road, then south via Farringdon Road and Farringdon Street to Ludgate Circus. This walk, however, takes a more picturesque and historic route to Ludgate Circus (based on one recommended by The Ramblers).

Turn left into Upper Woburn Place and a few yards on the left is:

18. SITE OF CHARLES DICKENS' HOME (BMA House, Tavistock Sq, WC1H 9JP) A plaque confirms that Charles Dickens lived in a house on this site from 1851 to 1860, during which time he wrote *Bleak House* and other novels. A lover of amateur dramatics, he also had his own private theatre here where he put on productions with his friends including fellow novelist Wilkie Collins and artists George Cruikshank, who illustrated *Oliver Twist* and *Sketches by Boz*, and Augustus Egg. Egg shared digs with Richard Dadd, the artist who killed his own father in 1843, on which Dickens based his novel *Martin Chuzzlewit*, serialised from 1843 to 1844. The site is now the head office of the British Medical Association (BMA).

☛ Cross the road and look through the railings into Tavistock Square Gardens to see:

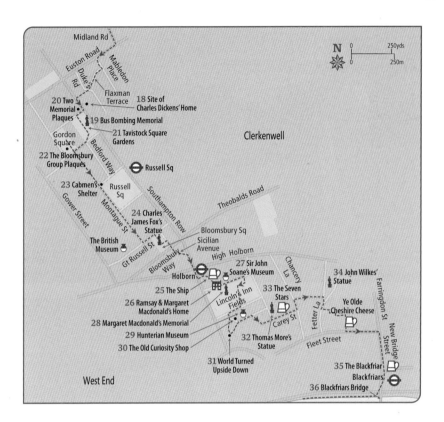

19. MEMORIAL TO THE BUS BOMBING OF 7 JULY 2005

(Tavistock Sq, WC1H 9BQ) This memorial, unveiled in September 2018, honours the names of the 13 people who were killed when the number 30 bus exploded in front of BMA House. Four suicide bombers struck London's transport network during the morning rush hour that day, killing 52 people and injuring more than 770 others. One of the bombs was on the tube between King's Cross and Russell Square which led to the diversion of the 30 bus to here. An earlier memorial plaque is now in the London Transport Museum.

☛ Retrace your steps a short distance to the corner of Tavistock Square and Upper Woburn Place, where you will find:

20. TWO MEMORIAL PLAQUES (Woburn House, 20–24 Tavistock Sq, WC1H 9HQ) The older plaque, on the wall of Woburn House, reads: 'In memory of auxiliary Firemen Stanley Harold Randolph and Harry Richard Skinner who died from injuries received as a result of enemy action near this site on the night of 16th–17th April 1941, while serving under Station 73 Euston.' The second

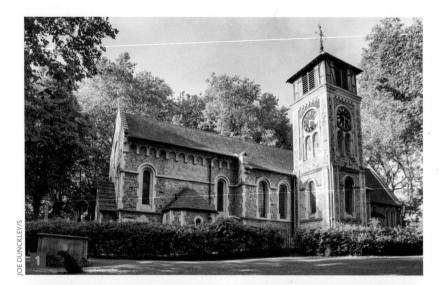

JOE DUNCKLEY/S

JOSH BROWN PHOTOGRAPHY/S

NEIL MATTHEWS

TRANSPORT FOR LONDON/A

1 St Pancras Old Church. **2** Gandhi statue in Tavistock Square. **3** A plaque marks the spot of the Unity Theatre. **4** Memorial to the Bus Bombing of July 2005.

plaque, on the adjoining wall, dates from 2019 and notes that Otto Schiff CBE (1875–1952), founder and director of the Jewish Refugees Committee, lived here between 1933 and 1939.

☞ Go a few yards up Tavistock Square and turn left into:

21. TAVISTOCK SQUARE GARDENS (Tavistock Sq, WC1H 9BQ)

Tavistock Square was built in the early 19th century as part of the Bedford Estate. The dukes of Bedford's eldest sons used the courtesy title Marquess of Tavistock, hence the name. Many of the artefacts in the gardens share themes of peace and peaceful resistance. On the right as you enter from Tavistock Square is a memorial dedicated to conscientious objectors. To the right of the path as you walk towards the centre is a cherry tree planted in memory of the victims of Hiroshima.

In the centre is a statue of Mohandas Gandhi (1869–1948), who became known as Mahatma (meaning 'great soul') after his campaign of civil disobedience and passive resistance finally won independence for India. He studied at nearby University College London in 1888. The statue was sculpted by Fredda Brilliant and unveiled by the Prime Minister, Harold Wilson, in May 1968.

In the far right corner of the gardens is a bust of novelist Virginia Woolf (1882–1941; page 208) who lived at 52 Tavistock Square, now the site of the Tavistock Hotel, with her husband Leonard for 15 years while they ran the Hogarth Press. Virginia was one of the Bloomsbury Group of intellectuals and creatives.

☞ Leave Tavistock Square Gardens by the gate opposite the Tavistock Hotel and turn right. Continue straight into Gordon Square and turn right to find:

22. THE BLOOMSBURY GROUP PLAQUES Three buildings in

Gordon Square sport four plaques relating to the Bloomsbury Group. The plaque at No 50 notes that several members including Virginia Woolf lived here and in neighbouring houses. There are two plaques at No 46: one remembering economist John Maynard Keynes who lived here for 30 years; and the other Virginia's sister, the artist Vanessa Bell, and her partner and fellow artist Duncan Grant. Finally, No 51 was home to the writer, biographer and critic Lytton Strachey.

☞ Retrace your steps to the corner of Gordon Square and cross the road into Woburn Square, which becomes Thornhaugh Street, passing the Institute of Education on the left and the School of Oriental and African Studies (SOAS) on the right. Outside the SOAS building is a statue of Thiruvalluvar, one of

Tamil culture's most notable literary figures. The Government of Tamil Nadu presented the statue in 1996. Continue into Russell Square where there is a small green hut on your left:

23. CABMEN'S SHELTER (23 Russell Sq, WC1H 0XG) This Victorian shelter was one of over 60 built from 1875 onwards to keep the drivers of horse-drawn carriages out of pubs. Especially during rain and snow, drivers would be tempted into pubs rather than sitting on the uncovered part of the carriage and getting soaked, and this made it difficult to find a cab in such conditions. It was also the time when the Temperance Society was at its height, and a Cabmen's Shelter Fund was set up, erecting the huts with 'good and wholesome refreshments at moderate prices' to lure them away from the taverns and keep them on the job. By law they had to be no larger than a horse and cart. Many were destroyed in the Blitz or later demolished during road widening, so this is one of only a handful that remain. It was originally in Leicester Square from 1901 until pedestrianisation in the 1960s and, restored on this site in 1987, it continues to serve snacks to cabbies and members of the public.

☞ Continue straight on, passing on your right the rear of University of London's Senate House (which George Orwell's *Nineteen Eighty-Four* depicted as the Ministry of Truth). Continue into Montague Street; if you wish to visit the British Museum, the less busy North Entrance in Montague Place is on your right. At the end of Montague Street, turn left into Great Russell Street. On the right in Bloomsbury Square Gardens is:

24. CHARLES JAMES FOX'S STATUE (Bloomsbury Square Gardens) The radical Whig MP known as 'the Intrepid Fox' (1749–1806) had a huge capacity for alcohol. Finding him surrounded by seven empty port bottles, a friend asked if he had drunk them all unassisted. He replied: 'No, I was assisted by a bottle of Madeira.' Such heavy drinking meant he had rather a portly figure so, when his second in a duel advised him to stand sideways to reduce the target area for his opponent, Fox chuckled: 'Why? I am as thick one way as another.' The opponent, William Adam, invited Fox to shoot first, but, showing remarkable courtesy in the circumstances, he replied: 'After you.' Both missed, then Fox was hit in the groin, after which he again showed incredible civility by firing in the air. They then became firm friends. Politically, Fox supported many progressive causes such as the extension of the franchise (when less than a quarter of a million people had the vote out of a population of six million) and the abolition of slavery. He proposed the bill that became the 1807 Slave Trade Act, abolishing the trade in slavery (but not slavery itself), though he did not live to see the bill become law.

☛ Go into the gardens and take the exit to the left about halfway down, then turn right and go over the road into Sicilian Avenue (a pedestrian arcade with some interesting shops) opposite. Turn right at the end into Southampton Row. Go past Holborn underground station on the left, and just past it turn left into Gate Street (a pedestrian alley). Here on the corner of Little Turnstile is:

25. THE SHIP (12 Gate St, WC2A 3HP ♂ theshiptavern.co.uk) A great traditional alehouse hidden away in this back alley, The Ship dates back to 1549 and serves six 'Cask Marque' accredited real ales (two each week on a rotating basis). It dishes up old-fashioned pub grub, as well as a more formal menu in the Oak Room on the first floor.

☛ Continue along Gate Street into Lincoln's Inn Fields, where Lord William Russell was publicly executed in 1683 for plotting the assassination of Charles II. Turn left and a short distance on the left is:

26. RAMSAY & MARGARET MACDONALD'S HOME (3 Lincoln's Inn Fields, WC2A 3AA) James Ramsay MacDonald, the first Labour Prime Minister (page 40), lived here from 1896 to 1916. He also attended regular debates in the Rainbow Tavern nearby at 15 Fleet Street.

☛ A few doors down is:

27. SIR JOHN SOANE'S MUSEUM (13 Lincoln's Inn Fields, WC2A 3BP ♂ soane.org ◔ 10.00–17.00 Wed–Sun & bank hols, last entry 16.30) Soane (1753–1837), the son of a bricklayer, was one of the great British architects, and this is his startling home, preserved by private Act of Parliament after his death so it would be retained as a museum and left unchanged (partly so his sons couldn't get their hands on it); it's free to enter, too. Three houses at Nos 12, 13 and 14 were knocked down to build the museum in two phases between 1808 and 1824. So many curiosities and relics are packed in that you hardly know where to look: all manner of things – Greek and Roman relics, thousands of drawings, paintings, stained-glass windows and even mummified cats – are stashed on the walls and in display cases. In the room where originals of Hogarth's celebrated paintings (the series *The Rake's Progress* and *The Election)* hang, the attendant unhooks the panels to reveal more works hidden behind, including a painting combining a number of Soane's architectural schemes that never reached fruition, plus a scale model of the Bank of England which he designed. In the central courtyard, itself cobbled with wine bottle bottoms, arches recycled from

CHRISDORNEY/S

NICOLETA RALUCA TUDOR/DT

NICOLETA RALUCA TUDOR/DT

ARNDALE/S

1 The Cabmen's Shelter, Russell Square. **2** The extraordinary Sir John Soane's Museum.
3 Exhibits in the rather gory Hunterian Museum. **4** Ye Olde Cheshire Cheese pub.

the House of Lords surround a melodramatic mausoleum to 'Alas, poor Fanny!' – his beloved dog. Soane's tomb is in St Pancras Old Church (page 45).

☛ Retrace your steps a few yards and turn left into Lincoln's Inn Fields gardens, then take the path immediately right, where on the right is:

28. MARGARET MACDONALD'S MEMORIAL Margaret (1870–1911), who married James Ramsay MacDonald in 1896, founded the Women's Labour League and was a deeply committed feminist. Her memorial here is a bench topped with a sculpture depicting Margaret with nine children (she had six).

☛ Go to the opposite (southern) exit of the gardens, and facing you is the:

29. HUNTERIAN MUSEUM (ROYAL COLLEGE OF SURGEONS)
(35–43 Lincoln's Inn Fields, WC2A 3PE ⊘ hunterianmuseum.org ⊙ 10.00–17.00 Tue–Sat, recommended last entry 16.00) A must for lovers of the ghoulish and macabre, but definitely not for the squeamish (there are skeletons of foetuses and bottled organs), this free museum is one of the oldest anatomical collections in the world. Revealing 400 years of medical history, right up to the latest advances in surgery, its basis is the collection and life's work of John Hunter (1728–93). The first section, covering anatomy and physiology, considers the relationship between body structures and functions; the second covers pathology, with examples of disease and injury. The exhibits range from the fascinating to the grotesque. Perhaps the most striking are the Evelyn tables, which the writer John Evelyn (1620–1706) brought back from Padua in Italy. They consist of human tissue – blood vessels and nerves – that a professional dissector removed from body tissue and pasted on to wooden boards.

After no early formal education, John Hunter trained as a surgeon and became very proficient at dissection and experimental research. He became surgeon to George III and surgeon general to the British army, but his experiments were not always a success. In 1777 he tried to resuscitate the body of Rev William Dodd, who had just been hanged for fraud and forgery. Hunter had previously revived people who had been drowned. Dodd's friends bribed the hangman to cut him down early and rushed the body to Hunter whose attempt to revive him in a hot bath failed. Dodd had written prolifically in prison during his last two weeks, prompting his friend Samuel Johnson's famous remark: 'When a man knows he is to be hanged in a fortnight it concentrates his mind wonderfully.'

Hunter's older brother William, who guided and trained John early in his career, had a medical school which received corpses from body-snatchers at

8–10 Windmill Street, off Tottenham Court Road. Over a hundred bodies were found hidden in a shed in 1776. William donated his collections to the University of Glasgow where they remain on public display – also under the title of The Hunterian.

☛ Turn left out of the museum, and take the first left into Portsmouth Street, where on the left near the junction with Sheffield Street, is:

30. THE OLD CURIOSITY SHOP (13–14 Portsmouth St, WC2A 2ES)
The novel of this name by Charles Dickens was serialised from 1840 to 1841 and was so popular in America that the ship carrying the magazine with the last instalment from London was besieged when it arrived in New York. The building, which dates from the 16th century, has been, in its time, a tailor's shop, a bookseller, a print and paper shop, an estate agent's office, a souvenir shop and, most recently, a shoe and hat shop for a Japanese designer. It is now owned by the London School of Economics (LSE) which, at the time of writing, is holding a Dragon's Den-style competition to attract business propositions from student entrepreneurs, with the winner receiving a lease.

☛ Turn around, with your back to the Shop, and walk down Sheffield Street (still on LSE's campus) towards:

31. 'WORLD TURNED UPSIDE DOWN' (Sheffield St) This globe
sculpture (2019) is the work of Mark Wallinger. The title comes from a 17th-century English ballad. Wallinger depicts the world as resting on its North Pole. The art attracted controversy by depicting Taiwan as a sovereign entity, independent of China. After various protests, LSE opted to add an asterisk and a placard explaining Taiwan's position. Students have vandalised the sculpture in response to its omission of the state of Palestine, which is a non-member observer state in the UN.

☛ Turn left into Portugal Street, then right into Carey Street. On the next corner is:

32. THOMAS MORE'S STATUE (cnr Carey St & Searle St) More (1478–
1535) wrote the classic Utopia (meaning Nowhere Land) in 1516, in search of the best form of government. It describes an imaginary island of communal ownership, education for all men and women and religious toleration. Sadly, the latter was not extended to him, and he was beheaded on Henry VIII's orders for refusing to recognise him as head of the Church in place of the Pope. More

1 & **3** The Blackfriar pub – a rare Art Nouveau gem. **2** The Old Curiosity Shop. **4** John Wilkes' statue, Fetter Lane. **5** Thomas More's statue, on the corner of Carey and Searle streets.

studied at nearby Lincoln's Inn between 1496 and 1502 and became a successful barrister. He later became an MP, Speaker of the House of Commons and then Lord Chancellor.

☛ Continue along Carey Street where a few yards on the left is the:

33. THE SEVEN STARS (53 Carey St, WC2A 2JB ⌂ thesevenstars1602.co.uk) One of the oldest pubs in London, dating back to 1602, this was one of the few buildings to survive the Great Fire of London. It is just behind the Royal Courts of Justice, so gets a fair passing trade of barristers and their clients (there is a selection of barristers' wigs and legal paraphernalia in the window). A small and busy free house, it offers pub grub and real ales (including Adnams). You may also find, as we did, a black cat wearing a white ruff with feline insouciance.

☛ Continue to the end of Carey Street, then turn left into Chancery Lane, then first right into Bream's Buildings. This takes you to Fetter Lane where you turn right. Here is:

34. JOHN WILKES' STATUE (New Fetter Lane, EC4A 3AT) Wilkes (1727–97), like Thomas More, was a defender of religious toleration, as well as freedom for all. The cry 'Wilkes and Liberty' was often heard in the streets of London. He was thus a thorn in the side of the establishment and was locked up in the Tower of London for sedition and blasphemy from 1768 to 1770. While he was incarcerated his supporters formed the Society for Supporting the Bill of Rights. Earlier he had been elected three times as MP for Middlesex, but was expelled each time by the House. One of his greatest opponents in Parliament was the Earl of Sandwich, who said Wilkes would die 'on the gallows or of the pox'. Wilkes famously rejoindered: 'That depends, my lord, on whether I embrace your principles or your mistress.'

TADEUSZ IBROM/S

↑ Blackfriars Bridge, with St Paul's Cathedral and the City behind.

☛ Continue along Fetter Lane and take the first left into West Harding Street, and left into Pemberton Row. On the right go through an archway into a cobbled alley (signposted 'Dr Johnson's House') to Dr Johnson's House in Gough Square (page 192), then to the opposite exit from the square into Wine Office Court, turning right at the cannon. A few yards on the left is **Ye Olde Cheshire Cheese pub** (🖰 ye-olde-cheshire-cheese.co.uk; page 192), originally the Horn Tavern when built in 1538 and rebuilt after the 1666 Great Fire of London. Continue down Wine Office Court a few yards to Fleet Street, named after the famous river-turned-sewer. Turn left and continue towards Ludgate Circus.

When you reach Ludgate Circus, turn right into New Bridge Street down towards the Thames, and on the left on the corner of Queen Victoria Street is:

35. THE BLACKFRIAR (174 Queen Victoria St, EC4V 4EG
🖰 nicholsonpubs.co.uk) A rare Art Nouveau interior, complete with stained-glass windows and furniture, and on the site of an old Dominican monastery, this pub features many jolly friars in sculptures, mosaics and reliefs. Real ales including Nicholson's Pale Ale and a seasonal selection of local and national beers, along with basic pub grub, are available and there is seating outside.

☛ Cross the road, passing Blackfriars station. Continue to:

36. BLACKFRIARS BRIDGE This bridge opened in 1869, replacing an
earlier bridge from the 1760s. Its ends mimic the shape of a pulpit, a reference to Black Friars.

☛ Go down some steps on the left. Somewhere under this bridge, the Fleet joins the Thames. From here, retrace your steps to Blackfriars tube station.

7 EPIC FOREST FIGHT

A MIRACULOUS SURVIVAL OF SEMI-WILDERNESS IN THE NORTHEASTERN SUBURBS, PRESERVED THANKS TO AN EPIC STRUGGLE AGAINST ENCLOSURE

Epping Forest wasn't always called that. For centuries it was Waltham Forest. And despite its name it's not all wooded; there are also patches of heath, wetland, grassland, numerous rivers and streams. It's large enough to lose yourself in comprehensively: this green corridor of elevated, rather infertile gravelly land extends from Manor Park to beyond Epping, a total of more than nine square miles. More than half of it is designated as a Site of Special Scientific Interest, and it comprises ancient woodland which has been covered with trees since Neolithic times. Parts of the forest are still grazed by cattle; rare-breed pedigree English longhorns keep the grass down to allow more flowers to flourish. These flowers in turn preserve butterflies and other insects.

↑ Autumn in Epping Forest. (FreedomFungPhotography/S)

In medieval times it was a royal hunting forest, allowing only the king to hunt there; locals were allowed to exercise their commoners' rights and collect wood and food from it. That's where things turned nasty in the 19th century as matters came to a head between landowners and commoners, and the then Lord of the Manor started enclosing parts of the forest. In this walk we pay homage to local hero Thomas Willingale whose bold lopping saved the forest from suburbanisation. Although much of the forest was lost, an Act of Parliament preserving the remainder was passed in 1878, since when the ownership of Epping Forest has passed to the Corporation of London.

Earlier, Henry VIII hunted in the forest and breakfasted in it while the second of his six wives, Anne Boleyn, was being beheaded. Another murderer, police killer Harry Roberts, used it as a hideout in 1966, as did highway robber Dick Turpin a couple of centuries earlier.

WHERE: London/Essex, Epping Forest: Chingford to Loughton
STATS: 6 miles; 2½hrs; easy
START POINT/GETTING THERE: Chingford railway station /// game.lion.trails
🚃 To Chingford from Liverpool Street (26–28mins; 4 an hour) or 🚇 to Walthamstow Central (Victoria Line), then train to Chingford (11–12mins; frequent); turn right out of Chingford station into Station Rd.
FINISH: Loughton station (Central Line) /// proud.safely.trap
MAP: OS Explorer map 174
TAKING A BREAK: Butler's Retreat, The Original Tea Hut, Victoria Tavern

👉 After turning right into Station Road, follow it as it becomes Ranger's Road for about seven minutes or so to the Royal Forest pub. A bit further along on the left are two sites of interest next to each other:

1. EPPING FOREST VISITOR CENTRE (6 Ranger's Rd, Chingford E4 7QH 📞 020 7332 1911 🌐 cityoflondon.gov.uk/things-to-do/green-spaces/epping-forest 🕐 10.00–16.00 Tue–Sun) This friendly centre incorporates a gift shop where you can buy maps and leaflets to help you enjoy your time in Epping Forest. A programme of exhibitions explains key points in the forest's history. Under the Normans, 'forest law' meant that the local people had rights 'in common' to gather wood, graze livestock and fatten pigs. The forest has been a tourist destination since the 18th century, benefitting from ideas of the 'picturesque' and the Romantic movement. Many of the campaigners who saved the forest from development in the 1870s remembered picnics from their childhoods, or had come here on church or works outings.

2. QUEEN ELIZABETH'S HUNTING LODGE (Ranger's Rd, Chingford E4 7QH 🌐 cityoflondon.gov.uk/things-to-do/green-spaces/epping-forest 🕐 11.00–

13.00 & 14.00–15.00 Tue–Sun) This three-storey lodge was built by Elizabeth's father, Henry VIII, in 1542. It was designed to enable the royals to stand with their crossbows on the lodge balconies on the first floor and shoot at captured deer which were driven to them by beaters. If they missed, the deer were brought down by hounds, so the beasts didn't stand much of a chance. After each wave of deer had been slaughtered the carcasses were collected by cart to make way for the next set of victims.

The lodge exterior now sports a traditional white limewash, a more modern method of preservation compared with Victorian predilections for staining timbers black. Displays of artificial food and Tudor recipes (boiled mallard with onions, anyone?) illustrate the use of part of the ground floor for the kitchen. The nobility were protected from the cooking smells of the venison wafting upwards into the banqueting room, because the kitchen ceiling was specially filled with plaster containing human hair which acted as a filter.

☞ After turning left out of the hunting lodge on to Ranger's Road, you will find **Butler's Retreat** (⊘ larderlondon.co.uk/the-larder-at-butlers-retreat), a restored barn offering locally sourced refreshments. Go through the grounds, passing an obelisk with a water fountain to a fingerpost signposted 'Connaught Water'. Follow the grassy path northeast and downhill. When you reach the bottom, cross the surfaced ride and continue straight ahead until you reach:

3. CONNAUGHT WATER
Once a swampy pool fed by rainwater, Connaught Water was constructed in 1883 as an ornamental lake for paddling and boating. It derives its name from the first Ranger of the Forest, the Duke of Connaught, and is one of Epping Forest's busiest sites. The abundant local wildlife includes fallow deer, bats, and birds such as tree-creepers and woodpeckers. There is also a large variety of wildfowl – swans, coots, moorhens, mallards, great crested grebes and Canada geese.

☞ Turn right at the water and follow the path around it past a car park, then take the first path off to the right, following it in a northerly direction. At the end turn left into another track, Fairmead Road (not marked as such) which ends at **The Original Tea Hut** (⊘ originalteahut.com), a favourite haunt of bikers, on the junction with Cross Roads (again unmarked).

Turn left and after about 200 yards turn right into a road (signposted to 'High Beach'); this is Paul's Nursery Road. Parallel with the road are bridleways or tracks through the forest which you can use. After about 15 to 20 minutes you will come to High Beach village and the:

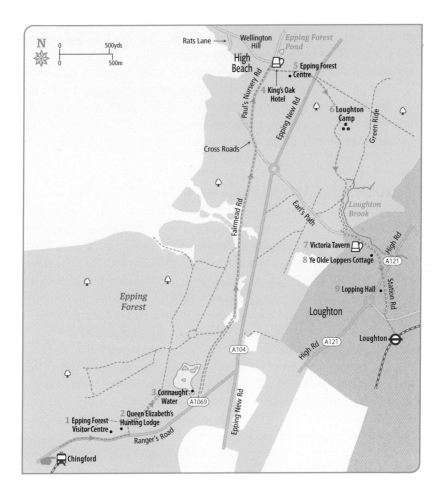

4. KING'S OAK HOTEL (Paul's Nursery Rd, High Beach IG10 4AE 🖉 kingsoakhotel.com) Henry VIII had breakfast in this hotel, which was then a tavern, on 19 May 1536 while he waited for news that his wife Anne Boleyn had been executed.

☛ Go through the hotel's car park to find on the right:

5. EPPING FOREST CENTRE (Paul's Nursery Rd, High Beach IG10 4AF 🖉 020 8508 0028 ⊙ 10.00–15.00 Wed–Sun) Built on the site of Britain's first speedway track, the centre has a range of maps and guidebooks about the forest, and souvenirs made from local wood. Next door to it, the Epping Forest Field Studies Centre caters for groups, including families, and provides outdoor education programmes.

☞ After leaving the visitor centre, turn right into a path between signs for the Corporation of London and the City of London. This path takes you past a pond on your left; turn immediately right into a ride. Follow this for a while. After passing three paths off to the left, you will see another path to the left leading to a gate on to a road. (This is visible from the path you are on.) Take this path down to the road, which is Epping New Road. Cross the road and take the path immediately opposite. Follow this path ahead and round to the right to reach:

6. LOUGHTON CAMP Loughton Camp is one of two ancient earthworks in Epping Forest and may date from c300BC or earlier. It was used as an animal fold in times of attack, and as a boundary marker and lookout post between two tribes, the Trinovantes and the Catevellauni. It is one of the highest points of the forest.

While there are at least two other locations in the forest with the same claim, this may also have been the place where Dick Turpin had a hideout while on the run from the law. The infamous highwayman (1705–39) had a butchery business at Waltham Abbey, just two miles northwest of here. He used to steal cattle or deer grazing in the forest, and then sell the meat in his shop until he was caught and forced to go on the run. He became a burglar and highwayman, and lived for a while somewhere in the forest with another highway robber called Tom King, until they were captured by the law. Turpin was aiming to shoot one of the constables but hit and killed King instead, before escaping and riding on his horse Black Bess all the way to York, only to be hanged there for shooting a cock after confessing to a murder and several robberies.

Another highwayman to use the forest was John Rann (1750–74), better known as 'Sixteen String Jack' on account of the eight silk ribbons he wore on each of the knees of his breeches, representing one for each of his acquittals until he was finally hanged.

A more recent fugitive who took refuge in the forest was Harry Roberts (born 1936), who, in 1966, shot and killed two police detectives in Shepherd's Bush, west London. His accomplice killed a uniformed constable. Roberts, who had been trained in the army on how to survive in the wild, spent 3½ months in the forest before being captured. He was sentenced to life imprisonment with a minimum of 30 years. After he had served 48 years, making him one of the UK's longest-serving prisoners, the Parole Board approved his release in 2014.

☞ Continue along the path south from Loughton Camp, following the yellow waymark arrows. Eventually you will come to a wide path known as Green Ride. Turn right and follow this down to the junction with the road, which is Earl's Path. At the junction, continue into Forest Road till you reach the:

1 Connaught Water. **2** Queen Elizabeth's Hunting Lodge. **3** Fallow deer can be seen in Epping Forest.
4 The ancient earthwork of Loughton Camp. **5** Rare breed English longhorn cattle graze parts of the forest.
6 Lopping Hall.

7. VICTORIA TAVERN (🏠 165 Smarts Lane, Loughton IG10 4BP

⌀ thevictoriatavern.co.uk) A free house, the Victoria Tavern serves real ales including Timothy Taylor's Landlord and Sharp's Doom Bar. It describes itself as 'a nice place to sit and chat with friends'; there is 'no music, no televisions, no fruit machines'. The pub was built about 1868 as a beerhouse with extensive tea gardens and a field between Forest Road and Smarts Lane, which also housed visiting circuses and other entertainments for the thousands of visitors who came to Loughton by train to enjoy the forest. The field was sold in 1908 for housing.

☛ Return to Forest Road and turn right to continue down it. After a while on the right you will come to:

8. YE OLDE LOPPERS COTTAGE (56 Forest Rd, Loughton IG10 1EQ)

Until recently, a descendant of Thomas Willingale, the great defender of commoners' lopping rights in the forest against enclosure, lived here. She was Gwendoline Gatherclowe, Willingale's great-great-granddaughter. There are more details of his campaign at the next stop.

☛ Continue along Forest Road until you come to a staggered crossroads with High Road. Go ahead into Station Road and a few yards on the right is the back entrance (once the front entrance) to:

9. LOPPING HALL (187 High Rd, Loughton IG10 4LF) With its sculpted

terracotta relief of loppers, this is a pilgrimage spot to pause and thank the saviour of Epping Forest as we know it. Thomas Willingale (1798–1870) led the battle in the 1860s to stop the further enclosure of the forest and protect the lopping rights of commoners to collect firewood from trees in winter. His good deeds are commemorated by this hall, built in 1883.

The ancient rights of commoners to graze their cattle and other livestock, as well as lopping, were threatened in the 19th century by the lord of the manor, Rev John Whitaker Maitland. The not very reverend Rev enclosed for his private profit all the woodland in the parish (some 1,300 acres), using fencing to exclude the public, and began clearing the trees in preparation for converting the land into building plots. To protect their right of lopping (so the story goes), the commoners had to lop one branch at midnight on 11 November each year and present it to the lord of the manor. According to local legend, Maitland tried to prevent this one night by inviting all the commoners to a supper at the King's Head pub, getting them all drunk and locking them in before the midnight hour. Willingale, however, had kept his senses – and his axe, which he used to break out at 11.30pm. He supposedly ran up to nearby Staples Hill and, on the stroke of midnight, lopped off a branch and returned in triumph with it to the fuming Maitland.

It's a great story. What we do know for certain is that, on 11 November 1865, Willingale (with help from his son and nephews) broke down the fencing and resumed lopping as usual. Maitland took the family to court; Willingale's son and nephews were fined and imprisoned. Willingale then began lengthy legal action, with help from the Commons Society, attempting to get injunctions preventing further tree felling. In retaliation Maitland obtained a legal order ejecting Willingale from his cottage. Despite having difficulty finding a new home, and being refused work by many local landowners, Willingale persisted with his legal action. The case dragged on, allowing the Commons Society to prepare its case and the Corporation of London to get involved in action against the forest's lords of the manor. Eight years after Willingale's death, the Epping Forest Act of 1878 protected the forest from further enclosures. As the *Oxford Dictionary of National Biography* entry puts it, his 'sheer old-fashioned cussedness was later much embroidered and romanticized, but it was seminal in the open-space movement.'

The right to lopping was finally abolished on conservation grounds, but compensation was granted and was used to build this hall – a fine legacy for Willingale. His name also lives on locally through Willingale Road and Willingale School.

☛ Continue down Station Road to a roundabout at the bottom, the other side of which is Loughton tube station. You can also return to Chingford from here, via the 397 from bus stop C (15–20mins; 2 an hour).

8 THE CANAL, THE OLD RAILWAY & THE QUAKER

WILD FLOWERS, KINGFISHERS & A NOD TO WILLIAM PENN IN AN EXPEDITION ALONG THE GRAND UNION CANAL & EBURY WAY

We've carefully plotted this route to cover the most scenic aspects of this green swathe near Watford. On the way you'll pass three rivers – the Chess, the Gade and the Colne – and encounter two nature reserves (Croxley Common Moor and Lairage Land). There are satisfying stretches along the towpath of the Grand Union Canal as well as the Ebury Way, which is a disused railway track that acts as a green corridor for wildlife. And there's the opportunity to visit the home of William Penn (founder of Pennsylvania) and to see a stained-glass window by the Pre-Raphaelite artist Edward Burne-Jones.

Foraging and fishing could reap some pleasing rewards. Large carp and chub can be caught in the River Colne. There are plentiful rosehips, blackberries and (if you pick them while they're young, and use rubber gloves to do so) good standard edible nettles.

WHERE: Hertfordshire: Rickmansworth to Bushey
STATS: 7 miles; 2½–3hrs; easy
START POINT/GETTING THERE: Rickmansworth tube station (Metropolitan Line) /// rise.monks.film ⊖ To Rickmansworth; turn immediately right out of the station, past the bus stops
FINISH: Bushey railway station (London Overground) /// pin.stage.gets
DROP-OUT POINTS: After 3 miles & 4 miles

↑ The Grand Union Canal at Croxley. (Raf Pro/A)

MAPS: OS Explorer maps 172 & 173
TAKING A BREAK: The Pennsylvanian, Café@Lock 81, Tasty Bean Café, The Railway Arms

☞ After turning right out of the station, turn right again under the railway bridge (Station Road), then left into the High Street. On the right a short distance away is:

1. THE PENNSYLVANIAN (115 High St, Rickmansworth WD3 1AN
🖉 jdwetherspoon.com) This Wetherspoon pub has all the usual Wetherspoon real ales. It depicts on its sign a portrait of William Penn (page 69) and displays much information about him inside.

☞ Continue along the High Street. Just past the junction with Church Street turn left by the library to:

2. THREE RIVERS MUSEUM (Basing House, 46 High St, Rickmansworth
WD3 1RL 🖉 trmt.org.uk ⊙ 14.00–16.00 Wed–Fri, 10.00–14.00 Sat) William Penn (1644–1718), the Quaker who founded Pennsylvania, lived in this house from 1672 to 1677 after marrying local resident Gulielma Springett.

It was in his early twenties when he was in Cork, doing business on behalf of his father, that he became a Quaker and so was disowned by his family. A plaque outside the free museum describes him as a 'Quaker statesman and man of vision, founder of Pennsylvania and planner of Philadelphia, friend of the Indians, crusader for civil and religious liberty, designer of European peace.'

During his life in England, Penn was jailed several times for his beliefs. While incarcerated in the Tower of London he wrote a book, *No Cross, No Crown* (1669), arguing against organised religion and royalty and for religious toleration. The following year, he and a fellow preacher, William Meade, were arrested. A recently passed law forbade gatherings of more than five people for worship, unless it was a Church of England service. During the case, Penn and Meade received fines for refusing to remove their hats. The judge directed the jury to deliver a guilty verdict and, when they refused to do so, he locked them up in Newgate Prison until they changed their minds. Then he jailed Penn and Meade. A higher court, however, ordered their release and established the precedent that juries could deliver their own verdicts without being coerced by judges.

Penn wrote: 'True godliness doesn't turn men out of the world but enables them to live better in it, and excites their endeavours to mend it.' This comment has inspired Quakers ever since.

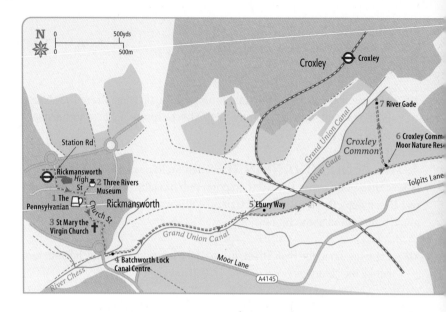

You can pick up leaflets in the museum about Penn and other famous people from the area, including Feargus O'Connor (1796–1855), who set up the nearby Chartist colony of O'Connorville (now Heronsgate) in 1847 which gave farm land to workers through a lottery. Apart from providing the opportunity to work for themselves this also gave them the vote (which at this time was only given to those who owned a significant amount of property). The authorities wound up the arrangement by Act of Parliament in 1851 and sold the freeholds by auction in 1857. The colony is commemorated by a pub in Heronsgate village called The Land of Liberty, Peace and Plenty (⌀ landoflibertypub.com).

Another notable resident commemorated in the museum is Dr Henderson (who, in addition to running his medical practice, started the local volunteer fire brigade). Look out also for Daisy the two-person manual vacuum cleaner from 1910, and a 17th-century wall painting from the old Bell Inn in Rickmansworth High Street.

☞ After coming out of the museum, turn right, go along the High Street and cross the road. Turn left into Church Street and soon you will reach:

3. ST MARY THE VIRGIN CHURCH (Church St, Rickmansworth WD3 1LB) This church is of medieval foundation, but was rebuilt in 1826 and again in 1890. In the early 16th century, parishioners angry at ecclesiastical malpractice caused serious damage. Cardinal Wolsey, who was living at the nearby Manor of the Moore (Moor Park) at the time, granted freedom from 100 days in Purgatory to anyone who gave their goods to aid the restoration. More recently, for many

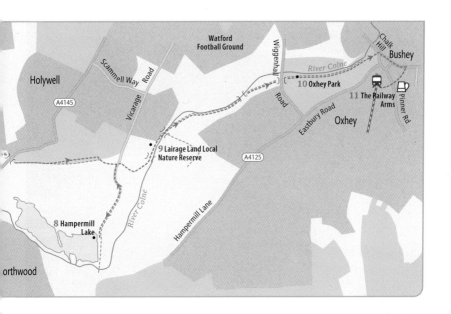

A MIGHTY PENN

In 1682 William Penn travelled with some fellow Quakers to the American colonies and settled by the Delaware river. This was land given to them by Charles II in payment of a debt to Penn's father – or so Penn claimed. His main motive was probably to secure a space where Quakers could live free from persecution. He wanted to call it Sylvania (meaning 'wooded place') but Charles insisted on 'Penn' being added to the name. Although the king had given them the land, Penn recognised it really belonged to the native Americans, so he insisted on paying them and signing a treaty with them. Voltaire later wryly observed that this was the only treaty that was 'never sworn to and never broken'.

Penn believed divine providence had provided them with the colony and so he had an obligation to make it into a model community. Laws were passed guaranteeing freedom of conscience and religious toleration. The capital, Philadelphia, was built and became known as 'the city of brotherly love'.

He returned to England for a while but fell out of favour in 1688 when William and Mary ousted James II (whom Penn had supported). Penn was accused of treason but not prosecuted. In 1699 he went back to Pennsylvania but mismanaged his finances, forcing him to sell his land, and before long he ended up in a debtors' prison. A group of supporters paid off his debts and he returned once more to England, where he suffered two strokes in 1712 which left him disabled for the rest of his life. He was buried in an unmarked grave at the Quaker cemetery in the village of Jordans, five miles west of Rickmansworth.

HELEN MATTHEWS

PETER FLEMING/S

PETER ARKELL

HELEN MATTHEWS

1 Walking the towpath beside the Grand Union Canal. **2** The Three Rivers Museum. **3** Stained-glass window by Edward Burne-Jones in St Mary the Virgin Church. **4** View over the River Gade.

years St Mary's was the subject of an unusual sharing arrangement between the Church of England and the Methodists.

At the east end of the church is a magnificent stained-glass window installed in 1896. It is by Pre-Raphaelite artist Edward Burne-Jones and depicts Christ hanging from the Tree of Life.

☛ After coming out of the church, turn right and go through the churchyard, which rejoins Church Street, and takes you to a roundabout. Go straight over it to Batchworth Bridge which crosses first the River Chess, which you can see over the wall to the left (it goes north to Chesham and merges into the River Colne to the south), then the Grand Union Canal. Take the steps on the left down to the river and the canal where on the left is:

4. BATCHWORTH LOCK CANAL CENTRE (99 Church St, Rickmansworth WD3 1JD ✆ 01923 778382 ⊘ rwt.org.uk ☺ Easter–Oct; call to check) You can pick up plenty of information leaflets in this fascinating little place, including some relevant to this walk, especially maps of the Ebury Way and Croxley Common Moor.

☛ Cross the short bridge over the river to the canal and follow the towpath. On the left is **Café@Lock 81** (⊘ rwt.org.uk), a traditional tea stall with a seating area overlooking the River Chess on one side and the canal on the other. There now follows a 10- to 15-minute walk alongside the canal where many colourful houseboats are moored. We spotted one with a cabin made from an old Volkswagen. Then you come to the first bridge, with a sign to 'Ebury Way' pointing left. Go up the steps, then turn right and cross over the bridge. You are now on:

5. EBURY WAY (DISUSED RAILWAY TRACK) The railway track between Rickmansworth and Watford was built by Lord Ebury in 1862, and carried passengers (until 1951) and freight until it finally closed altogether in 1981.

Running between the River Gade (north of the track to the left) and the River Colne (south to the right), lined by a variety of trees (notably ash, oak, apple and horse chestnut), the three-mile track is now reserved for cyclists and ramblers. Both rivers wander away from the track and are mostly not visible from it. But you have a chance to see the Gade soon in Croxley Common Moor, and the Colne during the last part of the walk.

☛ Shortly after going under a railway bridge, where you can see a graffiti portrait of George Michael, you will see on the left a nature reserve (fenced off at this stage). After a few minutes you come to the first entrance (through double kissing gates); the main entrance (signposted 'Public Footpath No 17') is a bit further along Ebury Way. You have now arrived at:

6. CROXLEY COMMON MOOR NATURE RESERVE

(croxleycommonmoor.org.uk) Designated as a Site of Special Scientific Interest and periodically used by model aircraft enthusiasts to fly their machines, this is a wonderfully unspoilt hundred-acre area of grassland within the floodplain of the River Gade. It is renowned for its wild flowers, with some 130 grassland species, as well as invertebrates and some rare insects. The considerable number of anthills support plants such as large thyme, and the ants themselves are food for green woodpeckers.

☛ A five-minute walk along the footpath through the moor takes you to the:

7. RIVER GADE Kingfishers are a common sight on its bank here, and numerous fish can be seen darting between the reeds. You may see egrets – there are a few.

✋ The bridge over the river ahead is the first drop-out point, for Croxley (Metropolitan Line) tube station.

☛ Otherwise return to Ebury Way and continue along it. After about 10–15 minutes you will come to a bridge under a road (Tolpits Lane).

✋ Two minutes later you will reach a path on the left signposted to Watford (Metropolitan Line) tube station.

☛ Otherwise continue straight ahead along Ebury Way. After a further 10 minutes you will come to a crossing of paths. On the left is a path to the bottom of Vicarage Road (home of Watford Football Club), and on the right is 'Public Footpath No 2' to Hampermill Lane, which is a detour to:

8. HAMPERMILL LAKE This is a haven for wildlife, especially birds such as great crested grebes, pochards, shovelers, tufted ducks, Canada geese, herons and swans. It has excellent views across the wide valley. The lake is owned by Merchant Taylors' public school so there is no right of access to it, but you can view the wildlife, including an abundance of common mallow and meadow brown butterflies, from the public path.

PAWEL NIEMCZYK/A

HELEN MATTHEWS

PETER ARKELL

1 Croxley Common Moor Nature Reserve at sunrise. **2** A portrait of George Michael marks the route beneath a railway bridge on the Ebury Way. **3** Cyclist on the Ebury Way.

☞ Retrace your steps to the crossroads and continue along Ebury Way. After about 2 minutes, a path on the left is signposted to:

9. LAIRAGE LAND LOCAL NATURE RESERVE Lairage means 'grazing land': these meadows and reedbeds attract abundant wildlife, including butterflies, damselflies, dragonflies, and green and great spotted woodpeckers, and are home to masses of yellow water lilies. Go quietly and you may spot a fox, as we did. The path off Ebury Way leads to a kissing gate on the right, then a bridge over a stream to the nature reserve. The River Colne and marshland prevent you from returning to Ebury Way at the far end, so after you have wandered around you will have to retrace your steps.

☞ Back on the Ebury Way, continue across several bridges, and past the Riverside Recreation Ground, until you reach Wiggenhall Road, which you cross to enter:

10. OXHEY PARK (⏁ oxheyactivitypark.co.uk) This park comprises approximately 34 acres of wooded parkland with a wooded dell and grassy slopes, and contains kingfishers, blue tits, chaffinches, coots, woodpeckers and ducks; trees include poplars and willows. It has won a Green Flag Award and was voted one of the UK's ten favourite parks in 2022. The family-friendly **Tasty Bean Café** (⏁ tastybean.co.uk) is here, too.

☞ On the right side of the park, walk parallel to Eastbury Road (A4125). When you reach a roundabout, turn right on to Chalk Hill, then right again into Aldenham Road. As you approach the railway station, look on the opposite side of the road for:

11. THE RAILWAY ARMS (🏛 1 Aldenham Rd, Bushey WD19 4AB ⏁ railwayarmsbushey.com) This pub has a good selection of cask ales including Abbot Ale, Timothy Taylor's and Greene King IPA.

☞ At Bushey station, go to Platform 2 to use your Freedom Pass on the London Overground (43mins to Euston, 3 an hour). Faster mainline trains to Euston (about 20mins) stop here but the Freedom Pass is not valid on them (although you can pay a small charge to take you to the valid zone).

→ A sculpture of a monk in the grounds of Lesnes Abbey. (Helen Matthews)

9 HOLLY, IVY & CHESTNUTS

PAST A STRIKING MONASTIC RUIN, THROUGH WOODLANDS & ACROSS A HEATH PATROLLED BY BIRDS OF PREY

If you like roast chestnuts with your Christmas feast the woodland here is the place to get them, as well as holly and ivy for the decorations. When we went in October the sweet chestnut shells were seemingly everywhere on the ground. You may also find some of the largest mushrooms and toadstools (at least a foot tall) you have ever seen. Apart from the holly and ivy there are also various berries and wild flowers and you may well spot kestrels or hear the tapping of green woodpeckers. You can also linger in the ruins of a monastery that owed its creation to a famous murder.

WHERE: Southeast London: Lesnes Abbey Wood, circular
STATS: 4 miles; 1½–2hrs; easy except for two quite steep climbs of about 200 & 350 paces
START POINT/GETTING THERE: Abbey Wood railway station /// deny.test.mount
⊖ To Abbey Wood (Elizabeth Line); or 🚌 Abbey Wood from Charing Cross, Waterloo East or London Bridge (30–35mins; 2 an hour). Arriving by either train or tube, go out of the station, cross the road & turn right along Harrow Manorway.
DROP-OUT POINT: After 2 miles
MAP: OS Explorer map 162
TAKING A BREAK: Chestnuts Kiosk, Abbey Arms

☛ After a short distance walking along Harrow Manorway, you will reach an ornamental gateway to Lesnes Abbey Wood on the left. Go through, but instead of following the path ahead, turn right and continue uphill and parallel to the road for a short distance until you reach the:

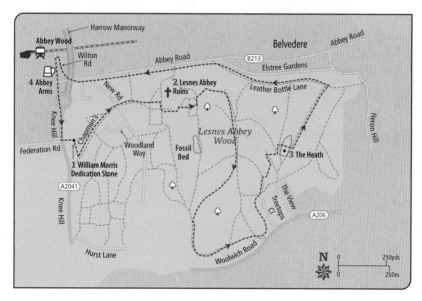

1. WILLIAM MORRIS DEDICATION STONE The socialist poet, designer and craftsman William Morris (1834–96) passed this spot regularly in the 1860s when walking between Abbey Wood station and his home, Red House in Red House Lane in Bexleyheath, about three miles away.

To visit Red House, now managed by the National Trust, you can take the B11 bus from opposite Abbey Wood station towards Bexleyheath, getting off at the Upton Road/Broadway stop (18mins) and then walking (5–10mins).

☞ Turn left on to a footpath and continue uphill a short distance. When you reach a waymark post with a black arrow and a white background, turn left and continue to follow the path downhill. When you reach New Road, cross it. Ahead is an entrance to Lesnes Abbey Woods. On your right you will pass a tree carved into a statue of a monk then reach **Chestnuts Kiosk** (⌀ lesnesabbeywoods.org), which serves hot and cold drinks and snacks. To the right is the Monks' Garden and to the left are:

2. LESNES ABBEY RUINS (⌀ lesnesabbeywoods.org) The abbey which once stood here owed its creation to one of the most notorious murders in English history. Henry II appointed Thomas Becket as Archbishop of Canterbury to increase his own influence over the Church, only for Becket to defend religious power with a fierceness that would lead to his death. Henry and his senior officials, including Richard de Luci (1089–1179) who was Sheriff of Essex, strove to make clerics who committed crimes liable for punishment by secular authorities, rather than by the Church. Becket resisted their efforts, excommunicating the king, his bishops and his advisors including de Luci. Henry's reputed exasperation ('Will no one rid me of this turbulent priest?') led four knights to go to Canterbury Cathedral where they killed Becket on 29 December 1170. Within three years Becket had become revered as a martyr across Europe, and the Pope canonised him. Henry eventually backed down, performing penance and confirming the supremacy of Pope over King in Church matters.

De Luci, who was Henry's Chief Justiciar (in effect running the country when the king was abroad), came to regret his involvement in the dispute. He built Lesnes Abbey in 1178 as his own form of penance – and as somewhere he could receive care and hospitality as his life neared its end. After his death, and burial in the grounds, the abbey endured eight centuries of fluctuating fortunes, including dissolution under Henry VIII, before Bexley Council took it over in 1986.

Today the abbey ruins lie before you, from the remains of the church and chapter house to the dormitory, refectory and brewing house. It's a pleasant place in which to linger and imagine monastic life in medieval England. A plaque in one of the chapels marks the burial of the heart of Roesia de Dover, who inherited

HELEN MATTHEWS

JOHN GOMEZ/S

HELEN MATTHEWS

PETER ARKELL

Si Je Puis

WILLIAM MORRIS
1834 - 1896
CRAFTSMAN, DESIGNER, POET, SOCIALIST

He lived at Red House, Bexley Heath,
from 1860 to 1865
and passed this spot regularly
to and from Abbey Wood Station

BEXLEY CIVIC SOCIETY
MILLENNIUM YEAR

1 The ruins of Lesnes Abbey. **2** The Monks' Garden, Lesnes Abbey. **3** The William Morris dedication stone. **4** A wooden sculpture marks the fossil beds at Lesnes.

the estate some years after Richard de Luci's death. She married an illegitimate son of King John and fought hard to retain her part of the estate as her husband racked up debts, selling off land to repay creditors. The ghost of Roesia is one of three spirits which, according to legend, haunt the ruins; the others represent a horseman and a monk who was murdered after being caught in a compromising position with a woman.

Major restoration works in 2018 included the creation (or recreation) of the Monks' Garden. Here the monks grew herbs to assist their healing work in the infirmary, such as sage (for getting rid of pestilence), hyssop (for treating chest infections and bruises) and cumin (for eye and skin problems). There is an old mulberry tree north of the ruins. This very old tree is said to have been commissioned by James I, who wanted to set up his own English silk industry. However, the trees that the king was sold were the wrong type of mulberries (black, not white).

☛ Follow the path round to the left past the ruins and uphill to the Viewpoint, from which you can see the Shard and other notable modern London buildings. On the Viewpoint's framework of window arches, designed by a local metalsmith, is a poem written by members of the local community. Shortly afterwards, turn right. When you see a waymark sign, follow the arrow pointing straight ahead to 'The Heathland'. Continue ahead, and after a while you will see a sign indicating the fossil beds to your right, along with a wooden sculpture of a prehistoric creature. Metal discs in the ground show designs depicting fossils. The fossil pit is a designated Site of Special Scientific Interest. Digging for fossils is permitted within a fenced area, provided you follow the rules on the noticeboard. You may find sharks' teeth and shells.

Continue ahead along the path (don't turn off along the Green Chain Walk). You will see holly trees either side. After a while the path will curve around to the left, with fenced back gardens to your right. Eventually you will reach some steps on your right leading to a metal gateway.

✋ If you want to end the walk here, go up the steps and turn left to find the bus stop for buses towards Erith, from where trains to London Liverpool Street or Cannon Street take 30–35 minutes.

☛ Otherwise, turn left down a path. Ignore the steps going uphill to your right and continue to follow the path as it goes steeply downhill and slightly left. In autumn, take care not to slip on the many sweet chestnuts on the ground. At the bottom, turn right. After a short distance you will see the fenced-off Chalk Pit or quarry to your left. This quarry provided chalk for various purposes including the production of lime. Continue ahead until you reach a crossing of paths, signposted 'Green Chain Walk'. Turn right and follow the path uphill to reach:

3. THE HEATH

This was common grazing land for ponies, cattle and sheep for many centuries, between the marshes of Woolwich, Erith and Bexley. In those days, heather turfs were cut for fuel, fodder and livestock bedding. The open heath is now a favourite spot for birds of prey.

☛ Continue following the Green Chain Walk signs around the site of the excavation of a Bronze Age burial mound or tumulus and continue along the path until you exit on to Leather Bottle Lane (named after a nearby pub, now sadly demolished). Turn left and continue along Leather Bottle Lane. After passing a playground on the left, turn left into Abbey Road. Continue along Abbey Road, head under the flyover and turn right into Wilton Road. At the end of the road opposite some stairs leading to the station is the:

4. ABBEY ARMS (31 Wilton Rd, Abbey Wood SE2 9RH abbeyarmsse2)

This family-friendly pub, popular for its pizzas, has had three makeovers in the past decade; there's a large garden at the back.

10 A RACING CERTAINTY

VARIATIONS ON AN EQUESTRIAN THEME, WITH A WANDER PAST THE DERBY COURSE & A CHANCE TO GO RIDING

P retty much everything on this walk is related to the art of racing and training horses. You'll see the historic course where the famous Derby has been run since 1780, and – even if there's no race in progress – racehorses can be seen training from early morning to noon on any of the three sand gallops laid out on the side of the downs. They make a spectacular sight. And you get a decent view of the racecourse from the featured pub. The scenery opens up to magnificent views of the rolling countryside, which is made full use of by leisure riders and dog walkers.

↑ Epsom Downs racecourse. (Greg Balfour Evans/A)

WHERE: Surrey: Epsom Downs
STATS: 6 miles/3hrs; easy–moderate
START POINT/GETTING THERE: Epsom Downs station /// leaves.pens.intent 🚆 To Epsom Downs station from London Victoria (38mins–1hr; 4 an hour); turn right out of station into Bunbury Way.
FINISH: Tattenham Corner station /// score.limp.couch
DROP-OUT POINT: After 5½ miles
MAP: OS Explorer map 146
TAKING A BREAK: Tattenham Corner

☞ Continue along Bunbury Way, which is quite a long cul-de-sac with a couple of mini-roundabouts, for about six or seven minutes. The road name is almost certainly a reference to Sir Charles Bunbury, who tossed a coin with Lord Derby to decide the name of a new race that Lord Derby started at Epsom in 1780 for three-year-old horses. The Derby was nearly called the Bunbury! At the end is Longdown Lane South where you cross to the other side and turn left into a public bridleway (signposted with blue arrows) round the edge of a golf course. The path crosses one of the tees, so beware of low-flying golf balls. When you come to a road (Burgh Heath Road) cross it and continue following the bridleway round the golf course, coming to a roundabout where you turn right on to Grandstand Road. You will see the Epsom Racecourse Grandstand ahead. When you reach a roundabout, there is a pub on the right called the Derby Arms (established 1875). Directly opposite is:

1. EPSOM DOWNS RACECOURSE (KT18 5LQ ⊘ thejockeyclub.co.uk/Epsom) Epsom's early claim to fame was the chance 17th-century discovery of the health-giving properties of the local waters (hence the product known as 'Epsom salts'). Horseracing was a well-established activity here by then. Cromwell's regime banned horseracing, but the first post-Restoration race meeting took place at Epsom in 1661. Meetings became a regular Epsom feature in subsequent years and, more than 200 years after Lord Derby's successful coin toss (see above), the Derby is one of the world's most famous equestrian events.

The racecourse's entrance gates have medallions featuring famous Derby winners Mill Reef and Hyperion. Access within is for ticket-holders only, though the staff are extremely helpful if you get lost. In any case, you're about to get unbeatable views of the course and grandstand.

☞ Continue along the road past the grandstand then turn left along a public footpath. Follow the path round the track to the front of the Rubbing House pub, and turn left into the downs by a noticeboard proclaiming 'Welcome to Epsom and Walton Downs' and warning you that racehorses train there (🕐 06.00–noon Mon–Sat, 08.00–09.30 Sun), and that it is dangerous to get too close to them. If you have a dog with you, please keep it on a lead.

When the path forks, go to the right for a short gradual climb which takes you over the racetrack and past another warning notice about racehorses travelling at speed in the mornings.

Follow the path down the other side, over two more gallops and a track, into Walton Downs ahead. Keep going ahead over another gallop until you reach white railings over the track and the far edge of the Downs. Follow the track ahead which goes slightly uphill for a long way through fields and hedgerows, and widens into a lane (Ebbisham Lane). You're passing through Langley Vale Wood, the Woodland Trust's World War I Centenary Wood for

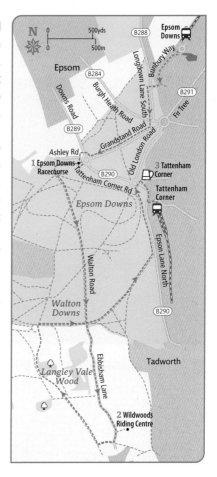

England, which commemorates the contribution of various communities to the war effort. The Walton and Tadworth end of the site hosted military training and there were trenches, a rifle range, a gas training school and a camp. The Trust bought the land in 2014. The wood, which comprises 640 acres of previously farmed land, is a mix of ancient woodland, arable fields, chalk grassland and created woodland. It is home to the nationally rare red hemp nettle, five types of bat, over 30 butterfly species and more than 80 species of bird.

This route takes you eventually past Downsview Farm and then Wingfield Farm, both on the right, and then on the left is:

2. WILDWOODS RIDING CENTRE (Ebbisham Lane, Walton-on-the-Hill, Tadworth KT20 5BH ✎ wildwoodsriding.co.uk) 'Picnic rides' (🕐 from

WENN RIGHTS LTD/A

NEIL MATTHEWS

HELEN MATTHEWS

PT PICTURES/S

1 & **3** Langley Vale Wood is a mix of ancient woodland, arable fields, chalk grasslands and created woods; it's home to the nationally rare red hemp nettle. **2** The gates at Epsom Downs pay tribute to former greats. **4** Enjoy the view from this appropriately themed bench.

11.00 Tue–Fri, prebooking required) are a speciality. Anthea, who runs the centre, started at the age of 12, working at Ewell Riding Stables in return for rides. She also worked at other jobs to save enough to buy her first pony at the age of 14, which was stabled in her back garden. She started the school here at 17, now has over 25 horses and ponies, and gives riding lessons at all levels. Her mother has written a book about the centre, *Legs! Legs! Legs!*, under the name Justine Dowley-Wise.

☛ Continue along the lane a few yards and turn right through a gap in the hedge and over a stile with a yellow-arrowed 'Public Footpath' sign. This takes you through a paddock, and over another stile to the left, into a public bridleway where you turn right and go downhill. This goes between more paddocks, trees and hedgerows, and becomes a chalk path with rosehips, old man's beard and deadly nightshade bushes either side. Hazelnuts and crab apples can also be found in season, along with blackberries and sloes. On this part of the walk, you are once again passing through Langley Vale Wood. The bridleway continues downhill through arable fields, thickets, holly bushes and woods, until there is a cottage at the bottom on the left. A few yards further along, on the right, you are back on the downs. Turn right and follow the edge by the gallops for a mile or so, bearing left. You can pause on a bench with horse motifs and admire the many butterflies, before continuing to Epsom Lane North on the right. Turn left along Epsom Lane North into Tattenham Corner Road.

✋ Turn right into Tattenham Crescent for shops, cafés and the railway station, or continue to the:

3. TATTENHAM CORNER (Epsom Downs, Epsom KT18 5NY
⌂ tattenhamcornerpub.co.uk) This large pub, overlooking the race track, has been recently bought by Young's which, at the time of writing, was refurbishing it for reopening in late 2024.

☛ After coming out of the pub, retrace your steps to Tattenham Corner station for a train to East Croydon or London Bridge.

11 HAPPY VALLEY

VINTAGE SURREY DOWNLAND, & A VISIT TO A SAXON CHURCH WITH AN ASTONISHINGLY SPOOKY MEDIEVAL WALL PAINTING

You couldn't be much closer to Croydon, but this walk on the North Downs is remarkably rural in character, and was a favourite stamping ground of the novelist DH Lawrence. Happy Valley is indeed a feel-good patch of land, comprising downland and ancient woodland acquired by the local authority under the Green Belt Scheme back in 1937, and evidently saved from the developer's bulldozer in the nick of time when so much of London's fringes had succumbed to suburbanisation. When it snows, it's a veritably happy valley for children as the steep grass slopes become ideal toboggan runs. Farthing Downs, purchased by the Corporation of London in 1883, adjoins it and has many of the same qualities. Despite both areas' municipal ownership, they are very much managed as open countryside.

Two historical bonuses come in the form of an exceptional Saxon church with a remarkable wall painting, and a 300-year-old pub.

WHERE: Surrey, North Downs: Coulsdon Common, circular
STATS: 6½ miles/2½–3hrs; easy except for two short, steep climbs
START POINT/GETTING THERE: Coulsdon South station /// cook.lung.snows 🚌 To Coulsdon South station from London Bridge (24–27mins; 4 an hour) direct, or from London Victoria changing at East Croydon (25–30mins; 4 an hour, 2 an hour on Sun). Take Farthing Downs exit from Platform 2 of the station.
DROP-OUT POINT: After 3½ miles
MAP: OS Explorer map 146
TAKING A BREAK: The Fox

👉 Turn left from the 'Farthing Downs' exit into Reddown Road. When you reach the end turn right (Marlpit Lane) and immediately right into Downs Road. After a few yards bear left off the road and into:

1. FARTHING DOWNS

Stone Age hunters, Iron Age farmers and Saxon warriors all roamed this 235-acre area. There are low banks where fields were ploughed 2,000 years ago, and circular mounds of 7th-century Saxon graves. Novelist DH Lawrence and his friend Helen Corke also rambled on these downs in 1911 when they were both teachers in Croydon. She likened them to 'the smooth, rounded back of a huge animal' which they walked along 'in mutual isolation from humankind'. During World War II, anti-glider ditches were dug to prevent enemy invaders landing by glider. You may still glimpse these ditches today.

Sussex cattle graze with sheep all year round to enable wildlife to flourish on the chalk downland and keep invasive scrub at bay; dogs must be kept under control, and on certain bridleways walkers are asked to give way to horseriders. There's also a burgeoning deer population, which has trebled in recent years.

← Coulsdon's Church of St Peter & St Paul. (Neil Matthews)

The chalk grassland supports a wide range of plants (including pyramidal orchids and dropwort), insects (including half of all English butterfly species, and ants which make nests up to three feet tall), birds, lizards and slow-worms; look out, too, for skylarks in summer. Information boards around the site give the details.

☛ Take the footpath which forks left going slightly uphill. When you reach the top of the hill you will see seven trees in a circle. This is:

2. THE FOLLY
First named 'the Folly' on a 1783 map, this circle of seven beech trees marks the highest point on the Farthing Downs (600ft above sea level). Nowadays only one of the original trees remains, several replacements having been planted. A signpost points to Coulsdon to the north, Purley to the east, Hooley to the west and Chaldon to the south. Interpretation boards explain the 4,000-year history of the Farthing Downs landscape, which includes a group of Saxon burial mounds to the south.

☛ Just past The Folly, a few yards to the left of the footpath is the:

3. MILLENNIUM CAIRN
This flint cairn was constructed by volunteers in September 2000. A plaque on the top reveals that the church in Chaldon is 2.53km (1.57 miles) ahead, Happy Valley is 0.79km (half a mile) to the left and The Folly is all of 0.04km (131ft) behind you. It also identifies other places you can see.

☛ Continue along the footpath. At Farthing Downs Car Park there is a circular seating arrangement, with more interpretation boards, where you can pause before turning left down a grassy path with Farthing Downs cottages on the right, and then right where the path is signposted 'Public Footpath 71 Happy Valley' and also 'Downlands Circular Walk' and 'London Loop'. Later, bear left to Happy Valley, then follow the 'Permissive Path, Chaldon Church, 1 mile'. Bear right round the edge of fields (not straight on through the middle) alongside woods, through a gap to the right into the woods, and left to 'Public Footpath, Chaldon Church, 1 mile', into fields, then right into woods again at the 'Public Footpath, Chaldon Church ½ mile' sign. This takes you through fields into a lane. Turn left and after a few yards bear right to:

4. ST PETER & ST PAUL'S CHURCH
(Church Lane, Chaldon CR3 5AL ⓐ chaldonchurch.co.uk) The Saxon foundation of this restored church was recorded as being there in AD727, and the present building was started in the late 10th or early 11th century. The remarkable feature here is the stupendous wall painting on the west wall, dating from about 1200, and surely guaranteed to

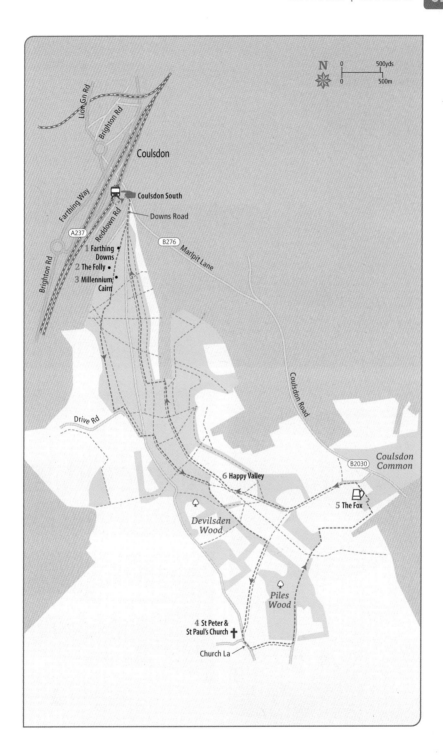

SS

HELEN MATTHEWS

PETER ARKELL

PETER ARKELL

1 Happy Valley. **2** The Millennium Cairn on Farthing Downs. **3** The astonishing wall painting in St Peter & St Paul's Church. **4** Sledging at Happy Valley.

put the holy wind up the medieval congregation; there is nothing else like it in England. It depicts the 'Ladder of Salvation of the Human Soul' with 'Purgatory and Hell' and was painted by a travelling artist monk. Sinners being punished include a blacksmith making a horseshoe without an anvil, a mason without a chisel, a potter without a wheel and a usurer held by pitchforks in flames by demons. Other demons are encouraging a couple to surrender to lust. But there are also gates for the righteous to enter.

The pulpit of 1657 is one of the few surviving from the time of Cromwell. Plaques commemorating local names include one on the west wall for Lt Col William Edward Shaw, a churchwarden who served in the Indian Mutiny of 1857–59 and died in 1900.

The closed circuit television seems incongruous in such an ancient church, but increased security proved necessary after a 750-year-old bell was stolen in 1970 for scrap metal. A plaster cast of it stands in the south aisle.

☞ Turn left out of the church back to the lane, then turn right and immediately turn left into the public footpath signposted to 'Piles Wood'. This takes you through a field and soon between woods on the left bordered by a long and high holly hedge and horses on the right. Follow this when it goes left into a track between gardens on the right and woods on the left. Follow it ahead into woods, signposted 'Public Bridleway, Happy Valley'. At the next fork bear right, following a 'Downland Circular Walk' arrow. At a crossing of paths continue ahead following the public bridleway signposted 'Coulsdon Common ¼ mile'. This takes you up a steepish hill for a short climb and emerges into a lane. Go through a kissing gate a few yards on the left by a 'Coulsdon Common' noticeboard. Take the grass track which forks to the left, then after a short distance go through a kissing gate on the right. This takes you to a village green. Turn left and on the left is:

5. THE FOX (Coulsdon Common, Caterham CR3 5QS ⊘ vintageinn.co.uk/thefoxcoulsdoncommon) This pub dates back to 1720 and has a log fire for winter and a beer garden for the summer (or for frozen smokers). It offers hot meals and real ales including Fuller's London Pride and Young's, plus guests including Sharp's Doom Bar. Dogs (on a lead) and children are allowed, and there is an old anvil outside to which to tie them (the dogs, not the children).

A plaque on the pub wall reveals that this was the site of the Joint Services School for Linguistics listening post for covert national security work from 1952 to 1954. The plaque erected in 2007 states that the linguists at Coulsdon Common Camp were 'trained for covert work, their vigilance contributing to national Security during the Cold War'.

✋ If you want to finish the walk here, turn right out of the pub and cross the village green to a bus stop for the 404 to Coulsdon South station (18mins; 1 an hour) or the 466 to Purley Oaks station (20mins; 4 an hour) or East Croydon station (35mins; 4 an hour).

☞ To continue the walk turn left out of the pub to the public footpath signposted 'Farthing Downs' as well as 'London Loop' and 'Happy Valley', taking you naturally to:

6. HAPPY VALLEY

This ancient woodland and downland grass area is designated a Site of Special Scientific Interest and is run by Croydon Council. A notice tells us that coppicing of the trees since 2001 has helped to dramatically increase the number of butterflies (and led to the return of the silver-washed fritillary), and to preserve dormice which are now rare and a protected species. The coppicing allows light to reach the woodland floor, which helps bluebells and other plants to flourish, creating glades for butterflies and other insects and an ideal habitat for birds and small mammals. This takes place on a 15-year-rotation basis. After the cutting, temporary fencing is erected to deter deer from eating the hazel as it grows.

☞ Follow the path which becomes arrowed 'Downland Circular Walk' again. The path comes out into open fields with a sign 'Public Footpath, Farthing Downs ¾ mile'. A little further on is a public footpath sign 'Drive Road ½ mile'. Go down the hill (very popular with sledges and toboggans in the snow). At the bottom, fork right along the flat. At a crossing of paths, follow the path ahead signposted 'Chaldon Way 260 yards' and through a kissing gate. Just before you reach the houses ahead, turn left up the hill, which is steep for a short distance, through another kissing gate, and through woods a few yards to another gate on the right which takes you back into Farthing Downs. Follow the footpath ahead uphill.

Near the top of the hill turn right along a bridleway just before the narrow road which runs parallel with it. The bridleway becomes marked with red arrows for the 'Happy Valley & Farthing Downs Nature Trail' and the green arrows of 'Corporation of London Permissive Ride'.

This takes you through a gate and back to Downs Road. You can turn into Reddown Road and then turn right, back to Coulsdon South station.

12 A TRAIL OF TWO FORTS

EXPANSIVE SKIES ABOVE THE ESTUARY-SIDE PATH

With the salty whiff of the Thames estuary to accompany you, this is a breezy, cobweb-blowing walk along the river, and beside the Essex marshes – a desolate landscape reminiscent of Pip's first encounter with the convict in *Great Expectations*, and of the opening scene of *Heart of Darkness*. This is certainly a walk for those seeking solitude, passing as it does a derelict power station and with views of shipping across to the Kent side. Seals make regular appearances in the water – a survey by the Zoological Society of London recorded over 700 grey and harbour seal sightings hereabouts. At either end are the two imposing forts, presented in very different style. Tilbury Fort, admirably maintained by English Heritage, is a fascinating journey back through time, in a building that began in Henry VIII's day and played a role in both World Wars. In contrast, Coalhouse Fort is a volunteer-run labour of love, well worth catching if you can.

WHERE: Essex, River Thames: Tilbury Riverside Terminal to Coalhouse Fort Park
STATS: 3½–4 miles/1½–2hrs; easy
START POINT/GETTING THERE: Tilbury Riverside Terminal /// dish.smiled.agreed
🚌 To Tilbury Town station from Rainham, Essex (26mins, change at Grays; 2 an hour; NB: This is not covered by the Freedom Pass). Then 🚌 99 from the station to Tilbury Riverside station (10mins; 2 an hour). The Riverside Terminal is adjacent to the station.
FINISH: Coalhouse Fort Park /// detect.force.monday
MAPS: OS Explorer maps 162 & 163
TAKING A BREAK: The Worlds End, Coalhouse Fort Park

↑ Coalhouse Fort marks the end of this walk. (Helen Matthews)

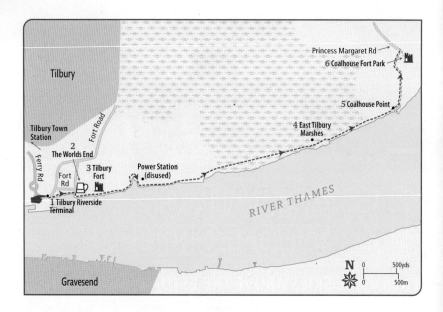

1. TILBURY RIVERSIDE TERMINAL

Nearly 500 West Indian immigrants landed at Tilbury on 22 June 1948 from the ship *Empire Windrush*. This historic occasion was illustrated by now-famous photographs of the newcomers walking down the gangplank; we also know that there was some hostility to their arrival. The ship had been on its way from Australia to England when it docked in Kingston, Jamaica, to pick up several locals who had fought in the RAF during World War II. An advert offered a fare of £46 to those who wanted to work in England and many took up the offer, including calypso star Lord Kitchener. Cy Grant was another; having been a prisoner of war in Germany, he was a fully qualified lawyer but had to perform as a calypso musician to earn a living in London. The footbridge from the ferry features an art installation, *Walkway of Memories* by Eve Wright, telling the stories of some more of those who arrived here in 1948.

☛ Turn right out of the ferry terminal, following signs to:

2. THE WORLDS END

(Fort Rd, Tilbury RM18 7NR ♂ twe.pub) A historic timbered pub with a real fire, The Worlds End is designed in the style of a ship's hold. Samuel Pepys (1633–1703) visited a tavern on this site in 1660 and wrote about it in his famous diary. He was on his way to Holland to help bring Charles II back to England and restore the monarchy. Charles II did not reward his loyalty and Pepys was locked up in the Tower in 1679 for treason and piracy before the charges were dropped. During Pepys' lifetime the Dutch made further raids on this area, and he lived to see William III of Orange and his wife Mary take the throne.

There are some allusions to Pepys in the pub, with a quotation on one wall from his diary giving his reaction to the outbreak of the Great Fire of London. Real ales on offer include Abbot and Sharp's Doom Bar, and the chicken curry is good.

☞ Leaving the pub, continue along the path and turn left through a kissing gate for:

3. TILBURY FORT (Tilbury RM18 7NR ✆ 0370 333 1181; English Heritage ◷ Apr–Oct Wed–Sun; Nov–Mar Sat & Sun; for hours see EH website £ 💰) In 1539 Henry VIII built a blockhouse (known originally as Thermitage Bulwark) here, with a rampart and ditches, to defend against a French invasion. The fort was rebuilt and strengthened with new ditches and ramparts from 1670 to 1685 by workers from Essex and Kent. From around 1716 it was used to store and supply gunpowder, with a special wharf being constructed for that purpose; by 1830 it could store over 19,000 barrels of gunpowder.

After the defeat of Bonnie Prince Charlie at Culloden in 1746, more than 300 Jacobite prisoners were rounded up and shipped here from Inverness. But 57 died en route from starvation and disease, and within a month of arrival another 45 died of typhus. The survivors were tried in London in 1747. Some were executed, but most were transported to Barbados and Antigua to be used as slave labour on sugar plantations. A memorial stone to their suffering is in the river wall outside the Water Gate.

As battleships took over the role of defending the estuary early in the 20th century, the fort became a barracks for soldiers on their way to the front in World War I. It was also used for storing explosives and ammunition. When air raids

TILBURY FORT & THE ARMADA

On 9 August 1588 Elizabeth I made what is perhaps her most quoted speech at Tilbury Fort, addressing her makeshift 'Citizen Militia' army in advance of their battle against the Spanish. Wearing a breastplate and sword, she told the troops that she was 'resolved, in the midst and heat of the battle, to live or die amongst you all; to lay down for my God, and for my kingdom, and my people, my honour and my blood, even in the dust. I know I have the body of a weak and feeble woman; but I have the heart and stomach of a king, and of a king of England too, and think foul scorn that Parma or Spain, or any prince of Europe, should dare to invade the borders of my realm: to which rather than any dishonour should grow by me, I myself will take up arms.' A few days later news reached Tilbury that the Armada had been beaten and was retreating in flight. The army was disbanded on 17 August.

by German Zeppelins started in 1915 the fort was equipped with anti-aircraft guns and searchlights, and was soon known as 'Screaming Lizzie'.

During World War II the building became an anti-aircraft operations room, directing fire from guns along the river against German bombing raids, but some of the barracks still suffered from bombing. To prevent enemy troops being dropped, a series of trenches were dug in the surrounding marshland.

The army kept Tilbury Fort until 1950 when the Ministry of Works took it over as a historic monument. Major restoration work was carried out in the 1970s. It was opened to the public in 1982 and is now cared for by English Heritage.

Highlights of a visit include one of the oldest surviving chapels to have been built in an artillery fortress. An exhibition in the East Magazine explains how gunpowder was stored as well as the history of the fort. You can also explore the Magazine passages. Hot drinks are available in the ticket office/gift shop.

☞ Leaving the fort, go up the steps immediately in front of the impressive Water Gate; this takes you on to the Two Forts Way, which features several interpretation boards. Turn left and continue past the fort. After passing horses grazing by the moat of the fort you will come to the wall around Tilbury Power Station. This is labelled as 'Footpath 146', which you follow to the right around the wall by the river, past blackberry bushes, teasel, thistles and rosehip bushes. Note that this path is underwater at high tide and may be slippery at other times. Continue past more beaches and keep to the river, ignoring any tracks off to the left (especially where there are warnings of quicksand). On the left, fenced off, are:

4. EAST TILBURY MARSHES These are a favourite with migrant wading birds, hawks, kestrels and other birdlife as well as hosts of rabbits.

☞ As you continue along the riverside, the fence around the marshes gives way to farmland and more rabbits. This is good foraging territory in August, especially for blackberries and sloes. Common blue, large white and gatekeeper butterflies are your constant companions. Eventually you will reach:

5. COALHOUSE POINT (East Tilbury RM18 8QD) This area of the foreshore has Scheduled Ancient Monument status. The invading army of Emperor Claudius is believed to have crossed the Thames at East Tilbury in AD43 during his conquest of Britain, and recent research suggests Julius Caesar may also have crossed here in 54BC. The remains of a Romano-British settlement from the 1st to 2nd centuries AD were discovered about a mile away. In medieval times East Tilbury to Higham

1 Aerial view of Tilbury Fort. **2** Coastal path on East Tilbury Marshes. **3** Tributes to Samuel Pepys at the Worlds End pub. **4** A display at Coalhouse Fort.

was a popular crossing point for pilgrims en route to Canterbury, and a hermitage or hospice was situated here until the Dissolution of the Monasteries, when Henry VIII chose to use the site for a small artillery fort. There has been a timber jetty here since the Middle Ages and in the 18th century there was a coal wharf, which gave the nearby fort its name. During World War II the jetty was protected by a Lewis gun. Much of the saltmarsh and foreshore is protected as a wetland site of international importance and special protection area for the habitat of migratory birds. In autumn and winter you may see avocet, black-tailed godwit and dunlin; curlew and oystercatcher are visible throughout the year.

☞ Follow the tarmac path away from the river to:

6. COALHOUSE FORT PARK (Princess Margaret Rd, East Tilbury RM18 8PB ᎞ thurrock.gov.uk/coalhouse-fort-park) The fort here was built between 1862 and 1874 to combat the threat of an invasion from France. It was one of many built following Prime Minister Lord Palmerston's Royal Commission to review Britain's defences. During World War II the fort was designated as an anti-invasion emergency gun battery and also housed a minefield control tower or XDO post which was responsible for an electronically controlled minefield aimed at preventing enemy vessels travelling up the Thames. The surrounding public park provides interpretation boards, trails and the old radar tower. There are plenty of benches for picnicking, and refreshments available in the **Engine Room Café** (10.00–16.00 daily), which also has a timeline of the fort and memorabilia.

☞ You can end the walk here, taking the 374 bus from the car park for a 25-minute journey to Grays rail and bus station. (The bus also stops at the Ship Inn, 10 minutes' walk up the road past St Catherine's Church.) From there you can pay for two stops on the train to Rainham (where your Freedom Pass will take you the rest of the way).

→ Carshalton Ponds. (Charles Bowman/A)

13 WANDERING ALONG THE WANDLE

A RIVER EXPLORATION THROWBACK TO AN ERA OF COUNTRY ESTATES, WATERMILLS & WILLIAM MORRIS

owadays the Wandle makes a distinctly leisurely nine-mile journey through the southwestern suburbs from Croydon to the Thames at Wandsworth, but a century or so ago its current was much stronger, enough to power up to 49 waterwheels. You'll see evidence of these at Merton Abbey Mills, now a market, and within Morden Hall Park, one of two striking former country estates on the route. As so often, London reveals its villagey side, particularly at the gorgeous scene around Carshalton Ponds and in the form of the abundant wildlife in local nature reserves such as the exotically named Wilderness Island.

WHERE: Southwest London, River Wandle: Colliers Wood to Croydon
STATS: 9 miles/3½hrs; easy
START POINT/GETTING THERE: Colliers Wood station (Northern Line) /// loaded.
theme.merit ⊖ To Colliers Wood; turn left out of the station
FINISH: Hare & Hounds pub, Croydon /// native.cuts.claims
DROP-OUT POINTS: Numerous throughout the walk
MAP: OS Explorer map 161
TAKING A BREAK: Merton Abbey Mills Market, The William Morris, Deen City Farm, Surrey Arms, The Palmerston, Honeywood Museum café, The Greyhound, Pavilion Café (Beddington Park), Hare & Hounds

☞ Proceed along Merton High Street past the Charles Holden pub on the right and keep going straight, over a dual carriageway (Priory Road) past Merton bus garage (on the right) until you see the river on the left and then a footbridge over it to Sainsbury's. Instead of crossing the bridge, turn right along the riverbank (signposted for the Wandle Valley Walk). Almost immediately you will come to a plaque embedded in the ground on the left, informing you this is:

1. THE SITE OF WILLIAM MORRIS' PRINTING WORKS Here

the socialist author and artist William Morris (1834–96) took over a calico printing works in 1881. This he turned into a craft workshop. His aim was to produce 'honest, original work, done with enjoyment, not mechanical imitation done by routine… executed in a pleasant and healthy surroundings, not in squalid dens… and properly rewarded, not sweated'. He created stained glass, textiles, tapestries, carpets, dyed and printed chintz, silk and wool products, much of which he sold to Arthur Liberty of Regent Street.

Morris lived about four miles away on the riverside at Hammersmith where, in 1881, the year he took over the workshop, on seeing homeless people outside his comfortable house he observed: 'It was my good luck only of being born respectable and rich that has put me on this side of the window among delightful

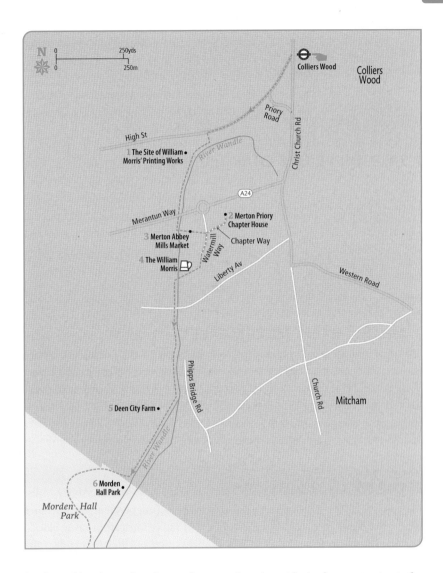

books and lovely works of art and not on the other side, in the empty street, the drink-steeped liquor shops and foul and degraded lodgings.'

He aimed for work to be an enjoyable experience at his workshop: 'If I were to work ten hours a day at work I despised and hated, I should spend my leisure time I hope in political agitations, but I fear – in drinking.'

☞ Continue along the path over two roads and then across a footbridge (signposted 'Merton Abbey Mills & Phipps Bridge') over the river to find the Paul Bowness Memorial Garden, named in memory of the Chairman of the

Wandle Heritage Trust. An interpretation board gives information on textile production at Merton Abbey Mills and the history of nearby Merton Priory. There are two micro-libraries, one of books and the other of toys – the latter had an outsize teddy bear in attendance when we visited. Cross the footbridge and walk through Merton Abbey Mills to Watermill Way. Cross the road into Chapter Way and go left to find the foundations of:

2. MERTON PRIORY CHAPTER-HOUSE (Chapter Way, Merton SW19 2RX ⏱ mertonpriory.org ⊙ Apr–Oct 11.00–16.00 Sun) This was part of a major Augustinian priory which was the location for the 1236 Council of Merton. The foundations have recently been excavated and a museum and arts centre has been constructed around them. The trust that runs the site also plans to create a physic garden as a public amenity on the site of the infirmary cloister.

☛ Now retrace your steps to:

3. MERTON ABBEY MILLS MARKET (Watermill Way, Merton SW19 2RD ⏱ mertonabbeymills.org.uk) This lively indoor retail place occupies a former textile mill established by Huguenot weavers in the early 18th century; it later became the site of the works of Liberty & Co (1904–82). Many of the buildings have display boards explaining their history and former use. The Wheelhouse is the last surviving working mill on the Wandle. Today the site houses a variety of craft workshops, a children's theatre and various **places to eat**. Here you will also find:

4. THE WILLIAM MORRIS (20 Watermill Way, Merton Abbey Mills, Merton SW19 2RD ⏱ wmpub.co.uk) This modern, independent pub occupies the former Block Shop, built by Liberty in 1910 to store intricate printing blocks. As the information board puts it, it is 'highly typical of [the] Arts and Crafts movement, being a factory built resembling a pleasant domestic house.' It serves classic pub meals and ales including Sharp's Doom Bar and Atlantic, and Camden Pale Ale, and you can drink on the patio overlooking the river.

☛ Cross the footbridge by the pub over the river and turn left along the opposite bank, following the 'Wandle Trail' signs. After a while you will come to a road, and after you cross it you will see the Deen City Farm and Riding School ahead. Go past a notice about Phipps Bridge (the original of which dates back to 1572).

Continue ahead and after a short distance on the right is:

HELEN MATTHEWS

LUIGI PETRO/DT

MAGICBONES/S

HELEN MATTHEWS

WILLIAM BARTON/S

1 The River Wandle. **2** The waterwheel at Merton Abbey Mills. **3** Deen City Farm. **4** The toy library at the Paul Bowness Memorial Garden. **5** Merton Abbey Mills now houses craft workshops and independent retailers.

5. DEEN CITY FARM (39 Windsor Av, Merton Abbey, Merton SW19 2RR ⌖ deencityfarm.co.uk ⊙ farmyard: 10.00–16.30 Tue–Sun; riding school 09.00–19.00; café 10.00–16.00 £ – free but £2 donation recommended)

Children may get seriously distracted here: along with animals including geese, turkeys, ducks, pigs, horses, cows, goats, llamas, rabbits, guinea pigs, hamsters, gerbils, ferrets and an owl, there are pony rides on offer and a maze. There's also a farm shop, a plant and vegetable stall and a **café**. The only dogs allowed in are guide dogs. 'Aviary Avenue' is one of the amusing faux street names on display.

☞ After the farm, follow the riverbank until you come to a crossing over a tramway. Keep going and take a path to the left, through bogs and swamplands, to a noticeboard announcing this is:

6. MORDEN HALL PARK (Morden Hall Rd, Morden SM4 5JD ⌀ 020 8545 6850; National Trust) A surprisingly large expanse of wetlands, woodland and meadows, this former country estate is a tad wilder than its name suggests. You might find kingfishers, newts and grey herons here, and mallards and moorhens on what's probably the river's most scenic spot. A restored waterwheel stands redundant as a reminder of the Wandle's industrious past, beside a modern hydro-electric turbine. The walled garden centre has an aquarium and pet departments, craft workshops with furniture restoration and handmade pottery. Special events, including an annual country show, are held frequently.

☞ Follow the path to the left with a sign for the wetland boardwalk. This elevated path winds through bulrushes and reeds in which wetland species thrive. At a wide path and a signpost in the shape of a dragonfly, turn left (passing a metal bridge) towards the:

7. SNUFF MILL & ROSE GARDEN These historic snuff mills were owned by the philanthropist Gilliat Hatfield, who left them to the National Trust in 1941. The former snuff mill centre, now a children's and young people's centre, has a grindstone in front of it. From May to September, more than 2,000 roses bloom in the spectacular rose garden.

☞ Return to the metal bridge, cross over it and follow the avenue of trees.

✋ When you come to a fork you can go left (signposted 'Phipps Bridge Gate'), for trams to Wimbledon or Croydon.

👉. To continue the walk take the right fork, signposted 'Surrey Arms Gate'. This takes you to Morden Road. A few yards to the left on the same side of the road is the:

8. SURREY ARMS (Morden Rd, Mitcham, Merton CR4 4DD ✆ 07583 569848) This traditional and friendly pub has two bars, a pool table, a dartboard and a jukebox but no cask ales.

👉 Turn right out of the pub.

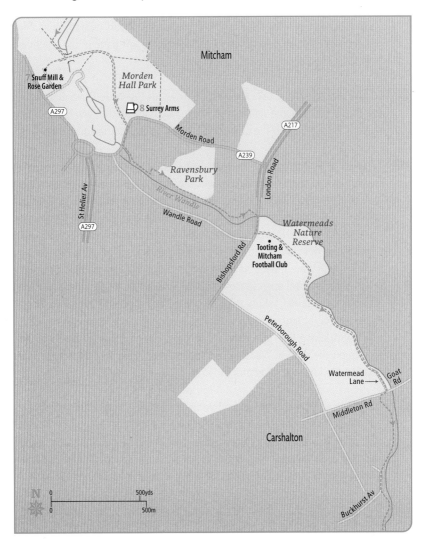

🤚 In a few yards on the same side is Bus Stop Q for the 201 to Mitcham, Herne Hill and Morden.

👉 To continue the walk, go past the bus stop along Morden Road, and after a hundred yards or so cross the road and turn left (signposted to 'River Wandle'). Cross over a footbridge, and take the path to the left (by a large grinding stone) between the river on the right and a stream on the left, keeping to the riverbank, into Ravensbury Park.

Do not cross the next bridge over the river (which leads to a dead end), but follow the path to the left, keeping on the left bank. After a couple of hundred yards cross a steel bridge (No 70) and you will have rivers on both sides. They merge where you cross another footbridge to the left bank of the combined river. When you approach a road the path forks.

🤚 To end the walk here, take the left fork towards Riverside Drive. Turn left to Bus Stop Y on the same side for the 280 to Mitcham, Brixton and Tooting. Turn right to Bus Stop W on the other side for the 280 to Morden and Sutton.

👉 To continue the walk take the right fork to Bishopsford Road, cross over it, turn right and then immediately left into a footpath, with a wooden post labelled 'Wandle Valley' on the left. This goes past Tooting and Mitcham Football Club's ground on the right. When you come to the end of the football pitches, fork to the right around them and you will soon be back on the right bank of the river. (Alternatively you can go through a gate on the left and walk through Watermeads Nature Reserve, which the National Trust received in 1913 from a local open spaces committee launched by the trust's founding member, Octavia Hill. Follow the path along the right bank of the river and, at the reserve's far end, cross a footbridge and go through a gate to rejoin the other path along the right bank.) When you come to the 'Willow Cottages' terrace on the right in Watermead Lane, go past them to a T-junction (Goat Road to the left, and Middleton Road to the right).

🤚 Turn left and walk a few hundred yards to the main road, Carshalton Road, with The Crown of Mitcham pub on the corner. Here you can get the 127 bus to Tooting Broadway and Purley stations, or the S1 bus to Banstead station and Mitcham. Alternatively, Mitcham Junction railway station is just a few minutes' walk away (turning left out of the pub along Carshalton Road).

👉 To continue the walk when you come out of Watermead Lane, turn right (into Middleton Road) and immediately left over a pedestrian crossing signposted to 'Buckhurst Avenue'. Take the path and cycle track ahead to the left, then left again at the signpost to Buckhurst Avenue. When you reach a bridge on the left, don't cross it but keep to the right bank of the river. You will come to Culvers Avenue (with Millside ahead).

🖐 To the left on the other side of the road is Bus Stop V for the 80 to Belmont, Sutton and Morden South station.

👉 To continue, turn left into the road, then take the first right into Culvers Retreat (signposted 'Wandle Trail, Poulter Park'). At the end of this cul-de-sac take the path to the left (signposted to 'Hackbridge Road'), cross over a footbridge, then turn right past a weir to reach another road (Hackbridge Road).

🖐 To the left on the other side is Bus Stop H for the 127 to Purley and Tooting Broadway stations, and the 151 bus to Worcester Park and Wallington stations.

👉 To continue the walk, cross the bridge to the right and turn left into a community garden with a footpath sign to 'The Causeway'. When you get to River Gardens, turn left and continue to the junction with Strawberry Lane, opposite which is a bridge to:

9. WILDERNESS ISLAND (Mill Lane, Carshalton, Sutton SM5 2NH ⊘ wildlondon.org.uk) This tranquil nature reserve has a good number of different habitats for a small site, including woodland, scrub, meadows, wetland and a sedge bed. A notice warns: 'Only kingfishers are allowed to fish on the island.' The kingfisher population has increased in recent years.

👉 After visiting the island, cross back over the bridge and turn left along Mill Lane, under a railway bridge, to Butter Hill bridge on the left. You can cross it for a short cut, but we preferred the longer route so continued along the right bank of the river (signposted to 'Carshalton Ponds'). After a short distance take a path off to the left from Mill Lane to follow the river (signposted 'Wandle Trail').
If you need refreshing, turn right when you come to Papermill Close, then turn left and on the right is:

10. THE PALMERSTON (31 Mill Lane, Carshalton, Sutton SM5 2JY ⊘ 020 3638 5963) This traditional two-bar pub has been refurbished in recent years and has a new beer garden, with heated booths.

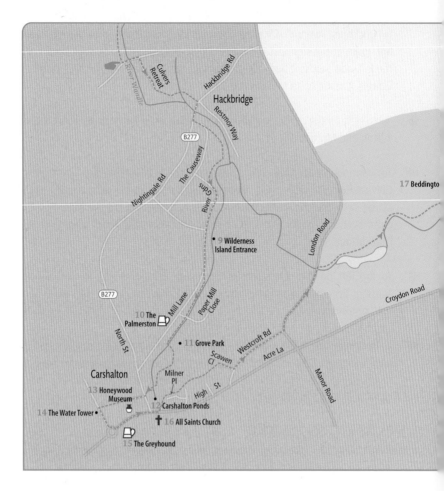

☞ Back at the river, continue along it until you come to a bridge over it (signposted 'Carshalton Ponds'), which leads into:

11. GROVE PARK (Carshalton, Sutton SM5 2JR ⌁ wandlevalleypark.co.uk)

This was once part of the grounds of a medieval manor house. The mansion, Grove House, and some outbuildings now serve as council and education department offices. Other features of the park include a restored waterwheel and an extensive recreation area with crazy golf, a bowling green and ball park among other facilities.

☞ Take the path forking right and follow the left bank of the river. At the ponds turn right (signposted 'Carshalton Ponds & Beddington Park') and left when these signs are repeated. This takes you to:

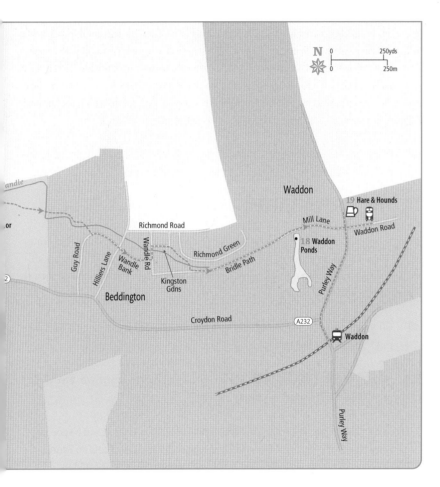

12. CARSHALTON PONDS (High St/Honeywood Walk, Carshalton, Sutton SM5 3NX ⌀ wandlevalleypark.co.uk) These two ponds were a single pond once, before a 15th-century decision to divide it into two, one for public use and the other in private ownership, as a power source for a local mill that ground corn. They add a picturesque air to the surroundings.

🖐 For those so inclined, there is a bus stop here for the 157 to Morden station.

☞ Around the ponds the following four places are worth visiting if you have time:

13. HONEYWOOD MUSEUM (Honeywood Walk, Carshalton, Sutton SM5 3NX ⌀ friendsofhoneywood.co.uk ⊙ 10.00–17.00 Thu–Sat) The exhibitions in this marvellous Edwardian house explain how the local area prospered by

growing lavender, mint and watercress, and how Carshalton evolved from a village into a suburb. Francis Carew built the first English orangery at nearby Beddington in the 16th century. Quirky items on display include Terence, a rainbow trout which a local angler caught in the Wandle in 1890. There's a billiard room downstairs and a childhood-themed room upstairs, full of Victorian and Edwardian toys, as well as a **café** next door to the main building.

☞ From the museum, turn left, then left again into Festival Walk. At the junction with West Street, turn left and look to your right to see:

14. THE WATER TOWER (West St, Carshalton, Sutton SM5 3AP
⌖ carshaltonwatertower.co.uk ⊙ Apr–Sep 14.30–17.00 Sun £) A listed early-18th-century garden building, where a water-powered pump supplied water to the fountains and garden, the tower also has an orangery and a remarkable 18th-century bathroom complete with a tile-lined plunge bath. In the garden is a Hermitage and Folly Bridge.

☞ Go to the top of West Street and turn left into Pound Street (which becomes High Street). On the right is:

15. THE GREYHOUND (High St, Carshalton, Sutton SM5 3PE
⌖ thegreyhoundhotel.com) A plaque states:

> This public house was known as the Greyhound as early as 1700. It was a sporting centre and the venue where racehorses were inspected prior to competing on Banstead Downs. The old inn was rebuilt around 1840 and a separate existing building, 'The Two Rooms' incorporated.

Allegedly, the ghost of a traveller who froze to death on the doorstep in the 1800s haunts the Swan Bar, which is part of the original coaching house. The bar, inside what is now a hotel, has a log fire (which the ghost presumably appreciates, rather belatedly).

☞ Further along the street on the right is:

16. ALL SAINTS CHURCH (High St, Carshalton, Sutton SM5 3PD) This
occupies what was originally a pagan site. Although the building was much restored in 1891, the tower was built before the Norman Conquest. It has several magnificent stained-glass windows including one dedicated to the locals who died in World War I, with their names listed below, and another created in 1743 showing the

Magi worshipping the baby Jesus. There is also a table tomb from 1400 showing a Tudor knight by the north wall. On a corner outside, a plaque tells the story of 'Ann Boleyn's Well', which according to legend burst from the ground when Anne Boleyn's horse kicked against a stone there as she rode by. However, the name may have a more prosaic origin: 'Boleyn' or 'Bullen' may be a contraction of 'Boulogne', as the Count of Boulogne was lord of the manor here in the 12th century.

☞ To continue the walk, cross the road and return past the ponds into the park. Turn right and go past a children's play area on the left and a crazy golf course on the right. Take the path to the left and over a bridge at the end with Westcroft Leisure Centre ahead. Turn right and then left into Westcroft Road (signposted 'Wandsworth Trail, Beddington Park'). At the end of the road, round to the left is the Rose & Crown on the corner of Butter Hill. Opposite the pub is a small pond with a fountain in the middle, which you walk past with London Road on your right, following the signpost to 'Beddington Park'.

✋ To end the walk here, go to Bus Stop GM, on the main road (London Road), for the 151 to Wallington or Worcester Park stations.

☞ To continue the walk keep along London Road until you come to a road bridge over the river. Just before the bridge take the public footpath (signposted to 'Croydon Road') to the right which leads to, on the left:

17. BEDDINGTON PARK (⊘ wandlevalleypark.co.uk) This landscaped park was once a deer park, part of Carew Manor, a Tudor mansion. It has many attractive features including an avenue of trees, a long lake, and the **Pavilion Café** in the centre where you can get homemade cakes and other snacks (🕐 09.00–16.30 daily).

☞ Follow the footpath until the path forks and take the left fork. Then at a crossing of paths, turn left, down to a footbridge which you cross over a lake and then turn right (signposted to 'Waddon Ponds') along the left bank. Stick to the same side of the river (ignoring a footbridge) even though the track gets a little overgrown, through woodlands, until you come to the Riverside Animal Centre. Then turn right over the bridge and left along the right bank (signposted to 'Waddon Ponds'). Go through a car park and take a path through grass to the right (away from the river) with the back of Carew Manor (now a school) to the right. Cross over the next footbridge, then bear right though grass, and pick up a tarmac path going right, back to the river by a waterfall and continue along the left bank. Further along cross two footbridges close to each other and turn left into Guy Road (signposted

VANESSA ROSE/S

ANDY WASLEY/S

ROSEPETAL80/S

VANESSA ROSE/S

1 Beddington Park. **2** & **4** Look out for kingfishers at Morden Hall Park. **3** The snuff mill.

'Wandle Trail, Waddon Ponds'). (As an alternative to all the above, you can just go straight through the park, to the right of the lake, coming out opposite St Mary the Virgin Church, Beddington. Continue past the church into Church Lane where, in the late afternoon, we saw a flock of parakeets feasting on elderberries. From here, turn left into Guy Road.)

✋ You can opt to finish here: at the end of Guy Road on the junction with Hilliers Lane, turn right to Bus Stop B for the 455 and 463 to Croydon.

👉 To continue the walk, cross over Hilliers Lane and follow the footpath ahead (signposted to 'Bridges Lane') along the river's right bank to Bridges Lane, past a row of picturesque cottages and then left into Wandle Road. Cross over the river and turn right into Kingston Gardens, then cross another footbridge and follow the signs to Waddon Ponds. This will take you past Richmond Green Balancing Pond. Before long you will reach, on the right:

18. WADDON PONDS (Waddon Court Rd, Lodge Ave, Mill Lane & The Ridgeway, Croydon CR0 4RG ∂ wandlevalleypark.co.uk) Large willow trees surround the water gardens in this park, and a variety of waterfowl including ducks and coots can be seen on the water. The name Waddon comes from 'woad', which grew on the chalk hills and was used by ancient Britons to extract blue dye for use as body paint; traces dating from the Bronze Age and the Iron Age have been found here. The Domesday Book lists a mill at the northern end of the ponds used for grinding corn; this was in use up until 1928.

👉 After strolling around the ponds, continue along the path that you came from, along Mill Lane to Purley Way. Close to the junction you will see to the left on the other side the:

19. HARE & HOUNDS (325 Purley Way, Croydon CR0 4NU ∂ 020 8688 4131) This independently owned pub has a spacious interior with traditional décor, with pool and table football available.

👉 After leaving the pub, turn left and left again into Waddon Road, to Bus Stop EX where you can get the 410 to both West Croydon (about 8mins) and East Croydon railway stations (about 12mins). Or you can continue down Purley Way, past Waddon Road, a short distance to Epsom Road on the left for Waddon railway station, where you can catch trains to London Bridge (20mins direct or 41mins with changes; 2 an hour) and Victoria (40mins–1hr; frequent).

14 PICNICKERS' PARADISE

THAMES-SIDE PLEASURES IN LONDON'S FAR WEST

Munching a sandwich and pouring a drink while contemplating the beauties of the Thames makes a nicely laid-back way of passing an afternoon, and happily for picnickers there are plenty of seats and tables along the riverside as well as on Penton Hook Island. You can pick wild fruit and look out for a wide variety of birds besides the swans (you might be lucky to spot a kingfisher and then celebrate in the pub of that name). Salmon swim up the river with the aid of a special channel, and a wide variety of fish lures anglers.

WHERE: West London/Surrey, River Thames: Staines to Chertsey
STATS: 4½ miles/1½–2hrs; easy
START POINT/GETTING THERE: Staines bus station /// dish.flap.winter ⊖ To Hatton Cross station (Piccadilly Line, Heathrow Branch), then 🚌 203 to Staines (23mins; at least 3 an hour, 2 an hour on Sun) from Hatton Cross bus station (next to the tube station exit). Otherwise 🚆 Waterloo to Staines (35–50mins; extension ticket needed from Feltham); from Staines train station walk for 6mins via Kingston Rd & Station Path.
FINISH: Chertsey Bridge /// drive.cities.paper
MAP: OS Explorer map 160
TAKING A BREAK: Penton Hook Island, Laleham Park, The Kingfisher

↑ The River Thames at Laleham. (Hilsdon25/DT)

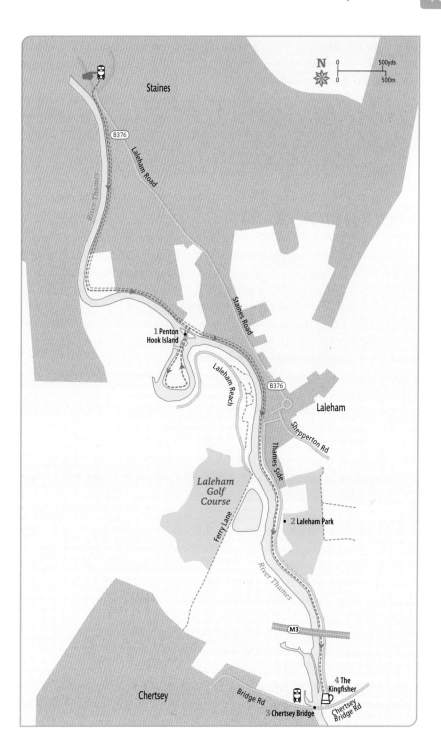

☞ With the shopping centre entrance behind you, turn right for the Friends Walk exit from the bus station, then turn left, go under the railway bridge and on the right is the River Thames. Continue on to the Thames Path. Garden lovers will appreciate the variety of flowers on display from the riverside cottages, chalets and bungalows. Wild flowers abound on the riverbank too. Purple loosestrife makes a particularly attractive display in summer.

After about half an hour you will come to Penton Hook Lock. Cross over the lock to:

1. PENTON HOOK ISLAND
This island is managed by the Environment Agency to protect wildlife and allow fish to spawn and travel upstream in a special channel that bypasses the weir. A salmon ladder was opened in 1995 (completing the link from Teddington to Whitchurch) and the fish-spawning channel in 1999 (which also acts as a nursery for young fish). Fishing is not allowed by the lock but is possible on the rest of the island, with a permit.

This is a good habitat to look out for the endangered water vole; kingfishers and herons nest here too. Be sure to look out for the beautiful banded demoiselle damselfly – attracted by the water crowfoot that grows in the channel – the gatekeeper butterfly and dragonflies. Five species of willow are visible around the island and on the river.

There are **picnic tables** on the island and fruit for foraging is plentiful, including blackberries, crab apples, wild plums and rosehips.

☞ After walking around the island, return to the Thames Path. You will see traditional boatbuilders' yards on the opposite bank of Laleham Reach, and before long you will come to:

2. LALEHAM PARK (Shepperton Rd, Staines-upon-Thames TW18 1SS)
This large open green, like the island, has **picnic tables**. It used to be part of the Laleham Manor grounds owned by the Lord Lucan family, which included the 7th Earl who went missing in 1974 after being suspected of murdering his children's nanny. The 3rd Earl didn't exactly cover himself in glory either, as he led the disastrous Charge of the Light Brigade in 1854.

Noticeboards highlight the bird species in the park, which include cormorants, great crested grebes and mallards. You might also spot rose-ringed parakeets. Originating from Asia and kept as pets in Victorian times, the birds proliferated in the 1970s (after being released by rock star Jimi Hendrix, according to one urban myth). There are now tens of thousands in this area around Kingston and Twickenham.

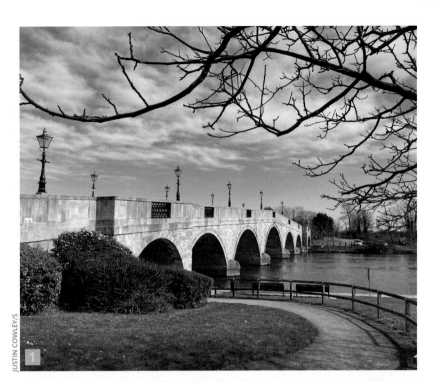

JUSTIN COWLEY/S

PETER ARKELL

1 Chertsey Bridge. 2 Fishing on the Thames.

☛ Continue along the river past Laleham Park Camping Site, under the M3 motorway, past Chertsey Lock to:

3. CHERTSEY BRIDGE
A bridge has spanned this point since around 1300, linking Dumsey Meadow on the Middlesex side with Chertsey in Surrey. When the present seven-arched span was erected in 1785, the bridge failed to reach the bank on either side, so the authorities had to fork out more money for its completion.

☛ Next to the bridge is:

4. THE KINGFISHER
(Chertsey Bridge Rd, Chertsey KT16 8LF ⌖ thekingfisherchertsey.co.uk) This traditional pub has an outdoor seating area by the river and a log fire inside. It serves hot food including Sunday roasts. Real ales on our visit included Fuller's London Pride, Adnams and Sharp's Doom Bar.

TWO ECCENTRICS ON THE THAMES

Dylan Thomas (1914–53), the fiery, alcoholic, tragic but hugely talented Welsh poet, lived on a houseboat on the river here at Chertsey on his first visit to London in 1933. It was owned by his older sister, Nancy, and he had come to meet fellow writer Pamela Hansford Johnson, who became his first serious girlfriend. He met his future wife, Caitlin Macnamara, a showgirl and dancer, in The Wheatsheaf pub in Rathbone Place, Fitzrovia; they got married at the third attempt after twice spending the marriage licence fee on drink. His masterpiece was *Under Milk Wood*, the only copy of the manuscript of which he inadvertently left in The George pub, Great Portland Street, Fitzrovia, after a drunken binge. Luckily it was rescued by the landlord.

Viv Stanshall (1943–95), the eccentric leader of the Bonzo Dog Doo-Dah Band, also lived on a houseboat at Chertsey from 1977 to 1983, from where he produced part of his album *Sir Henry at Rawlinson End*. Later he and Ki Longfellow, his second wife, lived on a floating theatre called The Old Profanity Showboat. Viv and his friend Keith Moon (drummer of The Who) were great pranksters. Viv once entered a tailor's shop and admired a pair of trousers. As planned, Keith followed him in and admired the same pair of trousers. In a struggle to gain possession of them, they tore them in half with one leg each, to the chagrin of the tailor. There then entered a one-legged actor they had hired who declared: 'Ah! Just what I was looking for!'

☞ Cross the bridge. The statue on the far side commemorates Neville Audley, condemned during the Wars of the Roses to be executed when the curfew bell rang at sunset. His life was saved by Blanche Heriot who held on to the clapper to prevent the bell from ringing.

Close to the statue is a bus stop where you can catch the 557 bus to Sunbury Tesco (20mins; 1 an hour) and then the 555 back to Hatton Cross (35mins; 1 an hour). Alternatively, walk around a mile to Heriot Road for a 446 bus back to Staines bus station (15–20mins; 2 an hour, 1 an hour at weekends) then the 203 back to Hatton Cross; or slightly further to Chertsey railway station for a train to Waterloo via Feltham (42mins; 1 an hour).

↑ The Kingfisher pub, a good stop for refreshments at the end of the walk. (Sandor Szmutko/S)

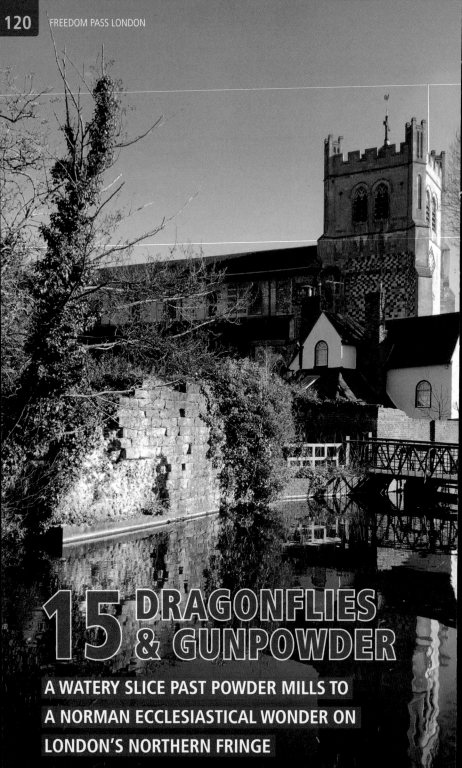

15 DRAGONFLIES & GUNPOWDER

A WATERY SLICE PAST POWDER MILLS TO A NORMAN ECCLESIASTICAL WONDER ON LONDON'S NORTHERN FRINGE

This river (variously spelled Lee or Lea) has been used for transport for over 2,000 years, carrying everything from gunpowder into London to horse manure from London to local farms. The story of gunpowder crops up twice on this walk, as you pass the factory site where Lee–Enfield rifles were made, and have the chance to visit the gunpowder mill that served some of the nation's military needs for several centuries.

Seeds blown off the barges have seen wild flowers from Asia and North America growing in the meadows along the Lea's banks. Another summer spectacle is the eye-catching bee orchid, so named because of its extraordinary likeness to that insect (nature's curious method to attract bees to the flower; the petals even smell like female bees, thus emitting enticing signals to male bees to come and mate).

On the way you'll also see colourful barges, and almost adjacent to the waterway are several huge reservoirs which supply a tenth of London's water, as well as providing a haven for aquatic birds and otters. Near the largest heronry in Greater London is a dragonfly sanctuary, while your binoculars might help you spot peregrine falcons, the rare Savi's warbler, kestrels and other species.

The walk ends at Waltham Abbey, where the superb Norman church is the burial place of King Harold after his demise at Hastings in 1066.

WHERE: North London/Essex, River Lea: Tottenham to Waltham Abbey
STATS: 10½ miles/4hrs; easy
START POINT/GETTING THERE: Tottenham Hale tube station (Victoria Line)
/// drape.firmly.bind ⊖ To Tottenham Hale or 🚌 from Liverpool Street (11–12mins; at least 5 an hour); turn left out of the station
FINISH: The Crown, Waltham Abbey /// lend.nearly.needed
DROP-OUT POINTS: After 2½, 4½ & 6 miles
MAP: OS Explorer map 174
TAKING A BREAK: The Waterside Café, The Greyhound, The Crown

☛ After turning left out of the station, take the first left into Ferry Lane. Just after Mill Mead Road take the second footpath on the left (down a short steep slope), signposted 'Lea Valley Walk' (the first one is Pymme's Brook), down to Tottenham Locks, and continue ahead on the bank of the River Lee Navigation on your right.

After about half a mile or so you will reach Stonebridge Lock. A few yards beyond it is:

1. THE WATERSIDE CAFÉ (Watermead Way, Tottenham Marshes N17 0XD ☉ 10.00–17.00 daily) Fortify yourself for the walk with a cup of coffee at this café run by the Friends of Tottenham Marshes (we also recommend the

bread pudding). Teddy and Millie, labradoodles with matching blue and pink bow ties, keep an eye on things.

☛ Return to the lock, cross over it and turn left. After passing Chalk Bridge, you will go past Edmonton bus garage and two business parks (opposite which we saw elders in flower, and coots building a nest) and then under the A406 North Circular Road.

✋ At Cooks Ferry Roundabout, Harbet Road, on the A406 North Circular Road, you can catch the 34 or 444 buses to Walthamstow, Chingford, Palmers Green or Turnpike Lane.

☛ Continue following the river, past a signpost 'Pickett's Lock 1 mile, Enfield Lock 4 miles'. After passing Pickett's Lock you will see to the left a golf course on the left bank, and plenty of ivy, wild roses, hazels and hawthorn hedges.

✋ When you reach Ponders End Lock, walk up the ramp from the canal to Wharf Road, turn right and walk a short distance to the junction with Lea Valley Road. Here there are bus stops on both sides of the road where you can get the 313 bus to Chingford station in one direction or Enfield station in the other.

☛ Continue along the river. To the right you will see a few horses grazing on the raised grass banks of King George's Reservoir. When you reach Enfield Lock, cross over a bridge and follow it to the other side of the canal. On the right is:

2. GOVERNMENT ROW (Enfield Island Village, Enfield) The Royal Small Arms factory was sited on the island (between the River Lea and the River Lee Navigation) in 1816, and was originally driven by waterwheel. Here the famous Lee–Enfield rifles were manufactured up to 1987. Government Row was built below the level of the canal bank in 1857 to house the arms factory workers, and the proximity of the waterway enabled barges to carry materials such as coal.

☛ A bit further along on the left is:

3. THE GREYHOUND (425 Ordnance Rd, Enfield Lock, Enfield EN3 6HR ⊘ mcmullens.co.uk/greyhoundenfield) A family-friendly pub owned by local brewery McMullens, the Greyhound serves real ale and food, and has a pool table and a dartboard. It was taken over by the Liquor Control Board during

World War I in order to restrict the sale of alcohol, presumably due to the nearby armaments facilities.

✋ Opposite the pub is the third possible drop-out point on this walk: from Causeway Bridge opposite the pub and up some steps, you can catch the 121 bus to Southgate and Palmers Green stations or the 491 to Edmonton. Or you can turn left out of the pub and walk along Ordnance Road a few hundred yards to Enfield Lock railway station (which is just within the Freedom Pass zone) for trains to Liverpool Street (27mins; 2 an hour).

☞ Otherwise continue along the canal past:

4. RAMNEY MARSH On your

left, this ancient pasture surrounded by river and marshes has been used since medieval times to graze sheep.

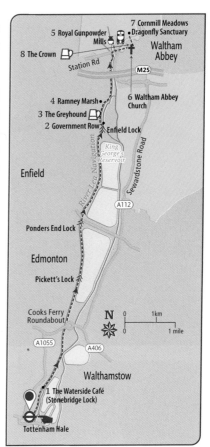

☞ Continue along the canal past Ramney Marsh Lock (built in 1768 and then rebuilt in 1864 from brick and stone from the demolished Westminster Bridge). If you would like to fish between here and Tottenham Lock, you need to join the River Lea Angling Club (✆ 07922 688060; a membership fee applies).

Follow the river under the M25. Cross over the next bridge on the right (signposted 'Waltham Abbey ½ mile, Royal Gunpowder Mill ¼ mile') over both the canal and Horsemill Stream into Highbridge Street, Waltham Abbey. Take the first turning on the left opposite the 24-hour McDonald's into Beaulieu Drive. After nearly half a mile you will come to the:

5. ROYAL GUNPOWDER MILLS (Beaulieu Drive, Waltham Abbey EN9

1JY ✆ 01992 707370 🖱 royalgunpowdermills.com 🕑 check website or call **£**) Discover 300 years of explosive history at this fascinating site. It all began in

CHRISDORNEY/S

HELEN MATTHEWS

HELEN MATTHEWS

1 The Royal Gunpowder Mills. **2** *Ancestor* by Helena Stylianides. **3** King Harold's Memorial at Waltham Abbey.

the 1660s when a mill producing vegetable oil was converted to the production of gunpowder during the second Dutch War. Following expansion in the 18th century the Mills became one of the first examples of an industrial factory system, and they were purchased by the Crown in October 1786 for £10,000. The Mills finally closed in 1943, only to reopen two years later as a research centre for military and rocket propellants before finally closing for good in 1991. The site is currently open only on specified dates, but there are hopes to increase access in the future. Note that this is also a nature reserve, the alder woodland attracting siskins which feed on alder cones.

☛ Return to Highbridge Street, turn left, continue past a roundabout and head on to:

6. WALTHAM ABBEY CHURCH (CHURCH OF HOLY CROSS & ST LAWRENCE) (Abbey Church Centre, Abbey Farm House, Abbey Gardens, Waltham Abbey EN9 1XQ ⊘ walthamabbeychurch.co.uk ☉ 11.00–16.00 Wed, 10.00–16.00 Fri & Sat, noon–16.00 Sun) There have been four churches on this site. The earliest was a 7th-century wooden building; its successor, a century later, was built from stone. In the early 11th century, the landowner brought a stone crucifix from his Somerset manor and pilgrims including King Harold came here in the belief that praying to the crucifix would heal their illnesses and injuries. Harold was cured of paralysis after praying here, and rebuilt the church, adding property which supported a community of priests to serve it and the surrounding parishes. The fourth church owed its creation to the Pope, who ordered Henry II to found three new monasteries as part of his penance for the murder of Thomas Becket (page 77). While the abbey suffered dissolution under Henry VIII, the church continued in use.

There have been various restoration efforts, in particular by the Victorians. The great east window – a rose window with three lancet windows beneath – was the work of Edward Burne-Jones in the 1860s. The wonderful painted ceiling, with diamond shapes enclosing depictions of Past and Future, the zodiac signs and the labours of the months, comes from the same period. Use the mirror on a mobile trolley to get a good look. The Lady Chapel houses a great rediscovery – a 15th-century Doom painting (depicting the Day of Judgement) which a false ceiling concealed for 400 years. We also enjoyed, in the north aisle, the bust of Francis Wollaston, which was originally white – until a cleaner in the 1930s applied boot polish to the bust's hair.

Pick up signposts to 'King Harold's Tomb' round the church to the back. Before the Battle of Hastings in 1066 the king vainly prayed at the church for victory, but instead was killed by (according to most interpretations of the Bayeux Tapestry) an arrow in his eye. According to a contemporary account by William of Poitiers, Harold's vanquisher William of Normandy ('the Conqueror') allowed the defeated forces to collect the bodies of their dead for burial. However, he refused an offer of gold from Harold's mother to return the king's body, for reasons which remain the subject of historians' speculation. Later, two canons from Waltham brought Harold's body here after his mistress Edith the Fair (also known as Edith Swan-Neck) identified it through certain marks that only she knew about. As well as the tomb and memorial stone behind the church, there is a statue of Harold on the southwest corner. He also paid for the herringbone masonry on the east wall.

Richard II took refuge at the church during the Peasants' Revolt, and Thomas Cranmer stayed here when discussing Henry VIII's desire for a divorce and the need to split from the Roman Catholic church.

The church is surrounded by extensive gardens with archaeological treasures, including a 14th-century gatehouse, along with seats, picnic tables and a green.

☛ From Harold's Tomb go away from the church diagonally left to a gap in the cloister wall, and follow the path to Abbey Church Centre. The cowled wooden figure you will pass on the way is *Ancestor* by Helena Stylianides. Turn left and then right round the side of the centre to a lane which goes across a wooden bridge over a stream, under a road subway, through a kissing gate and into fields with a 'Welcome to Lea Valley' sign. Bear right through a grass track to:

7. CORNMILL MEADOWS DRAGONFLY SANCTUARY (Waltham Abbey EN9 1XQ ⊘ visitleevalley.org.uk/waltham-abbey-gardens) At this Site of Special Scientific Interest, 23 species of dragonfly have been recorded (that's half the UK species). The meadows are seasonally flooded, and the site includes ponds, woodland and hay meadows, with an arboretum and heronry nearby. You can follow a waymarked trail of blue arrows to find out more.

☛ Return to the church, retrace your steps towards the canal, take the first right (Romeland) and tucked round the corner is:

8. THE CROWN (Romeland, Waltham Abbey EN9 1QZ ⊘ thecrownpubwa. co.uk) This friendly place has ancient timber beams and a dartboard, and serves food.

☛ Turn left out of the pub, then right into Highbridge Street. When you come to the roundabout turn right and on the right is the Highbridge bus stop where you can catch the 13 to Epping (Central Line; 26mins; 1 an hour) or the 66 to Loughton (Central Line; 33mins; 2 an hour).

The award-winning Slow Travel series from Bradt Guides

Over 20 regional guides across Britain.
See the full list at bradtguides.com/slowtravel.

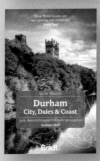
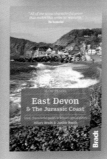
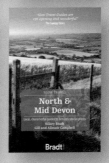

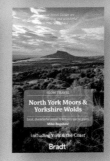

16 DEATH IN THE CHURCHYARD, LIFE BY THE LAKE

MULTIPLE MURDERS, WINNIE THE POOH & BRITAIN'S HOLLYWOOD

Death stalks the local churchyard in Elstree where three victims of infamous brutal murders are buried. It sets a sombre, even macabre tone for this entertaining walk, but things cheer up markedly after that. The route includes Aldenham Country Park, teeming with life in various ways, with wildlife abundant on and around the scenic reservoir, and a notable collection of rare breeds farm animals that visitors are allowed to feed. Children of all ages can enter the world of Winnie the Pooh in a themed woodland and play area. Elstree is a name that can't be uttered without evoking the world of film-making, and this walk's finale is a mural honouring the many film and television stars who have worked at the local studios.

WHERE: Hertfordshire: Elstree & Aldenham Reservoir, circular
STATS: 3½–4 miles/1½hrs; easy
START POINT/GETTING THERE: St Nicholas Church, Elstree /// bricks.that.rainy
🚇 To Elstree & Borehamwood station from St Pancras (22mins; 5 an hour, 2 an hour on Sun). In the station forecourt go to the bus stops on the left. 🚌 From Stop B, take the 107 (5mins; 3 an hour) or 306 (5mins; 3 an hour, 1 an hour on Sun) to the Watling Court stop on High St.
DROP-OUT POINT: After 2¼ miles
MAP: OS Explorer map 173
TAKING A BREAK: Winnie the Pooh's 100 Aker Wood, Rustic Rhubarb Café

↑ Aldenham Reservoir. (Fotomaton/A)

☞ Go back a few yards after alighting from the bus and on the same side is:

1. ST NICHOLAS CHURCH (High St, Elstree WD6 3EW ✆ 020 8905 1365)

Buried here are no fewer than three murder victims, and one of the country's most eccentric explorers was baptised here. The first murder victim was Martha Ray, born in Elstree in 1746, who was shot in the head by her spurned lover on 7 April 1779. She gave birth to five children by the 4th Earl of Sandwich, a member of the notorious Hellfire Club, who was 28 years older than her. She had a brief affair with a young army captain (later to become a vicar) called James Hackman. He later became excessively jealous and followed her to a Covent Garden theatre. When a stranger offered to escort her to her carriage, Rev Hackman (as he now was) stepped forward with two pistols, shot Martha through the crown of the head with the right, and aimed the left at his own head, but the bullet glanced off merely wounding him. He was sentenced to death and hanged in front of a large crowd at Tyburn, and his body publicly dissected. Many pamphlets and poems about the crime were published, as well as a novel, *Love and Madness* by Sir Herbert Croft, in 1780. Martha's body was entombed inside this church under the chancel floor. More than 40 years later, her coffin was discovered when the church was being renovated and she was reburied outside the vestry door (the back entrance), where it remains to this day. A 20th-century Earl of Sandwich

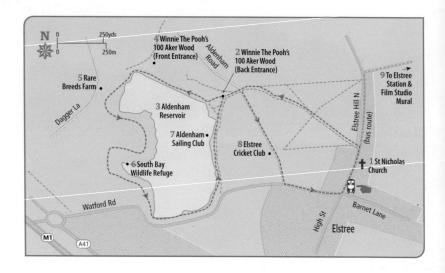

erected a tombstone for her, in memory of his ancestor's love for her. Stand with your back to the vestry door and walk forwards to find her.

The second victim interred here is William Weare, murdered locally in 1823 and buried about 20 yards to the east of the vestry door. He was a solicitor and a heavy gambler who won £300, a fortune in those days, from John Thurtell after a game of billiards or cards. Thurtell, who strongly suspected Weare of cheating, invited him to a cottage belonging to his friend William Probert, three miles from Elstree village, for 'a weekend's shooting'. They took Weare to the Waggon & Horses pub in Watling Street, Elstree, where he was shot in the face by Thurtell, but the bullet glanced off his cheek bone. Thurtell then cut Weare's throat with a knife, and battered him to death with his pistol. Thurtell, Probert and their accomplice Joseph Hunt dumped the body in a pond. Afterwards they enjoyed a supper of pork chops, drank, sang and shared out the victim's property. Probert gave evidence against Thurtell in return for immunity from prosecution. Thurtell faced the noose 'nonchalantly' in 1824, admitting to the crime on the gallows.

His was the last public execution in Hertfordshire. Hunt was also sentenced to death, but this was commuted to transportation to Australia because he co-operated with the authorities. He eventually became a police constable. Probert, meanwhile, was shunned for his treachery and hanged a year later for stealing a horse from a relative.

The third murder victim whose final resting place is here was Eliza Ebborn, from Watford. A married woman aged about 31, she was killed by a 24-year-old shoemaker, George Stratton, on 13 August 1882 in Elstree; she was buried four days later in the then new extension to the old churchyard. His death sentence was repealed and he was committed to an institution on grounds of insanity.

The eccentric explorer Richard Francis Burton (1821–90) was baptised in the church on 2 September 1821. During his career in the army of the East India Company, one of his assignments was to investigate (under cover) a brothel in Karachi believed to be used by soldiers, which led to his long-term interest in sexual practices. He became circumcised in order to disguise himself as a Muslim when going on a pilgrimage to Mecca as an explorer. In Somalia he was impaled by a javelin through his (facial) cheeks and had to escape with it still in his head, leaving him with a scar for the rest of his life. He could speak numerous languages, and translated the *Kama Sutra*. In his travel books he also described sexual techniques in different regions of the world, hinting that he had participated in them, so breaching sexual and racial taboos of the time. When baptised he was living with his uncle, Francis Burton, at Barham House (now called Hillside) in Allum Lane, which is on the bus journey from the station. The house was owned by Burton's grandfather (who is buried in the church).

☞ After visiting the church continue downhill a few yards and cross the road to the former Holly Bush pub (now a nursery). Down the side of the pub are signs for two footpaths through the fields.

Take the path to the right (signed 'Public Footpath 3 Aldenham Road 700 yards') through the centre of the fields going downhill. The path is a bit indistinct, but keep going diagonally downhill across the field until you reach a junction with a more clearly waymarked path. Turn left into this path, which takes you to Aldenham Road. Cross straight over through a kissing gate into a path by a noticeboard for 'Aldenham Sailing Club' and another 'London Loop' sign. A few yards on the right is a kissing gate and:

2. WINNIE THE POOH'S 100 AKER WOOD (BACK ENTRANCE) (⊘ aldenhamcountrypark.co.uk) This is not signposted as such, but you can enter 100 Aker Wood (page 132) here and follow its designated route backwards. You will see more of the lake if you continue along the path a short distance to:

3. ALDENHAM RESERVOIR Part of Aldenham Country Park, the reservoir was dug by French prisoners of war from 1795 to 1797 for the Grand Union Canal Company to control water levels after the building of the canal. Mute swans, mallard, coots and moorhens are often seen on the lake, and there are populations of damselflies and dragonflies. The lake contains massive roach, carp, pike, bream and tench; fishing activity is managed by the Aldenham Angling Club (✆ 07857 808442 ⊘ swimbooker.com/fishery/11338).

☛ Turn right by the reservoir and follow the lakeside path round its edge. This takes you across a footbridge. Turn right immediately for:

4. WINNIE THE POOH'S 100 AKER WOOD (FRONT ENTRANCE) (⌗ aldenhamcountrypark.co.uk) Free to enter and also part

of Aldenham Country Park, this woodland area is a themed attraction where children can explore many of the places described in AA Milne's classic stories. They have been recreated from the book's illustrations by EH Shepard (which themselves were based on real locations in Ashdown Forest in Sussex) and include Pooh Bear's House, the Sandy Pit where Roo plays, a Nice Place for Picnics, the Bee Tree, the way to the North Pole, an area with Big Stones and Rocks, Rabbit's House, Christopher Robin's House, the Pooh Trap for Heffalumps, Piglet's House, Where the Woozle Wasn't, a Floody Place, Owl's House, Eeyore's Gloomy Place and Pooh's Thoughtful Spot. It is indeed a nice place for **picnics**.

☛ Leaving the wood you will come to a car park which is a hub for various facilities including a minigolf course, a children's adventure playground and the **Rustic Rhubarb Café** (⌗ rusticrhubarb.com). A notice at the café proclaims 'Whilst we love a good boogie @RusticRhubarb NO Pole dancing is permitted. Thanks.' Follow the signs towards:

5. RARE BREEDS FARM (Aldenham Country Park, Elstree WD6 3BA

✆ 01438 861447 ⌗ aldenhamcountrypark.co.uk ◷ variable; check website **£**) The rarest breed here, among the assortment of pigs, turkeys and the like, is the whiteface woodland sheep, which is even rarer than the panda. They also have golden Guernsey goats, whose total numbers dwindled to just 30 at the end of World War II after most had been eaten by the islanders and German invaders. The modest entrance fee includes a bag of animal feed which you can give to the poultry, pigs and cattle; elsewhere you can observe bees in a special hive, ride on ponies (at weekends and holidays) and walk through an orchard of very special apples and pears. On certain days a cheery handler tells you about raptors such as the eagle owl, peregrine falcon and European goshawk and lets you get close to them.

☛ Retrace your steps a short distance and turn right into a footpath through the wood. After a while you come to:

6. SOUTH BAY WILDLIFE REFUGE A notice tells you this is the

quietest waterside area; fishing and sailing are not allowed here, so the plants and animals live undisturbed. The trees by the water's edge are mainly alder

1 Aldenham Sailing Club is one of the oldest in the country. **2** Aldenham Country Park is home to Winnie the Pooh's 100 Aker Wood. **3** The film-studio mural at Elstree.

and willow, and the smaller bankside plants include sedges and rushes. In the water are water bistort and water crowfoot. Swans, great crested grebes, water voles and shrews live and breed here. Summer sees damselflies, dragonflies, swallows, swifts and martins. In the autumn and winter there are Canada geese and cormorants.

☛ Further along the path it heads away from the reservoir to a farm. One signpost here is for the 'Nature Trail', which you have just taken; now follow the other, to continue in the same direction on the 'Lakeside Path'. Eventually you will come to a wooden kissing gate on the right which takes you into Watford Road.

✋ If you wish to end the walk here turn left along the road and walk a few yards round a bend, and cross the road to the bus stop for the 306 back to Elstree & Borehamwood station (7–9 mins; 3 an hour, 1 an hour on Sun).

☛ Otherwise continue along the Lakeside Path. After a short while you will come to:

7. ALDENHAM SAILING CLUB (Aldenham Country Park, Elstree WD6 3BD ☏ 020 8207 3782 ⌖ aldenhamsc.co.uk) One of the oldest sailing clubs in the country, this has operated since the 1920s. Among its most distinguished members was yachting author and journalist Ian Proctor (1918–92), who designed over a hundred sailing dinghies and cruisers, of which 65,000 were built. This earned him the title of 'Yachtsman of the Year' in 1965. As of July 2023, the Club had suspended operations because the water level was lowered to reduce pressure on the dam, but there are hopes for a solution that will enable sailing to resume.

☛ Continue along the Lakeside Path a short distance and on the right is the path to the right (signposted 'London Loop' and 'Aldenham Road') where you first came to the reservoir. Follow this back to Aldenham Road. The shortest way back to the bus stop for the return journey is uphill through the fields you came down originally. But if this is very muddy and/or you would like to watch some village cricket, then turn right along Aldenham Road. A short distance on the right is:

8. ELSTREE CRICKET CLUB (Aldenham Rd, Elstree WD6 3BD) There is a good chance of seeing a village cricket match here at the weekends, especially Saturdays. Elstree Cricket Club was formed in 1878 and has two teams, one

playing on Saturday, the other on Sunday. The ground is also used by Hatch End Cricket Club (founded in 1933) which plays on Saturdays. Both clubs welcome spectators.

☞ Continue past the cricket club to the end of the road, turning left and going uphill to the High Street, with a final left to get to the bus stop that takes you back to Elstree & Borehamwood station. In the train station forecourt is a:

9. FILM STUDIO MURAL (Outside Elstree & Borehamwood station, Allum Lane, Borehamwood WD6 3LS) Elstree is a name inextricably linked with film-making: the mural features stars Elizabeth Taylor, John Mills, Roger Moore and Vincent Price (as Dracula) who have all made movies here. It all started in 1914 when Neptune Studios (now the BBC Elstree Centre) was set up, and throughout the 20th century films and television brought thousands of jobs and millions of pounds to the area, which became known as the 'British Hollywood'. Early movies filmed here include some Alfred Hitchcock productions, and later the *Indiana Jones* and *Star Wars* series. The main studios are nearby at Clarendon Road (BBC) and Shenley Road, where more than 800 feature films have been made since 1927. Eventually six different studios operated within two miles of each other. Barbara Windsor, perhaps best known for her role as pub landlady Peggy Mitchell in the BBC TV soap *EastEnders*, earns a special display for her three films made here (*Too Hot to Handle* in 1960, *Crooks in Cloisters* in 1964 and *The Boy Friend* in 1971). Also, look down for the stars in the pavements celebrating the work of, among others, Jim Henson, Alec Guinness, Gregory Peck, Jack Nicholson and Harrison Ford.

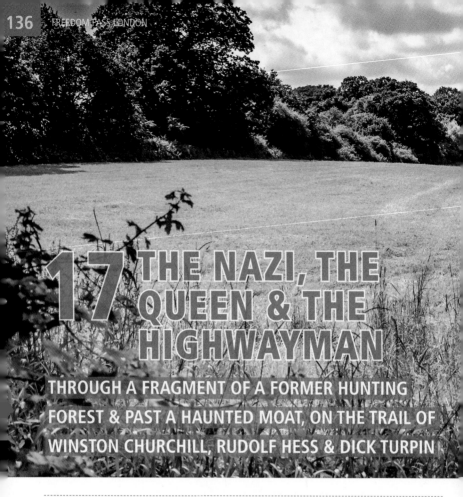

17 THE NAZI, THE QUEEN & THE HIGHWAYMAN

THROUGH A FRAGMENT OF A FORMER HUNTING FOREST & PAST A HAUNTED MOAT, ON THE TRAIL OF WINSTON CHURCHILL, RUDOLF HESS & DICK TURPIN

This walk in the old county of Middlesex takes a tour of Trent Country Park, once a royal hunting ground and more recently part of Middlesex University's campus. A colourful cast of characters has visited over the centuries: some involuntarily (the most famous highwayman in history, and a leading Nazi), others apocryphally or fictionally (King Arthur's queen, whose ghost is said to haunt an ancient monument, and a much-loved TV Time Lord). Nowadays, the park's residents include an array of animals and birds recovering from illness and injury, while young Tarzans enjoy a swinging time.

WHERE: Middlesex/Hertfordshire: Trent Country Park, circular
STATS: 4½ miles/1½–2hrs; easy with two short, moderate climbs
START POINT/GETTING THERE: Cockfosters tube station (Piccadilly Line) /// friday.rise.dozed ⊖ To Cockfosters station; leave by the Cockfosters Road exit
MAP: OS Explorer map 173
TAKING A BREAK: Japanese Water Garden, WRAS Wildlife Hospital & Animal Centre, Cock Inn

↑ Trent Country Park. (Abdul_Shakoor/S)

👉 After leaving by the Cockfosters Road exit, turn right, go past the cemetery and holly bushes, and after about four minutes turn right through gates by the 'Trent Country Park' notice, into:

1. TRENT COUNTRY PARK (Cockfosters Rd, Barnet EN4 0PS

🖈 trentcountrypark.com 🕒 08.30–16.00 Mon–Thu, 08.30–16.30 Fri, 08.00–16.30 Sat, 07.30–16.30 Sun) This land can claim almost a thousand years of recorded history; as the royal hunting forest of Enfield Chase, it merited a mention in the 1086 Domesday Book. Henry VIII, Elizabeth I and James I all hunted here. George III gave the estate to Dr Richard Jebb in gratitude for the doctor having saved the life of George's younger brother when the latter was in Trento in Italy – hence the estate's name. Dr Jebb had a house built in a Classical style. By the early 20th century the estate owner was Sir Philip Sassoon (cousin of the World War I poet), who bought three stone memorials from Wrest House in Bedfordshire for use here. He entertained, among others, Charlie

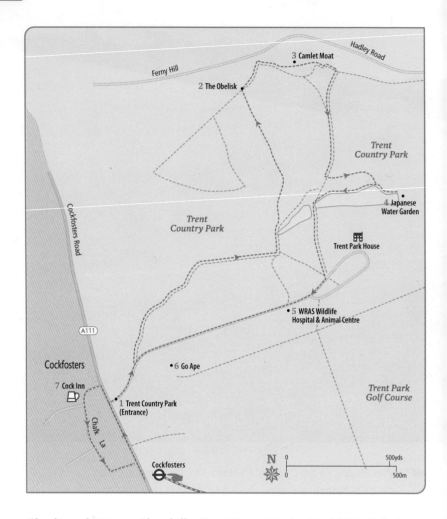

Chaplin and Winston Churchill at Trent House. During World War II the house was a (comfortable) holding cell for 84 captured German officers, including Hitler's deputy Rudolf Hess. Plying the officers with drink, and secretly bugging their conversations, uncovered some useful information, for example about the failed assassination attempt on Hitler in 1944. Nowadays the 413-acre estate is open to the public, who enjoy its varied woods containing ash, beech, rowan, silver birch and sweet chestnut trees, as well as a beautiful water garden (page 141). The ground floor of the house is due to open as a visitor attraction in Spring 2025.

☛ Continue through the park, passing a pond on your right. When you reach a monument commemorating the construction of the gardens take the left fork, which takes you towards a café (closed when we visited, but with two food/coffee trucks providing a replacement service). Immediately after the café, take the footpath to the left through the woods. Follow the path through the woods, which contain a number of pollarded trees. Just before reaching a field the path bends right. Continue on this path through the woods, emerging via a wooden bridge into a field. Follow the path along the field margin (there are lots of hawthorn berries in the hedgerow in autumn). Turn left just before reaching more woods and follow the path a short distance downhill. Immediately after passing a large oak tree, there is a fork, with a footpath to the left and a wider path to the right. Take the path to your left. Continue along this path, which takes you across an open area with views over the park and Trent Park House to your right. When you come to a crossing of paths turn left, cross a wooden bridge, and yomp up the hill to:

2. THE OBELISK This tall stone erection is engraved 'To the memory of the birth of George Grey, Earl of Harold, son of Henry and Sophia, Duke and Duchess of Kent, in 1702.' All is not quite what it seems: in fact George was born in 1732 and died less than six months later. *Doctor Who* fans will recognise the location from the 1983 story 'Mawdryn Undead' in which the Doctor (played by Peter Davison) finds himself in danger at a boys' school, and on an alien spacecraft, in both 1977 and 1983. Timey-wimey!

☞ Turn right into the woods. When the path forks, take the path to the right and after a short distance you will come to a kissing gate on your left, giving access to:

3. CAMLET MOAT This quiet, picturesque site, which is a scheduled ancient monument, has had a surprisingly turbulent past, if even only half the stories about it are true. Some evidence suggests origins from more than 2,000 years ago, a drawbridge in Roman times and habitation in the 11th century. The moat is also said to have two ghosts. The spirit of Geoffrey de Mandeville, Earl of Sussex and Hertfordshire (died 1144) guards some treasure which the stories say he hid down a deep well. The second spectre, according to Christopher Street's book *London's Camelot and the Secrets of the Grail*, is King Arthur's queen Guinevere. We do know from documentation from around May 1439 that there was a 'Manor of Camelot' nearby (the documents relate to instructions for the manor's demolition). According to Historic England, by the 18th century the ruins of a lodge here served as a hiding place for Dick Turpin while that infamous highwayman was on the run.

FELA SANU/S

HELEN MATTHEWS

HELEN MATTHEWS

1 The Obelisk dedicated to George Grey. **2** The Japanese Water Garden. **3** Camlet Moat.

☞ After visiting the moat, continue along the path downhill, past a signpost indicating the Animal Centre. Just before a bridge is another signpost. Turn left for the:

4. JAPANESE WATER GARDEN The plants in this idyllically peaceful place – the ideal spot for a **picnic** – may be local rather than exotic, but the inspiration is Japanese, a mini-world of harmony and balance, with water the key feature to promote feelings of serenity and well-being. It is the creation of Sir Philip Sassoon, who ensured the ensemble all fitted in with the natural contours.

☞ Follow the path around the perimeter of the water garden. When you are back at the entrance, take the footpath to your left which skirts the edge of the pond. Shortly after crossing a stream by a wooden bridge turn left over a bridge between the two ponds and follow the path through the woods (modern cuboid houses to the left) to emerge at the entrance to what was formerly the Trent Park Campus of Middlesex University and is now an upmarket housing development. Turn right past the memorial to Jemima Crewe, Duchess of Kent (died 1728), and continue along the road. On the left after a few yards is the:

5. WRAS WILDLIFE HOSPITAL & ANIMAL CENTRE (Trent Country Park, Enfield EN4 0PS ☎ 020 8344 2785 ⊘ wras-enfieldwildlife.org.uk ⊙ 10.00–16.00 Wed–Sun, also Mon & Tue in school hols; closes 30mins before dusk in winter £) The WRAS (Wildlife Rescue & Ambulance Service) is devoted to treating wounded and sick wild animals within their Wildlife Hospital, and the modest entrance fee goes to funding their work. Within the Animal Centre you can get close up to a range of creatures, including goats, Aylesbury ducks, ponies, parakeets, owls and others. A hedgehog garden demonstrates how you can help your local prickly friends. A sign by one aviary reads: 'If you see any Ring Necked Parakeets flying nearby don't panic, they don't belong to us!' Ring-necked parakeets are now the UK's most abundant naturalised parrot. The parakeets in the WRAS aviary are residents, having come here sick or injured. As they are classed as an invasive species, it is illegal to release them into the wild. The site also features a **tea shop** and a playground.

☞ Continue along the road (Lime Avenue). To the right is a hay meadow, managed for wildlife. On the left is:

6. GO APE (Trent Country Park, Cockfosters Rd, Barnet EN4 0DZ ⊘ goape. co.uk £££) Mainly for children and young adults, this treetop outdoor activity

centre offers a range of high-adrenaline experiences, using zip wires, Tarzan swings and rope ladders (strapped into a harness, of course).

☞ Follow the roadway back past the monument commemorating the construction of the gardens, out of the park, to Cockfosters Road. Turn right, then cross the road to take the first left into Chalk Lane. A short distance along, you will find the:

7. COCK INN (14 Chalk Lane, Cockfosters, Barnet EN4 9HU

⚭ thecockinncockfosters.co.uk) This large comfortable pub dates back to 1798, and was once named the Cock & Dragon after the alleged slaughter of a dragon in the 17th century by a local villager called Jason, who thus saved a Princess Louise. These days it serves Fuller's London Pride and is an upmarket dining venue ('No baseball caps after 7.00pm', according to one sign).

☞ Turn right out of the pub and bear left (following a 'London Loop' arrow) along Chalk Lane, past the playing fields of Cockfosters Bowling Club, Cockfosters Football Club and a cricket pitch all on the left, and back to Cockfosters Road. A few yards to the right is the subway to Cockfosters tube station.

↑ Go Ape in Trent Country Park. (DRG Photography/S)

18 MIDSOMER MURDERS TRAIL

INTO THE REALMS OF FICTION, WITH TV WHODUNNITS & THE WORLD OF ROALD DAHL, IN THE CHILTERNS LANDSCAPE

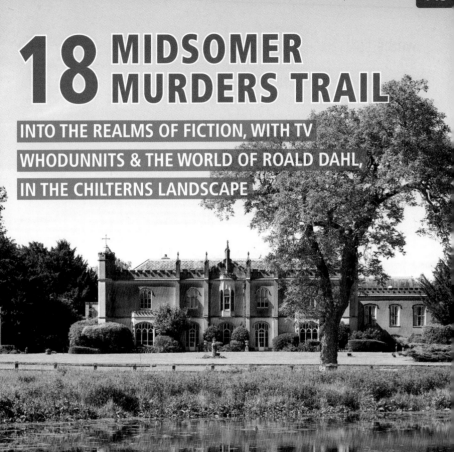

Beyond Amersham, this route runs village to village along the Misbourne valley, keeping company with the perch-laden River Misbourne ('bourne' meaning stream that disappears from time to time). Red kites are a regular sight over the farmland and lakes, and you may also spot buzzards and herons. Watercress grows here in one or two places, a reminder of what used to be a major industry on the river, along with fish and milling.

The scenery will be familiar to many viewers of ITV's *Midsomer Murders*, which is filmed in this area of the Chilterns. Indeed, *Missenden Murders* was considered as its original title. The series started in 1997 and is still going strong, and on the walk you'll pass many of its locations. Roald Dahl's connections with the area are celebrated in great style at the excellent child-oriented museum devoted to the writer and his works in Great Missenden, the village where he lived and died.

↑ Missenden Abbey and parkland. (Jason Ballard/A)

WHERE: Buckinghamshire, River Misbourne: Amersham to Great Missenden
STATS: 8½ miles/3½hrs; easy–moderate
START POINT/GETTING THERE: Amersham station /// wisely.costs.index
⊖ Metropolitan Line from Baker Street (50mins; 2 an hour) or 🚌 from Marylebone
(35mins; 1–2 an hour); turn left out of the station's main exit
FINISH: Black Horse, Great Missenden /// arriving.loaf.adventure
DROP-OUT POINT: After 4½ miles
MAPS: OS Explorer maps 172 & 181
TAKING A BREAK: The Eagle, Koko'S food trailer, Crown Inn, Red Lion, Kingshill
Kitchen, Full Moon, The George Alehouse, Roald Dahl Museum & Story Centre, Wild
Kite Bottleshop, Black Horse

☞ After leaving the station go downhill a few yards and turn left again under
the railway bridge, down Station Road. After a few minutes, cross the road
and take a footpath between two hedges, signposted 'Martyrs Memorial'.
When the path opens out into a field, turn right and walk a short distance
uphill to:

1. THE AMERSHAM MARTYRS MEMORIAL This tall stone
monument commemorates a time when the Chilterns was a key centre of
activity for a medieval form of religious dissent – before the Reformation

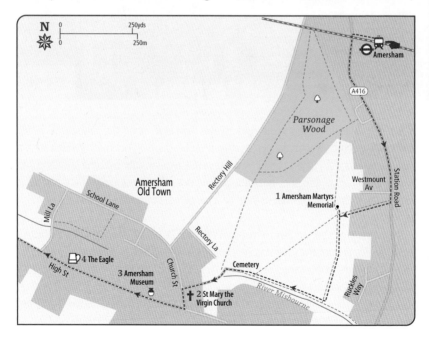

– known as Lollardy. Its name originates in a Dutch word for mumbling and is associated with 'lolling' of the tongue (not modern 'lols') and perceived stupidity. Lollardy rejected the trappings of traditional religion at that time, including the cult of saints, the veneration of images, confession to a priest, ashes and holy water. Some estimates suggest that by the early 16th century one in ten Amersham residents had Lollard sympathies. Between 1511 and 1521 seven people from, or connected to, the town were executed as Lollard heretics. In two cases the authorities forced the martyrs' children to light their pyres. In summer, period-costume-wearing volunteers from Amersham Museum (see below) lead guided historical walks to the monument.

☛ Retrace your steps and continue down the footpath along the field boundary. At the bottom of the hill turn right into a footpath leading between fields and Tesco's car park (and the River Misbourne, which is very narrow at this point). When you reach a cemetery (St Mary's), cross the small bridge over the river to:

2. ST MARY THE VIRGIN CHURCH (Church St, Old Amersham HP7 0DB ♂ stmaryschurchamersham.com) This church dates from about 1140, but long before then the site was used for baptisms by missionary monks of St Augustine (AD354–430), the patron saint of brewers and 'the alleviation of sore eyes'. A community play about the Amersham Martyrs has been performed many times in the church.

It was here that John Knox (1514–72), the leading Protestant and founder of Presbyterianism, preached his last sermon before fleeing from the new Catholic queen, Mary Tudor, in 1554. Many of the rectors were from the Drake family (descendants of admiral Sir Francis Drake's cousin).

Church funds have been raised by a variety of means over the years, the strangest perhaps being in 1539 when 'youngsters took turns tripping up passers-by, and tying them up until they agreed to make a payment' (from *St Mary's Church, Amersham: A Brief History and Guide*, by MJC Andrews-Reading).

☛ Nearby (left into Church Street and first right into Market Square then High Street) is:

3. AMERSHAM MUSEUM (49 High St, Old Amersham HP7 0DP ♂ amershammuseum.org ◷ noon–16.30 Wed–Sun £) Housed in a 16th-century building, but with a glass reception area complete with a large replica Underground sign, Amersham Museum provides local snapshots of different years or decades. You can imagine life as a merchant in the 1580s or sit in a

1930s living room and listen to local people's stories on a wireless (ahem, radio). The star exhibit is the preserved remains of a sulphur-crested cockatoo, whose squawks saved lives when a local hotel caught fire. There are also embroidered displays of front covers from the annual leaflet which the Metropolitan Railways Country Estates published to promote their housing developments along the line: a strong evocation of what John Betjeman called 'Metro-Land'. There is a herb garden to the rear, with an artwork commemorating the Amersham Martyrs on the wall.

☞ Continue along the High Street to:

4. THE EAGLE (145 High St, Amersham HP7 0DY ⊘ theeaglemersham. co.uk) Known in the 19th century as 'the poachers' pub' (because of its discreet rear exit), this traditional pub was licensed originally to sell only beer, cider and perry. Part of the building is 17th century but it did not become an alehouse until the middle of the 19th century. Offering real ale (including local IPA beers such as Neck Oil and Rebellion) and home-cooked food, it has a beer garden overlooking the river and meadow.

☞ Turning right as you leave, continue to the end of the High Street. Follow the road uphill and take the path on the left which goes away from the road between trees and takes you up to the A413. Then turn right and after a few yards turn right into a footpath marked 'South Bucks Way'. This takes you down to the river again. Turn left under the road bridge, and follow the path away from the river to another road (not open to the public). Go through the grounds of the Shardeloes estate, then fork right (following 'South Bucks Way' signs still), past the:

5. AMERSHAM CRICKET CLUB (Shardeloes, Missenden Rd, Old Amersham HP7 0RN ⊘ amershamcc.co.uk) This club dates back to the 1830s or even earlier. In the 1840s their star batter was Rev John Tyrwhitt-Drake and later his nephew, Rev Edward Tyrwhitt-Drake, went on to play first-class cricket for Cambridge University, specialising in slow left-arm underarm bowling; he was described as 'the prince of Buckinghamshire cricketers'. The club has four Saturday teams and welcomes visitors.

☞ Follow the perimeter fence until you come to a gate on the right (still marked 'South Bucks Way'). If you're in luck, the **Koko'S food trailer** (📘 KokoSanela) will be there, offering turkey toasties, tuna salad sandwiches and other snacks. You will soon rejoin the river which goes to (on the right):

1 Shardeloes Manor House. **2** The Amersham Martyrs Memorial. **3** St Mary the Virgin church, Amersham.
4 Amersham Museum.

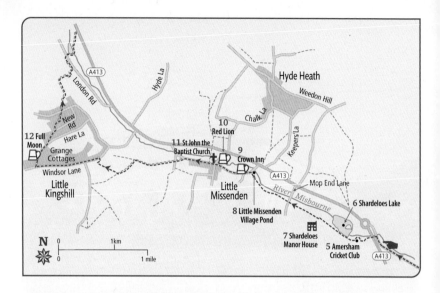

6. SHARDELOES LAKE

When the lake was being dug around 1750, remains of a Roman villa were found. In addition to swans it is visited by many species of bird: local twitchers have spotted water rail, reed bunting, spotted flycatcher, mandarin duck, fieldfare, common teal, grey heron, shoveler and carrion crow.

☞ As you go round the lake, up on the hill to the left you will see:

7. SHARDELOES MANOR HOUSE

The present building was constructed in 1758 for William Drake, MP for Amersham, with Robert Adam designing its interior, and stands on the site of an earlier manor where Elizabeth I stayed in 1592. The Drake and Tyrwhitt-Drake family were Lords of the Manor whose wealth increased up to the 19th century, only for their fortunes to decline; Squire Drake had to sell most of his property in 1928 and the house was auctioned off in the 1930s. It later became a maternity home, then fell into disuse and was scheduled for demolition in 1953 but a local campaign saved the day, and it was converted into flats which were sold off in the 1970s.

☞ Keep following the 'South Bucks Way' signs through the fields and farmland until you come to a country lane. A few yards to the right is:

8. LITTLE MISSENDEN VILLAGE POND

You can spot plenty of large trout in this duck-patrolled body of water. The village's name may come from a combination of an Old English word meaning 'moss' and 'den', an Anglo-Saxon word meaning 'valley'. One of its most infamous residents was Dr Benjamin Bates (1736–1828), who moved in about 1774 into the Manor House. A member of the notorious Hellfire Club, he was described as one of its leading members by E Beresford Chancellor in his 1925 book *The Lives of the Rakes: Volume IV, The Hell Fire Club*. Various debaucheries were allegedly practised by club members, whose motto 'Do what thou wilt' was later adopted by the satanist Aleister Crowley (1875–1947). What really went on was probably tamer than the legends suggest.

☞ Retrace your steps and continue along the lane to the:

9. CROWN INN (🍺 Little Missenden HP7 0RD ☎ 01494 862571) This

traditional pub of stone, with wooden floors – and an open fire in winter – serves Harvey's Sussex Best Bitter and three changing beers, often Oakham, Otter or Timothy Taylor's. A converted barn has three double en-suite rooms for accommodation.

☞ A few minutes' walk further along the lane, on the right, is the:

10. RED LION (Little Missenden HP7 0QZ ☎ 01494 862876) Featured in

several episodes of *Midsomer Murders*, this old pub claims to have been visited by many monarchs from George II to Elizabeth II, and Prince Harry once dropped in for ham, egg and chips.

The Red Lion dates back to 1649 when it was a coaching inn for the Uxbridge to Aylesbury route. When the railway was completed in 1900, many people travelled from Amersham to spend a few days in the countryside, often staying at this pub (it still does bed and breakfast). The evidence of these guests is seen in the form of the unique table mats that show entries from its visitors' book from those days. One from Dalston Rambling Club, dated 4 August 1913, states they 'had a very enjoyable tea, so much so that the members of the Choral Class could not refrain from singing some glees'. The pub still has a piano which attracts local musicians who play live on Saturday nights. Real ale includes Sharp's Doom Bar and Wadworth 6X, and there's a dartboard; walkers are requested to remove muddy boots.

Adjoining the pub is a large fish pond, which attracts swans, ducks and ducklings (one of which we witnessed stopping a lorry on the road).

☞ Continue along the road until you come (on the right) to:

11. ST JOHN THE BAPTIST CHURCH (Little Missenden HP7 0RA

☾ lmchurch.org) The River Misbourne flows past the back of this Saxon church,

PETER FLEMING/S

PETER ARKELL

DENIS KELLY/DT

HELEN MATTHEWS

1 Roald Dahl Museum & Story Centre, Great Missenden. **2** The petrol pumps that feature in *Danny the Champion of the World*, Great Missenden. **3** Little Missenden. **4** Little Missenden pond.

the oldest part of which dates back to AD975. King John, while Prince, gave two bells to the church. He often stayed in the nearby royal hunting lodge at Ashwell Farm, Little Kingshill, where reports of wild parties with loose women and alcohol were rife. Roald Dahl, who loved the church, was another who made a donation: a wooden figure of St Catherine (a copy of which is on the north wall). Two *Midsomer Murders* have been filmed here, and film star Diana Rigg (who appeared in the television series *The Avengers* and the James Bond film *On Her Majesty's Secret Service*) attended school services here.

Particularly striking is the stained-glass window 'Faith, Hope and Charity', in the style of William Morris and Edward Burne-Jones. In recent years a restoration project has revealed many of the church's wall paintings, the earliest of which dates from the 12th century. The paintings had been hidden under limewash following the Reformation, to save them from vandalism or destruction; the church's vicar discovered them by chance in 1931.

The church is also the main venue of the famous Little Missenden Music Festival which started in 1961 and is still going strong, every October. It includes classical music, jazz, folk, poetry, art lectures and children's events.

🖐 You can opt out here if you time it right – buses from the village run twice a week (Tue & Thu c 09.30 & 12.20; 35mins) to Chesham, where you can pick up the Metropolitan Line. Alternatively, you may wish to walk back to Amersham, stay overnight in one of the two pubs, or phone the local taxi firm, Kingshill Cars (✆ 01494 868699/07852 898699).

👉 To carry on, continue along the road, just past Highmore Cottages on the left, to a kissing gate on the left signposted 'Chiltern Heritage Trail'. Cross a paddock diagonally through to the far side and another kissing gate, head over a public bridleway and then keep ahead on the path marked 'South Bucks Way'. This takes you uphill with a hedge on your right and a field by a wood on the left. The path winds right, then left between a pylon and a hedge downhill towards more woods. After just a few yards there is an easily missed 'Public Footpath' yellow arrow quite high on a telegraph pole, pointing right through the middle of a large arable field. Go straight across the field, then on to a path through the woods, then left on to Windsor Lane, just to the left of the junction with Deep Mill Lane.

Turn left following the 'South Bucks Way' and 'Chiltern Heritage Trail Walking Route' signs along the lane for about ten minutes, past Little Kingshill Village Hall on the left, to the village green and playground on the right (by a bus stop). To the left is **Kingshill Kitchen** (⌂ kingshillbaptist.co.uk), an Italian coffee shop and deli housed in a Baptist chapel.

Turn right along the far side of the village green, marked 'South Bucks Way', to a path between houses, and turn right into Hare Lane. This takes you to the:

12. FULL MOON

(Hare Lane, Little Kingshill HP16 0EE, opposite Grange Cottages ⊘ thefullmoon.info) A traditional, independently run pub which serves, among other things, Fuller's London Pride, the local Rebellion IPA, guest ales and international lagers, along with hot food (Tue–Sun). It has a large car park and beer garden, with a heated tent ideal for walkers and families.

☛ Continue along the charming Hare Lane. After a short distance take the left fork into New Road. When you reach the junction with Wychwood, follow the path just to the left of the road between a holly bush and a fence marked 'South Bucks Way'. When you come to a road, cross it and continue along the path ahead between the fence to Cullen House and a holly bush. This takes you to a kissing gate into a field. Follow the path bearing right and ahead round the edge of the field. After a while the path goes right, through a gap in the hedge and under a railway bridge. Keep following the path, turning left at the 'Public Footpath' sign beside some fenced-off playing fields on the left.

Follow the path as it turns left round the other side of the playing fields to a kissing gate on the right to a road, which you cross, and follow the path ahead, which takes you to a kissing gate into a meadow. This is:

13. MISSENDEN ABBEY PARKLAND

William de Missenden founded Missenden Abbey in 1133. It was dissolved in 1538, when most of it was demolished. It was rebuilt in 1787 and bought in 1947 by Buckinghamshire County Council to use as an adult education centre. A fire in 1985 destroyed most of it but the council rebuilt it, uncovering part of its medieval structure in the process. Now it belongs to Buckinghamshire New University and opens for conferences, training events, weddings, lunches and afternoon tea, as well as offering 57 en-suite bedrooms for overnight accommodation. The grounds are the remnants of late 18th- and early 19th-century landscape and woodland. The main feature of the park is the pond known as Warren Water, which may be medieval in origin and is fed by the Misbourne.

☛ After entering the meadow, continue past the restored 19th-century iron footbridge by Warren Water on the left and follow the path round to the left to the far side of the parkland. When you come to another kissing gate with yellow arrows, take the few wooden steps up to a bridge over the main road. On the other side of the bridge is:

14. ST PETER & ST PAUL'S CHURCH (Church Lane, Great Missenden HP16 0BA ⌖ missendenchurch.org.uk) The world-famous author Roald Dahl (1916–90) is buried in the churchyard here. He had, according to his daughter, 'a sort of Viking funeral' as befitted his Norwegian parentage. On his insistence his snooker cues, a bottle of burgundy, chocolates, pencils and a power saw were all buried with him. The church itself was built in the 14th century and restored in the 19th century. Look out for a delightful stained-glass window that celebrates Great Ormond Street Hospital.

☛ Go back over the road bridge, follow a path downhill to the right and then go left into Church Street and up to the junction with the High Street. Across the High Street to the left is:

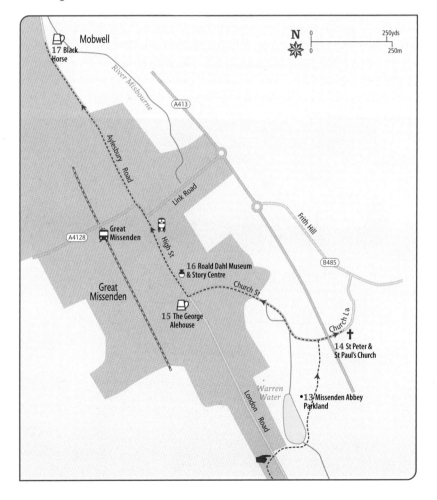

15. THE GEORGE ALEHOUSE (🍺 94 High St, Great Missenden HP16 0BG 🖉 01494 865185) This historic coaching inn dates back to the 14th century, and still has the coaching arch and courtyard. The timber beams were made from the remains of a wooden galleon.

The George narrowly escaped redevelopment into housing a few years ago. It reopened in 2018 as a dog-friendly, adults-only drinking pub and live music venue. It serves Harvey's Sussex Best Bitter and three other beers on rotation.

☛ Turn left out of the pub and a short way on the right you will come to:

16. ROALD DAHL MUSEUM & STORY CENTRE (81–83 High St, Great Missenden HP16 0AL 🖉 01494 892192 🖉 roalddahlmuseum.org 🕙 10.00–16.30 Thu–Sun, also 11.00–17.00 daily during local school summer hols & Aug Bank Hol Mon **£**) A wonderful homage to one of the most-read children's authors (not to mention his huge success with adult fiction too). This museum is aimed at 6- to 12-year-olds, but visiting adults have found their own creativity inspired by observing the children's interactive story-telling and craft sessions, and the colourful displays about the author's life interest people of all ages.

↑ The River Misbourne flows past the Black Horse pub. (Shen Stone/S)

Many characters in Great Missenden inspired Roald Dahl's books, which sold over 100 million copies in about 50 languages. In 1986 he turned down an OBE, wanting instead a knighthood so his wife could become Lady Dahl.

Born in Wales to Norwegian parents, Dahl served in the RAF during World War II, becoming a wing commander. He shot down five planes, earning the title of 'ace', and began writing in 1942. He moved to Gipsy House in Great Missenden in 1954, where he wrote in the small hut at the end of the garden, next to a traditional gypsy wagon he had bought as a playhouse for his children. The hut, now in the museum, was described as a dingy but cosy refuge. A dirty plastic curtain covered the window, and he sat on a faded armchair inherited from his mother, writing with pencils and paper as he could not type. Next to him on a table he kept a ball made from silver wrappings off the many chocolate bars he had consumed in his youth, which may have helped inspire one of his most famous books, *Charlie and the Chocolate Factory*, published in 1964.

There is an on-site **café** for refreshment before you move on.

☛ Continue along the High Street, on which there are three sights relating to Roald Dahl books: the petrol pumps which feature in *Danny the Champion of the World*; Crown House, which inspired the 'Norphanage' in *The BFG*; and the library which Matilda visits in the book that bears her name. There are several good restaurants and cafés, and the **Wild Kite Bottleshop** (⊘ wildkite.co.uk) is around the corner, too. Go past the sign to the railway station on the left and continue up Aylesbury Road where after about 15 minutes you'll reach the:

17. BLACK HORSE (Aylesbury Rd, Mobwell, Great Missenden HP16 9AX

⊘ theblackhorsegreatmissenden.com) The River Misbourne flows by this dog-friendly restaurant and pub which has a five-a-side football pitch, a dartboard and an open fire. There's also a large patio where barbecues are served in summer; real ales include Sharp's Doom Bar. Hot-air balloons (⊘ adventureballoons.co.uk/buckinghamshire-balloon-flights) take off and land regularly from the fields next to this pub in the summer.

☛ For your return journey follow the sign off the High Street to Great Missenden railway station, in Station Approach, and either take the 41 bus back to Amersham (15mins; 1 an hour), or pay for a train ticket (7mins; 1–2 an hour) to Amersham, from where your Freedom Pass is valid.

19 FROM DICKENS TO THE ROLLING STONES

ALONG THE DARENT VALLEY FOOTPATH
TO ENCOUNTER AN INTRIGUING CAST
OF KENTISH CHARACTERS

Although it ends in central Dartford, this walk enjoys some pleasingly rural stretches along the Darent as it winds through meadows, pastures, farmland and woodlands. What is special about it is that it follows the river practically the whole way, except for a few very short stretches, as it flows through the Darent (sometimes spelled Darenth) Valley. You'll see where Charles Dickens fished for trout, where Mick Jagger and Keith Richards of the Rolling Stones met, and where Wat Tyler gathered support during the Peasants' Revolt in 1381.

WHERE: Kent, River Darent: Farningham to Dartford
STATS: 7 miles/2½–3 hrs; easy
START POINT/GETTING THERE: Lion Hotel, Farningham /// walks.belts.lofts
🚃 To Swanley station from London Victoria (25–31mins; 3 an hour Mon–Sat, 1 an hour Sun). Exit station by Platform 1 into Station Approach, go to the end of the road to the junction, then turn right to the bus stop on the same side of road. Take 🚌 429 to Farningham (7mins; 1 an hour Mon–Sat only). Get off at the Lion Hotel stop.
FINISH: Dartford railway station /// stable.flags.notion
DROP-OUT POINTS: After 3 miles (two drop-out points) & 4½ miles
MAP: OS Explorer map 162
TAKING A BREAK: The Chequers (Farningham), Lion Hotel, The Chequers (Darenth), Brooklands Lakes, Wat Tyler, Churchyard Tearoom (Dartford Parish Church)

☛ Go back a few yards from where the bus stops, to the corner, where you will find:

1. THE CHEQUERS (87 High St, cnr Dartford Rd, Farningham DA4 0DT 🆗 thechequersfarningham) Rolling Stones memorabilia adorns this pub, in celebration of local boys Keith Richards and Mick Jagger who hail from nearby Dartford. Dating from 1797, the pub also features murals of local scenes and, less predictably, two candelabra and a suit of armour. The changing beers on offer typically include Harvey's, ESB and Mighty Oak. A piano is also on hand and there are regular open mic and quiz nights.

☛ Retrace your steps past the bus stop down to, on the left:

2. LION HOTEL (High St, Farningham DA4 0DP ⌀ vintageinn.co.uk/thelionfarningham) This pub dates back to the 16th century and was once visited by Charles Dickens when he was trout-fishing on the adjoining riverbank. The main beer is Sharp's Doom Bar, with alternating guest ales; you can drink in the garden overlooking the river, and hot food is available.

← The Glimmer Twins. (Helen Matthews)

☞ Opposite the pub is the:

3. FOLLY BRIDGE OVER THE RIVER DARENT

Built between 1740 and 1770 to prevent cattle from wandering downstream while crossing the ford, this bridge is a strikingly ornate example of its kind. Water mint and wild watercress grow by the banks of the Darent, and herons, swans and kingfishers may be seen on and around the river. The Darent's name derives from a Celtic word for 'oak river' and the area has been settled since 6000BC. Edmund Spenser (1552–99) refers to it in his poem *The Faerie Queene* as 'the still Darent, in whose waters cleane/ Ten thousand fishes play, and decke his pleasant streame'.

☞ Turn left along the river on its left bank (through the Lion Hotel's beer garden) following the 'Darent Valley Footpath' signs; there is a slightly dilapidated wooden sign, not easy to spot, just past the bridge. After crossing a wooden footbridge the route passes under the A20 then under another bridge beneath the M20. Shortly afterwards the path goes right over a footbridge then left through a stile between two fences. After a while, you reach Horton Kirby Cricket Club ground on the right. Here, turn left into a lane (Franks Lane) and go a short distance to a bridge over the river, then turn right and continue along its left bank, with trees by the river

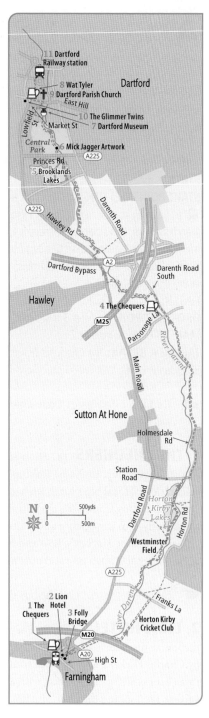

and fields on the left. Soon you go through a kissing gate into a football field (Westminster Field). By the pavilion, turn right through a gate back to the river and continue a short distance along the left bank. The path returns to the football field and then right, past Horton Kirby Lakes on the left, and back to the left bank of the river past rapids. Eventually you reach a road (Station Road) and a large railway viaduct parallel to it.

✋ If you want to leave the walk at this point, turn left along Station Road a short distance to Farningham Road railway station (a small charge will cover you to Swanley and back into the Freedom Pass zone).

☞ To continue the walk, turn right into Station Road to reach the T junction with Horton Road.

✋ Opposite the junction is a bus stop for the 414 to Dartford railway station (32mins; 2 an hour; no service Sun). You can use your Freedom Pass on the bus and the train.

☞ Otherwise turn left into Horton Road and under the viaduct. Continue along Holmesdale Road as it skirts the right bank of the river. As the road bends right, away from the river, turn left at The White House (signposted 'Darenth Valley Footpath'), over a stile between fences into an arable field. Take a path through the field to the left, close to the river. At the end of the field, continue to follow the path along the river to the left. After the path moves away from the river, it goes down steps to a path fenced off from a private lane on the left, which takes you to another road (Parsonage Lane). Go straight over it ahead into Darenth Road South. (If the river path is very overgrown, you can take a detour along the track to the right, turn left along Roman Villa Road and then take a footpath on the left to get back to Darenth Road South). Here you will find:

4. THE CHEQUERS (Darenth Rd South, Darenth DA2 7QT

🅵 thechequersdarenth) Another traditional, family-friendly pub with a beer garden, The Chequers was a 16th-century coaching inn. It does hot food, including a Sunday roast. Real ales include Sharp's Doom Bar, Fuller's London Pride and Harvey's Armada Ale.

☞ Continue along Darenth Road South to the end of the made-up road, then left through a kissing gate, signposted 'Darenth Valley Footpath', through a field and back to the river on its right bank. Follow it under the M25, sticking to the right bank of the river, for a short distance, then cross a wooden footbridge over the river to the left bank, then left away from the river to a road (Hawley Road, A225) with Mill Road ahead. Turn right along Hawley Road (signposted 'Darenth Valley Footpath').

✋ A short distance on the right is the Shirehall Road Bus Stop in Hawley for the 414 bus to Horton Kirby. You are now just 2½ miles from Dartford station. To get the bus there you need the bus stop on the other side of the road.

☞ Continue along the Hawley Road a short distance under the A2, and after a few yards turn right over a stile (signposted 'Darenth Valley Footpath') into a field and fork left, back to the river, and continue along its left bank on an asphalt path. After a short distance cross over a wooden bridge to the right bank of the river and through woodlands. When you come to a road, turn left, over the road bridge across the river, and then right, following the left bank of the river. This takes you on a path between the river and the:

5. BROOKLANDS LAKES This is a private fishing lake but has waterside trails open to the public, and is described by Kent County Council as 'a peaceful place for a lakeside stroll'. There is also a **café** (🕑 08.00–15.00 Mon–Sat). Those wishing to fish can buy a day ticket; carp up to 30 pounds have been caught here, but have to be returned to the water.

☞ Walk round the edge of the lake as it bends left, then turn off to the right through The Princes Tunnel. If this is locked take the steps on the left up to the road (Princes Road), cross the road diagonally right to the path on the other side, then follow it through zigzags down to Central Park and back to the left bank of the river. Here there is a:

6. MICK JAGGER ARTWORK (Central Park, Dartford) This ironwork stencil-style two-dimensional artwork portrays Rolling Stones singer Mick Jagger. Jagger was born in Dartford in 1943 and attended the local Wentworth Primary School, where fellow Rolling Stone, Keith Richards, was also a pupil but a year behind. Mick Jagger lived at nearby Denver Road, and later attended the local grammar school. The Mick Jagger Centre live music venue (⌀ themickjaggercentre.com), which the man himself officially opened at a ceremony in 2000, is in Shepherds Lane, Dartford DA1 2JZ.

☞ Continue along the riverbank, where we saw parakeets in a willow tree, until it is fenced off. Then take the path to the left, past a playground, through a gate, to an ornamental bridge, and then right to the park exit. Turn right into Market Street and drop into:

7. DARTFORD MUSEUM (Market St, Dartford DA1 1EU ⊘ dartford.gov.uk/museum ⊙ 10.00–17.00 Mon–Fri, 10.00–16.00 Sat) In just one room, this museum covers the area from prehistoric times to the present. Highlights include the late 4th-century Darenth Bowl, found in an Anglo-Saxon grave in Darenth Country Park, and the 'cash railway' from a historic draper's shop in the High Street.

☛ Leaving the museum, continue up to the corner of the High Street. Directly opposite (on the corner of Bullace Lane) is the:

8. WAT TYLER (80 High St, Dartford DA1 1DE ⬛ TheWatTyler) A historic pub named after the Peasants' Revolt leader of 1381, who drank here on the march to London. Dartford was one of the early towns to rise up on 4–5 June of that year, initially protesting against the hated poll tax.

A plaque on the pub wall proclaims Wat and his followers 'called at this ancient tavern (so it is said) to quench their thirst with flagons of ale' before marching to London to see the king and demand 'that you make us free for ever, ourselves, our heirs and our lands and that we be called no more bond or so reputed'. The young king, Richard II, playing for time, promised he would grant them freedom.

The king met Tyler again at Smithfield on 15 June. Accounts of this meeting vary considerably. According to a contemporary source, the *Anonimalle Chronicle*, Tyler outlined a list of demands including the division of church lands among the laity (after provision for the clergy and monks) and the abolition of serfdom. Richard said he would grant all that he fairly could, while retaining the 'regality' of the crown. There may have been an attempt to pick a fight with Tyler, who had kept his head covered, annoying the royal party. In the ensuing scuffle the Mayor of London, William Walworth, wounded Tyler in the neck before another member of the royal party killed him. After city militia surrounded the other rebels, Richard pardoned them, allowing them to go home. The authorities removed Tyler's body from the nearby hospital of St Bartholomew and beheaded him at Smithfield. The revolt collapsed after Tyler's death.

Four hundred years later, Thomas Paine (who fought in both the American and French revolutions) said of Tyler: 'All his proposals made to Richard were on a more just and public ground than those which had been made to John by the Barons… If the Barons merited a monument to be erected in Runnymede, Tyler merits one in Smithfield.'

Sadly the only legacy he has in Smithfield is the dagger which killed him, held in Fishmongers' Hall.

HELEN MATTHEWS

PETER ARKELL

HELEN MATTHEWS

THE ROLLING STONES
British Rock Band
Mick Jagger and Keith Richards met on platform 2 on 17 October 1961 and went on to form The Rolling Stones - one of the most successful rock bands of all time

DAVID DENNIS/S

1 The Folly Bridge over the River Darent. **2** Stencil-style Mick Jagger artwork in Dartford's Central Park.
3 A blue plaque in Dartford's train station commemorates the meeting of Mick Jagger and Keith Richards.
4 The River Darent in the Darenth Valley.

☞ Leaving the Wat Tyler, turn left for a look inside:

9. DARTFORD PARISH CHURCH (High St, Dartford DA1 1DE ✆ 01322 222782) This church has an impressive monument to Sir John Spilman (d 1626) and his wife Elizabeth (d 1607). Sir John was originally from Lindau in Bavaria; he became a goldsmith and jeweller to Elizabeth I and James I, as well as a paper-maker who established Dartford's first paper mill. You can get refreshments at the **Churchyard Tearoom** (⬙ thechurchyardtearoom.co.uk).

☞ Go out of the church and back along the High Street, noticing the blue plaque on the wall of Boots commemorating a stay by Jane Austen at the inn which once stood on the site. Continue along the street until you reach:

10. THE GLIMMER TWINS This new bronze artwork by Amy Goodman, depicting Mick Jagger and Keith Richards in mid-performance and taking its name from their nickname as a duo, was unveiled in 2023. The colourful mural on the wall behind depicts the area's first paper mill, an important part of the town's economic development. Next door is the Victoria and Bull pub which sports a blue plaque remembering Richard Trevithick (1781–1833). Trevithick, a pioneering engineer, invented the first steam-powered railway locomotive. He stayed here from 1831 (and, less happily, died here as well).

☞ From here, retrace your steps a short distance along the High Street and turn left into Bulls Head Yard. Go past the Orchard Theatre on the left, then up the steps and over the bridge to:

11. DARTFORD RAILWAY STATION This is where Mick Jagger and Keith Richards met, on Platform 2 on 17 October 1961. Mick, aged 18, was on his way to the London School of Economics where he was a student, and Keith, aged 17, was on his way to Sidcup Art College, which he attended after being expelled from Dartford Technical School for truancy. Keith was carrying his guitar and Mick his rhythm and blues records. They recognised each other from Wentworth Primary School and got chatting and discussed music on the train.

Richards joined Jagger's group, Little Boy Blue and the Blue Boys, but a year later they met Brian Jones and Ian Stewart to form the Rolling Stones.

A blue plaque on Platform 2 (London-bound) commemorates this meeting.

☞ From here you can get trains to Victoria (50mins–1hr; up to 8 an hour) or Charing Cross (48–55mins; up to 8 an hour).

20 BROOKSIDE & THE BIG GREEN SPACE

A BROOKSIDE EXPLORATION THROUGH WELL-HEELED SOUTHWEST LONDON, ON A REMARKABLY GREEN JOURNEY NORTHWARDS TO THE THAMES

W alk along the modest Beverley Brook and you can hardly fail to be impressed by the sheer size of southwest London's urban commons – vital green lungs in some very select suburbs and the longest joined-up parkland in London. That they join up to make one contiguous swathe means you can really stretch your legs on this quasi-country walk, which incorporates an eerie Victorian graveyard allegedly stalked by a devilish imp in the 1830s. If you want to extend the walk, there are almost infinite possibilities, with a vast network of official and unofficial paths over Wimbledon Common, where the windmill makes a useful objective, or into the breezy, rather wild expanse of Richmond Park with its lakes, herds of deer and splendid azaleas within the Isabella Plantation. Near Barnes Common, the centre of Barnes still evokes village origins, and soon afterwards the brook you've been following all these miles finally discharges into the Thames.

WHERE: Southwest London: New Malden to Putney Bridge
STATS: 8 miles/3hrs; easy
START POINT/GETTING THERE: New Malden railway station /// ports.forum.option
🚆 To New Malden from Waterloo (22mins; 5–8 an hour, 4 on Sun); turn right out of the station into Coombe Rd
FINISH: Putney Bridge underground station (District Line) /// calms.glare.poet
DROP-OUT POINTS: After 4, 6 & 6½ miles
MAPS: OS Explorer map 161
TAKING A BREAK: The Stag's Head, Vine Road Community Café, Duke's Head, The Eight Bells

☛ After turning right into Coombe Road, take the second turning on the right (Cambridge Avenue) and keep going to a woodland path ahead through a golf course. Continue through a subway under the A3, then left and left again on to the bank of the Beverley Brook. Continue along Westcoombe Avenue, then turn left into Coombe Lane and right into Beverley Avenue. At the end turn left into a path, then right by some playing fields. Follow the brook on your left through woodlands and past the:

1. BEVERLEY MEADS & FISHPONDS LOCAL NATURE
RESERVE This land was the property of Merton Abbey in the medieval era; the two ponds in Fishponds Wood may date from that time and their original purpose may have been to store water for a textile mill, or as fishponds for the abbey (hence the name). Wimbledon Borough Council acquired it in the 1950s and, though it was laid out for a pitch and putt course in the 1970s, it became a nature reserve in 1993. The woodland is mainly oak with coppiced hazel. Kingfishers and mandarin ducks are often to be seen here and, in spring, you may spot frogs, dragonflies and butterflies around the ponds.

← Beverley Brook, Wimbledon Common. (Nick Moore/A)

☞ The path takes you along the edge of:

2. WIMBLEDON COMMON (⊘ wpcc.org.uk/the-commons)

Encompassing a huge expanse of woodland as well as areas of heath with heather and gorse, this is one of London's largest open spaces. It is designated a Site of Special Scientific Interest and, as a Special Area of Conservation, is a habitat for many woodland birds and insects. In the 16th century, local men between the ages of 16 and 60 were obliged by law to practise archery regularly here, and the common was used for duels in the 19th century. The most famous was on 21 September 1809 between George Canning (1770–1827) and Lord Castlereagh (1769–1822). Both were senior members of the British government at the time, with Canning being Foreign Secretary and Castlereagh Secretary of State for War & the Colonies. Castlereagh challenged Canning to the duel after a prolonged dispute concerning the conduct of the war against Napoleon. Castlereagh shot and wounded Canning in the leg, and lost nothing but a shirt button. In the short term, the duel did neither of them much good, however, as they were both soon out of the government. In later years Canning would become Prime Minister and Castlereagh Foreign Secretary.

☞ The path is part of the Capital Ring for a short way. Just before reaching a sports pavilion turn left across a bridge over the brook, and then cross the A3 to Kingston Vale Road.

✋ The 85 bus to Putney can be caught in Kingston Vale Road.

☞ To continue the walk go through the Robin Hood Gate leading into:

3. RICHMOND PARK (⊘ royalparks.org.uk) This huge area of rough

pasture, woodland and ponds remains one of London's largest untamed expanses. It is the capital's largest Site of Special Scientific Interest and a designated National Nature Reserve. Its appearance can have changed little since Charles I enclosed it within a ten-mile boundary wall as a hunting park. The King introduced deer to the area in 1637; some 300 red and 350 fallow deer graze here today. The rutting season is in the autumn and the young are born in June. The park is a noted site for ancient trees, including a number of oaks planted before 1637. These in turn attract more than 1,000 species of beetle, including the rare cardinal click beetle and the spectacularly outsized and scarce stag beetle (known by some Londoners as a 'horny bug') – Britain's biggest beetle. Over a hundred species of bird can be seen in the park, including skylarks, kestrels and tawny owls. If you want to pause for a while, consider visiting the Isabella Plantation, a 40-acre woodland garden that is notable for its azaleas (at their most spectacular in late April and early May).

☛ Inside the park take the path to the right, and then bear right at a fork after a short distance. This takes you back to the brook where you turn left and follow it. Cross a wooden bridge over the brook and turn left over the road, going along the other bank through the park. Turn right at the next road bridge, to the Roehampton Gate exit. Turn left immediately following the park wall, back to the brook and over it, then turn right. This takes you through:

4. PALEWELL COMMON This
land appears in 16th-century manorial records and was owned by the Spencer family. It was taken over by the council in 1921 following a petition from local residents, and has since been developed as a public play area including pitch and putt, boules, football and cricket.

☛ Bear right along the brook, past the pitch and putt course on the left and the brook on the right, then by some allotments to Hertford Avenue. Turn right and keep going to Upper Richmond Road where you turn right.

✋ There are stops in Upper Richmond Road for the 33, 337 and 493 buses to Putney, Richmond and Hammersmith.

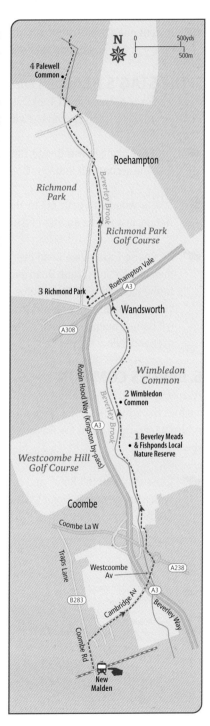

☞ To continue the walk turn left off Upper Richmond Road into Priests Bridge. Here you will find beside the brook:

5. THE STAG'S HEAD (24 Priests Bridge, SW14 8TA ⌀ stagsheadbarnes. co.uk ⊘ closed Mon; no food Tue) Dating back to 1863, this pub was renovated in 1938, serves Fuller's real ale and has a dartboard. Well-behaved dogs are welcome.

☞ Continue along Priests Bridge, turning left at the end back into the main road. Take the second left into Vine Road.

✋ Take a woodland path off to the right from Vine Road to Barnes railway station, less than a quarter of a mile away, for frequent trains to Waterloo.

☞ Otherwise follow Vine Road over two railway crossings close to each other, then turn left into Scarth Road and immediately right, parallel with Vine Road, to the junction with Station Road. If you are doing the walk at a weekend, you may be able to get refreshments at the **Vine Road Community Café** (⌀ barnescommon.org.uk) in the pavilion of the recreation ground. Cross over and follow the path ahead which bears left through:

6. BARNES COMMON (⌀ barnescommon.org.uk) This designated nature reserve is an excellent place to see birds such as green woodpeckers and flowers such as the white-flowered burnet rose (which blooms from May to July). It is also a feeding ground for the speckled wood butterfly and home to several species of bat.

☞ Cross over Mill Hill Road, and continue ahead until you return to the brook with a bridge over it. Don't cross the bridge but turn right before it, along the brook a short distance then follow the path to the right. Take the first path

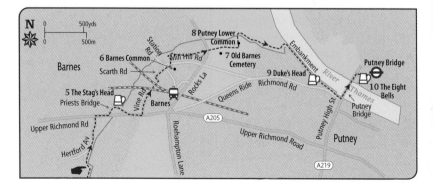

NOPPAWAN09/S

PETER ARKELL

ANNA MOORES

HELEN MATTHEWS

1 The windmill on Wimbledon Common. **2** Visit Richmond Park's Isabella Plantation in late April/early May to see the azaleas at their best. **3** Richmond Park is home to healthy numbers of both red and fallow deer. **4** Myths abound about Old Barnes Cemetery.

RAFAL SZOZDA/S

that forks off to the left and keep going until you reach Rocks Lane. Cross at the crossing, go past the Sports Centre car park and turn left past the tennis courts. On the right is:

7. OLD BARNES CEMETERY (Rocks Lane, SW13 9SA) Ghostly tales abound about this derelict and overgrown cemetery which was used from 1855 until the 1950s. A hovering nun is said to float over one of the graves, and Spring-Heeled Jack (a devilish imp with pointed ears and piercing eyes) supposedly carried out a series of attacks on people in Victorian times. He was able to jump extraordinarily high, and was first seen in this area in 1837. Witnesses described him as terrifying and frightful in appearance, with a diabolical face, clawed hands with sharp, metallic claws, eyes like red balls of fire and an ability to breathe out blue and white flames. He was never caught. The site is a wildlife haven. Thrushes, wrens, tits, finches, blackcap, chiffchaff, willow warblers and goldcrests breed here.

☛ The path takes you through:

8. PUTNEY LOWER COMMON (⌂ wpcc.org.uk/the-commons) The chiffchaff (a small olive-brown warbler which flits through trees and shrubs with its tail wagging) is among the birds that can be seen here in the summer. There are now hawthorn bushes where in Roman times it was open pasture and farmland. The winter of 2023 saw the planting of a new orchard with 12 new fruit trees (three cherry, three pear and six apple) as part of the Queen's Green Canopy scheme, and as a tribute to Her Late Majesty Queen Elizabeth II.

↑ Chiffchaffs can be spotted on Putney Lower Common in summer.

☞ The path continues by some playing fields and through woodlands, and to the left across a footbridge over the brook. Then turn right and follow the brook all the way to the Thames (almost opposite Fulham football ground). Turn right along the Thames to Putney Bridge which is half a mile away. Overlooking the river is the:

9. DUKE'S HEAD (8 Lower Richmond Rd, SW15 1JN ⊘ dukesheadputney.com) This Victorian pub is nearly 150 years old and serves Young's real ale and hot food.

☞ When you reach Putney Bridge, cross it over the Thames, take the steps down to the left, go under the bridge and follow the road past another pub:

10. THE EIGHT BELLS (89 Fulham High St, SW6 3JS 🅕 EightBellsFulham) Food is served along with Fuller's London Pride and Sharp's Doom Bar, which are the regular beers, with at least two real ales also available on rotation.

☞ A few steps further is Putney Bridge tube station.

21 COLNE RIVERSIDE RAMBLE

NATURE IN A WATERY LANDSCAPE ON THE BANKS OF THE COLNE

In the right season you might want to bring some fruit-picking equipment for this route along the River Colne. There may well be apples, sloes and blackberries. On our autumn visit, the stinging nettles were particularly clean and young – which makes them very edible for soup (boiled) or wine, though obviously you'll need rubber gloves and some scissors.

Here on Broad Colney Lakes nature reserve you're likely to see moorhens, dragonflies, coots and ducks on and around the water – and, if you're lucky, you may also spot otters and kingfishers. Irises, orchids, wild roses and water lilies proliferate.

This is only a short stroll, but you can make it a full day out by stopping for a pub lunch and visiting the child-oriented Willows Activity Farm.

↑ The River Colne. (Peter Arkell)

WHERE: Hertfordshire: London Colney, circular
STATS: 2½ miles/1hr; easy
START POINT/GETTING THERE: Willowside bus stop, London Colney /// hooks. loving.bids ⊖ To High Barnet (Northern Line). Leave by station exit on left, follow the short slip road to Barnet Hill, turn left downhill to Bus Stop W on the right; take 🚌 84 to London Colney, Willowside stop (about 35mins; 1 an hour). Or 🚌 to Watford High Street (London Overground), go up the High St to Bus Stop F for the 602 or 632 to London Colney, Willowside stop (about 50mins; 2 an hour).
MAP: OS Explorer map 182
TAKING A BREAK: Green Dragon, The Bull

☛ After getting off at the Willowside bus stop, continue in the same direction as the bus for a few yards past The Bull pub, and then across a bridge over the River Colne. On the other side turn left past the Green Dragon pub, to a footbridge on the left. Cross over it and then turn right.

Go over another small bridge, turn right and at a crossing of paths continue ahead (signposted 'Watery Lane to Shenley Lane'). When you come to a fork bear right, sticking to the side of Long Lake.

Just after a wooden bench (an ideal spot to sit and take in the view), turn right over a bridge (signposted 'Permissive off road bridleway link to Shenley Lane'), and then right again along the lakeside. You now have Long Lake on your right and Small Lake on your left. At a wooden footbridge fork right.

When you come to the end of the lake, follow it round the edge to the:

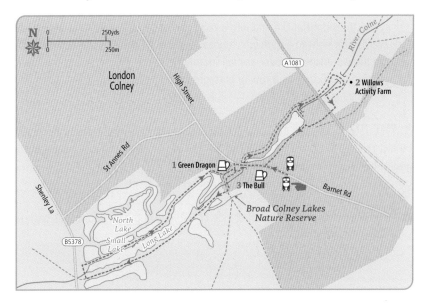

1. GREEN DRAGON (Waterside, London Colney AL2 1RB ⬜ the.green. dragon.lc) An early 17th-century coaching inn with a beer garden overlooking the green and the lake. It serves Fuller's London Pride, Timothy Taylor's Landlord and Tring Side Pocket for a Toad as well as various lagers.

☞ Continue along the river under the road bridge (built by Thomas Telford in 1775 and restored in 1998), then over a road and back to the waterside through a wooded area. When you come to a wooden footbridge over the river to the right, don't cross it but keep ahead instead on the left bank. Go under the bypass and follow the route signposted 'Public footpath to Colney Heath, 2 miles'.

Turn right at the next concrete bridge, where a noticeboard reminds you this is the River Colne and advises you to have a close look for a few minutes as there are often fish swimming beneath the tree there. You may also be lucky enough to see dragonflies, moorhens or kingfishers.

On the other side is:

2. WILLOWS ACTIVITY FARM (Coursers Rd, London Colney AL4 0PF ✐ willowsactivityfarm.com ⊙ 10.00–17.30 daily [last entry 16.30] ££) Farmyard animals such as sheep, goats, ponies and donkeys, as well as crops, are on display here. There are also funfair rides, children's shows, falconry displays and tractor rides.

☞ Turn right along the other riverbank back round the perimeter of the Activity Farm. Turn right at the end into a road and under a flyover. After about 100 yards turn right to a path which goes over a moat and then immediately left to the waterside. Go over a small footbridge to the left and round the water (going quite close to a row of cottages on the left), through the woods and on to a road. Turn right and ahead is:

3. THE BULL (Barnet Rd, London Colney AL2 1QU ✐ thebullpublondoncolney. co.uk) Dating back to 1726, this inn has low timbered ceilings, a beer garden and a children's play area, and serves home-cooked food (good and in generous portions). Real ales include Tring Side Pocket for a Toad.

☞ Opposite the pub on the other side of the road is the stop for buses back to Barnet or Watford.

22 ANIMAL WORLD

WHITE HORSES, BADGERS & RARE BEETLES AWAIT IN THE SURREY FRINGES

Chessington is a name mostly associated with its theme park and zoo, but this walk introduces you to some less celebrated gems. After a memorable mini-summit giving an unexpectedly wide view and passing within earshot of the children enjoying Chessington World of Adventures, you reach Ashtead Common. This is the largest of seven city commons in south London, and a National Nature Reserve, with Sussex cattle grazing and giving it a noticeably countrified character. These cattle help keep the scrub grassland sufficiently trim for invertebrates and flora to thrive; the common is a noted site for nesting birds and birds of prey.

WHERE: Surrey: Chessington, circular
STATS: 5½ miles/2–2½hrs; easy with a few gradual climbs
START POINT/GETTING THERE: Chessington South station /// hello.often. expand 🚃 To Chessington South station from London Waterloo (35mins; 2 an hour) or Clapham Junction (25mins; 2 an hour). Turn right out of the station into Garrison Lane.
MAP: OS Explorer map 161
TAKING A BREAK: The Barn at KT9, Barwell Café

↑ The pond at the top of Winey Hill. (Julia Gavin/A)

☛ Follow Garrison Lane to the junction with Leatherhead Road. Cross over diagonally to the left into Barwell Lane ahead. Go down this lane past some playing fields on the left, and then meadows on the right. Just after Chessington Recycling Station, the road bends to the right, and there is a kissing gate on the left with a sign stating: 'Warning, Animal behaviour is unpredictable, please do not feed them.' Go through this kissing gate into the path marked with the green and yellow 'Chessington Countryside Walk' arrows.

This path takes you through woods (including some fine cedar trees) up Winey Hill. Bear left near the top of the wood into a meadow and go slightly uphill, keeping left. Near the top of the hill is a:

1. BRICK STAND VIEWPOINT
This used to show the distances and directions of places, including the BT Tower (14 miles away), that you can see from this excellent viewpoint, 246 feet above sea level. Sadly the top part has disappeared. A bit further on by the very top of the hill is a pond with a fence going through the middle of it: we sincerely hope that any fish in it do not attempt to swim through to the forbidden side.

☛ Continue ahead past the pond, down the hill to some more trees, including huge oaks, where – during opening hours – you will hear the joyous screams of children in the Chessington World of Adventures to the left. Go through another kissing gate, past a meadow (where we saw three white horses galloping together), along a path with an electric fence on the right and a barbed wire one to the left. Turn left on to the public footpath signposted 'Leatherhead Road, $^1/_3$ mile'. This takes you to a track to the left (along the barbed wire fence of the Chessington World of Adventures) with signs for 'Explorer Glamping'. On the left is the entrance to:

2. CHESSINGTON WORLD OF ADVENTURES & ZOO & SEA LIFE CENTRE
(Leatherhead Rd, Chessington KT9 2NE ✆ 0871 663 4477 ⌂ chessington.com 🕙 end Mar–early Nov 10.00–17.00 or 18.00; check website for days; zoo also open w/ends in winter, 10.00–15.00 £££) This theme park offers various rides as well as the long-established zoo, which first opened in 1931, and a Sea Life Centre.

☛ Continue down the public footpath to the bottom of the hill, passing a line of car parks with animal-themed names (and amusing pedestrian crossing signs indicating a human and a bird or animal). Then cross over a stile ahead (signposted 'Public Footpath') and head through some woods.

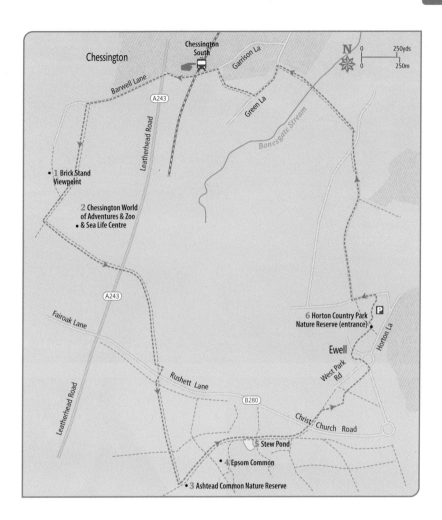

When you go over another stile and reach a road (Leatherhead Road), cross over it and go ahead on the bridleway signposted 'Ashtead Common 1 mile' through more woods, where hawthorn and blackberries abound and there is an oak wood on the right.

Cross a small wooden bridge and go through a green tunnel between arable fields over a stream into the open.

When you come to a road (Rushett Lane) turn left then, after a few yards, turn right through a kissing gate on to a public bridleway, signposted 'Ashtead Common ½ mile'. This takes you ahead through the middle of an arable field. If you need a rest and refreshment at this point, follow the signs to turn right and walk for a few minutes to **The Barn at KT9** (⌀ thebarnkt9. com), an outdoor café serving hot and cold drinks, pastries and some hot

1 Stew Pond. **2** Epsom Common. **3** Fair warning for drivers around Chessington.

food. Otherwise, continue to the other side where there is a gap in the hedge, through which the bridleway goes slightly uphill (past a sign pointing to 'Leatherhead Road ½ mile' to the right and 'Ashtead Common ¼ m' ahead) to some woods, which you enter through a kissing gate and a stile. This is part of:

3. ASHTEAD COMMON NATURE RESERVE This ancient wooded common, owned by the Corporation of London, has a good number of pollarded oaks whose branches are cut on a rotational basis. Bats nest in the trees, while rotting wood houses fungi and rare invertebrates, and nectar from the flowers in the spring supports hoverflies, rare beetles, bees and butterflies. Two scheduled monuments are on the site: a Roman villa and a triangular earthwork. These are owned by the Corporation of London. From medieval times up to 1890, the Corporation had the power to tax coal coming into the city and marked the boundary with white iron posts, some of which are nearby, indicating the points where the tax became due.

☛ Turn left along the bridleway (No 29) signposted 'Epsom Common ½ mile' past one of these white iron posts. Keep on the bridleway past another sign 'Epsom Common ¼ mile', to a crossing of paths (with a sign 'Rushett Lane ½ m' to the left) where you continue ahead following the bridleway to another crossroads signposted 'Christchurch Road, ⅓ mile'. This takes you through woods and then into the open. This is:

4. EPSOM COMMON Up until World War II this land was used for grazing, but then it was ploughed up to grow crops during the food shortage. Now, as a Site of Special Scientific Interest, grazing has been reintroduced in part of the common to conserve woodland and flora.

☛ After a while you will see on the right:

5. STEW POND (Christ Church Rd, Epsom) A stew pond is a fish pond for storing live fish before eating, and this pond was constructed by the Abbot of Chertsey in the 12th century, evidently for that very purpose. It is stocked with a variety of carp and coarse species (for day fishing tickets see calpacangling.com).

☛ Follow the 'Chessington Countryside Walk' arrow ahead through woods to a track. When it reaches a wooden gate, fork to the left, following the 'Chessington Country Walk' and 'Thames Down Link' arrows, to a road (Christ Church Road), which you cross using a handy pelican crossing where the lights are in the shape of a horse and rider. Follow the bridleway ahead signposted 'Horton Lane ¼ mile'. This takes you through a tree-lined avenue, over another road. Cross the road. On the other side of the road take a footpath to the left which runs parallel to West Park Road for a short distance, then turns right to enter:

6. HORTON COUNTRY PARK NATURE RESERVE (Horton Ln, Epsom KT19 8PL) One of the distinctive but less celebrated features of the Surrey landscape is the scattering of sanatoria and hospitals; this used to be an area of farmland providing food and work for patients from the nearby psychiatric institutions. In 1973, about 400 acres of it were purchased by Epsom and Ewell Borough Council to establish the country park and nature reserve, with fields, hedgerows, woods and ponds that provide habitats for a range of fauna, such as green woodpeckers, badgers, blue damselflies and butterflies. It makes notable blackberrying terrain in late summer.

☛ Cross over a narrow lane and continue ahead through woods, and then right into a fenced track round a paddock. Just after it bends to the left, turn right through a gate, and then turn sharp left around a car park. Then look on the left for a path with an easily missed 'Chessington Countryside Walk' sign.

Having made sure you have found the signposted path to the left, follow it as it goes right, near a cottage, then ahead and on to a track beside more horse fields. When you come to a fork in the tracks take the one to the left (arrowed), and when you reach a junction of tracks take a footpath ahead through more trees, to a kissing gate and stile into another arable field, where you will see houses ahead. Turn right following the edge of the field, to another field where you continue ahead to the other side, where there is a footbridge over a stream (Bonesgate Stream). Cross the bridge and go ahead on a tree-lined path between fields, with signs of badger activity and plenty of ladybirds, which eventually goes by back gardens of houses to a road (Green Lane). Turn left, signposted 'Chalky Lane ⅔ mile', along a path by Green Lane Farm Boarding Kennels and Cattery (birds and small pets also taken) through trees, and then rejoin the road, where after a few yards turn right up some steps into the public footpath signposted 'Garrison Lane ¼ mile'. This takes you past a wildflower meadow (formerly Chessington Golf Club) on the left. This path, Huntingdale Path, has wildlife features such as a bee garden. Finally you reach a road (Garrison Lane) where you turn left and see Chessington South station on the other side of the road. Just past the station, **Barwell Café** (202 Leatherhead Rd, Chessington KT9 2HU) offers traditional good-value food.

→ Shakespeare's Globe Theatre. (Aagje De Jong/DT)

23 LITERARY LONDON

A BIBLIOPHILE'S PILGRIMAGE THROUGH THE CAPITAL'S HEART

This walk visits the homes and workplaces of world-famous writers over six centuries from Geoffrey Chaucer and William Shakespeare to TS Eliot and Dorothy L Sayers, with the chance to go inside the homes of Chàrles Dickens and Dr Johnson, and to imbibe at a drinking-hole frequented by many writers, the classically unchanged Ye Olde Cheshire Cheese. You'll also see the places connected with some lesser-known figures such as the great wit Sydney Smith.
  The route takes in a memorable cross-section of urban scenery and non-literary attractions, starting in Southwark and moving past Borough Market and the admirably preserved George Inn, along the South Bank past the Clink Museum and over the Millennium Bridge from the Tate Modern to St Paul's, before continuing on over Fleet Street and through Clerkenwell into Bloomsbury.

WHERE: London: London Bridge to Bloomsbury
STATS: 4½ miles/1½hrs; easy
START POINT/GETTING THERE: London Bridge /// robot.feast.themes ⊖ London Bridge (Northern/Jubilee Line) or 🚃 to London Bridge station. Leave station by the exit for St Thomas St, passing the entrance to the Shard viewing gallery on the left.
FINISH: Russell Square (Piccadilly Line) /// longer.mimic.mild
DROP-OUT POINTS: Frequent, from bus stops or tube stations
MAP: Any A–Z
TAKING A BREAK: The George Inn, Cockpit Tavern, Ye Olde Cheshire Cheese, A Friend at Hand

☛ Emerge into St Thomas Street and turn right. A few doors down on the right is:

1. THE OLD OPERATING THEATRE MUSEUM & HERB GARRET (9a St Thomas St, SE1 9RY ☍ oldoperatingtheatre.com ◷ 10.30–17.00 Thu–Sun £💰) You enter this museum up 52 steepish spiral steps, which lead into the garret of St Thomas' Church, once used as a place to store and dry herbs used for medicinal purposes. Beyond is an intact early operating theatre. Most surgery performed here involved amputations, which had to be completed in a minute or less in those days before modern anaesthetics were invented. It has many fascinating exhibits including some fearsome-looking surgical instruments. The poet John Keats would have watched operations being performed here when he was a student at Guys and St Thomas' Hospital in 1815–16.

☛ Almost opposite is:

2. JOHN KEATS' LODGINGS (8 St Thomas St, SE1 9RS) The poet Keats (1795–1821) lodged here from 1815 to 1816 while studying at nearby Guy's

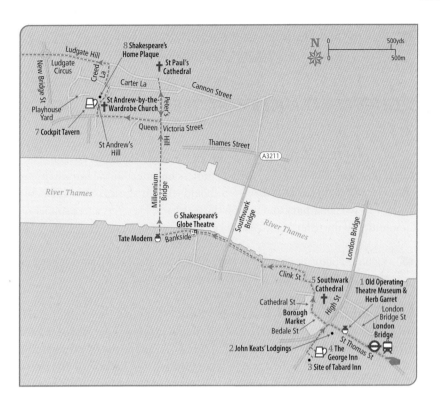

and St Thomas' Hospitals, as a plaque informs us. After being an apprentice apothecary-surgeon he became a surgeon's pupil at Guy's on 1 October 1815. Four weeks later he was appointed as a dresser to Mr Lucas, a surgeon at St Thomas', which was then in St Thomas Street. Mr Lucas had a reputation for rather bungling operations. Keats was then trained by Sir Astley Cooper, the great surgeon of Guy's who had been trained at St Thomas'. Keats became licensed to practise as an apothecary on 25 July 1816, but never got his surgeon's certificate and abandoned surgical practice altogether in 1817. 'My last operation was the opening of a man's temporal artery,' he recalled to his friend Charles Brown. 'I did it with the utmost nicety, but reflecting on what passed through my mind at the time, my dexterity seemed a miracle, and I never took up the lancet again.'

Keats became a poet instead and his poem 'O Solitude!' was published in 1816, but the following year he was savagely attacked by the critic John Lockhart for being of the 'low-born Cockney school of poetry' (his father was an ostler and tavern-keeper). This depressed Keats and he was soon beset with financial problems, and in 1819 he became very ill with tuberculosis. By then he was living in Hampstead (page 39).

☞ Continue to the junction with Borough High Street and turn left. The fourth turning on the left is Talbot Yard. Three doors down Talbot Yard on the left is a plaque commemorating:

3. GEOFFREY CHAUCER & THE TABARD INN
This is the site of the Tabard Inn, established in 1307 and demolished in 1873. The pilgrims set off from here in April 1386 in *The Canterbury Tales* as described by poet Geoffrey Chaucer (1342–1400), the son of a vintner. Chaucer wrote this around 1387, describing how 29 pilgrims of various professions meet in the inn where the host (Harry Bailey) suggests they each should tell four stories on the road, two on the way to Canterbury and two on the way back. He offers a free supper on their return to the teller of the best story.

☞ Return to Borough High Street and retrace your steps to the next turning on the right. This is George Inn Yard, where you will find:

4. THE GEORGE INN
(George Inn Yard, 77 Borough High St, SE1 1NH) William Shakespeare and Charles Dickens drank in this pub, which has existed since the late 16th century. It was rebuilt in 1677 and is the only remaining galleried coaching inn in London. Dickens featured it in his novel *Little Dorrit* (first serialised from 1855 to 1857). It is now owned by the National Trust and serves Greene King real ales. An excellent place for a pub meal inside or out in the courtyard.

☞ Return to the junction with Borough High Street and retrace your steps to the junction with St Thomas Street, past Borough Market on the left, and turn left into Bedale Street. Follow this under a railway bridge, until you reach:

5. SOUTHWARK CATHEDRAL
(London Bridge, SE1 9DA ✆ 020 7367 6700 🖥 cathedral.southwark.anglican.org 🕐 09.00–18.00 Mon–Sat, 08.30–17.00 Sun) There may have been a church here as early as the 7th century. Since then, it has been 'refounded' as an Augustinian priory with a hospital next door (the predecessor of St Thomas'), a parish church and, since 1905, a cathedral. There are several significant literary links for you to find.

As you enter, look at the stained-glass window above the northwest door. In a roundel is a portrait of Dr Samuel Johnson (whom we will meet later on the walk). The window dates from 1907. While you're in the cathedral, look out for the resident cat, Hodge, who shares his name with Dr Johnson's beloved pet.

In the north aisle lies the elaborate canopied tomb of John Gower (1327–1408), poet and friend of Chaucer. Gower lived at the priory for the last 30 years of his

1 The George Inn was frequented by William Shakespeare and Charles Dickens. **2** A plaque at the site of the Tabard Inn, from where the pilgrims in *The Canterbury Tales* set off. **3** Exhibits in the Old Operating Theatre. **4** The tomb of poet John Gower in Southwark Cathedral. **5** John Keats' Lodgings on St Thomas Street.

life. His main legacies are three long poems in French, Latin and English, of which the most famous is *Confessio Amantis*. The tomb depicts Gower's head resting on copies of these works.

Almost opposite Gower is an alabaster sculpture of William Shakespeare, created by Henry McCarthy in 1912. It shows the Bard lying outside the Globe Theatre, one elbow propping up his head. The pose may indicate remembrance; as Ophelia says in *Hamlet*, rosemary is for remembrance, and a sprig of rosemary sometimes appears in the playwright's hand. Next to the sculpture is a plaque giving thanks for the life of Sam Wanamaker, the actor and producer whose vision inspired the reconstruction of the nearby Globe Theatre (see below). Above the sculpture and plaque, like a giant thought bubble, is a stained-glass window made by Christopher Webb and unveiled in 1954. This depicts Shakespeare and some of his most famous characters such as Hamlet (with Yorick's skull in his hand), Prospero, Puck, Othello and Lady Macbeth.

Many of Shakespeare's contemporaries lived locally and used St Saviour's (as it was known then), including John Fletcher (1579–1625), a fellow playwright who collaborated with Shakespeare on *Henry VIII* and *The Two Noble Kinsmen*. In the choir there is a memorial ledger stone to him and another to Edmund Shakespeare (1580–1607), an actor and William's younger brother. Fletcher is buried in the churchyard.

☞ Return to the cathedral entrance, then bear left into Cathedral Street, which becomes Winchester Square. Passing St Saviour's Dock by the Thames, you will see a full-size replica of the *Golden Hinde*, the galleon in which Sir Francis Drake sailed round the world (1577–80). Turn left into Clink Street. On the left lie the remains of the great hall of Winchester Palace, once one of the largest and most important buildings in London, home to the Bishops of Winchester before its destruction by fire in 1814. The west gable, with its rose window, is the highlight of the remains, while the undercroft now hosts a shady sunken garden containing plants which were popular in late medieval gardens. Continue along Clink Street and then through Pickfords Wharf, where you pass the Clink Prison Museum, built on the site of the notorious medieval prison from which the phrase 'in clink' came. Continue along Clink Street to the end. Turn right by The Anchor pub – from where Samuel Pepys observed the 1666 Great Fire of London – into Bank End, and then left into Bankside along the Thames. Follow this under Southwark Bridge, and after a short distance, on the left, on the corner of New Globe Walk, is:

6. SHAKESPEARE'S GLOBE THEATRE (21 New Globe Walk, SE1
9DT ☎ 020 7401 9919 ⌖ shakespearesglobe.com ◷ see website for information

about tours & exhibitions) William Shakespeare (1564–1616) and his partners built the original open-air theatre a few hundred yards from this site in 1599 and staged his plays there.

The son of a glovemaker and alderman, the young Shakespeare travelled to London in 1592 to take up acting and often performed on beer barrels at inns. One anecdote has it that he was appearing in a play with fellow actor Richard Burbage, whom he overheard making an assignation with a woman who lived nearby. She told him to announce himself as Richard III to keep his real identity a secret. Shakespeare left before the end of the play, announced himself as Richard III and went to bed with her. Burbage turned up only to receive a message: 'William the Conqueror came before Richard III.' The playwright died of a fever following a drinking bout, according to John Ward, the Vicar of Stratford. Famously Shakespeare's will bequeathed his widow Anne Hathaway his 'second best bed' and furniture.

As well as the reconstructed open-air theatre here, there is a candlelit indoor playhouse in honour of Sam Wanamaker (1919–93). He was so moved by the theme of a play in which he was acting in Washington DC in 1943 that he joined the American Communist Party. After serving in the US Army from 1943 to 1946, he left the party and went to Hollywood. He was blacklisted there in 1952 during the McCarthy anti-communist witch-hunt. So he moved to England where he became director of the New Shakespeare Theatre in Liverpool in 1957, then joined the Shakespeare Memorial Theatre at Stratford-upon-Avon as an actor. He founded the Shakespeare Globe Trust in 1970 and raised over $10 million to reconstruct the theatre in its original form. His daughter, the actor Zoë Wanamaker, appeared in the BBC television programme *Who Do You Think You Are?* in 2009, which revealed that his activities were monitored in this country by MI5.

☞ Continue along the bank passing the Tate Modern gallery. Just opposite is the Millennium Footbridge, which you cross. On the other side go ahead up Peter's Hill to Queen Victoria Street. If you wish to visit St Paul's Cathedral (£££ 🥤) continue ahead up the path and steps that lead to it.

Otherwise turn left into Queen Victoria Street. Go past the College of Arms on the right, then a plaque marking the site of Doctors' Commons, the society of lawyers who practised civil law (which applied in the courts dealing with probate). Dickens mentioned it in *David Copperfield*, as did Wilkie Collins in *The Moonstone*. Just past St Andrew by the Wardrobe Church, so named because it was once a neighbour to the King's Wardrobe, which housed royal stores and ceremonial robes, turn right into St Andrew's Hill. A short way up on the left is the:

CLAUDIO DIVIZIA/S

FRANCOISE DE VALERA JAMES/DT

PRES PANAYOTOV/S

1 The replica of the *Golden Hinde* in St Saviour's Dock. **2** From the Tate, cross the Millennium Footbridge with views towards St Paul's Cathedral. **3** The Globe Theatre.

7. COCKPIT TAVERN (7 St Andrew's Hill, EC4V 5BY) There has been a pub on this site since the 16th century. It was a major venue for gambling on cock fights, and retains a gallery from where the gamblers watched the fights. Nowadays it is a small, friendly pub serving real ales such as Old Speckled Hen, Pedigree and Adnams. On the other side of the road is another drinking establishment: Shaws Booksellers, which once served as a set for a bookshop scene in the 1997 film *The Wings of the Dove*; some of the books remain.

☞ On the opposite corner to the Cockpit is:

8. SHAKESPEARE'S HOME PLAQUE (Ireland Yard) A plaque confirms: 'On 10 March 1613 William Shakespeare purchased lodgings in the Blackfriars Gatehouse located near this site.' This is where he lived after purchasing the Blackfriars Theatre in 1613 with fellow actors, as an additional venue to the Globe for their plays. This was also the main entrance to the theatre, which was in the vicinity of Playhouse Yard at the end of this alley.

☞ Continue up St Andrew's Hill, left into Carter Lane, then immediately right into Creed Lane, up to Ludgate Hill. Turn left and continue down to Ludgate Circus with Fleet Street ahead.
   On the right-hand corner of Fleet Street, set into the wall of Ludgate House beneath a clock, is the:

9. EDGAR WALLACE PLAQUE (Ludgate House, 111 Fleet St, EC4A 2AB) This prolific novelist, playwright and screenwriter (1875–1932) could have written a novel about his own life. He was abandoned at birth by his actor mother and raised by a porter in Billingsgate fish market. He first sold newspapers at Ludgate Circus at the age of 11 when playing truant from school. A year later he left school and got a job round the corner in Farringdon Street as a lowly print-reader's boy. A decade or so later, after working as a Grimsby trawler cook, milkman, building labourer and soldier, he was back in Fleet Street as the war correspondent of the *Daily Mail* (during the Boer War) and editor of the *Evening News*. The *Mail* sent him to the Congo to disprove stories of Belgian atrocities in 1907, but he found them to be true and reported his findings: these were suppressed, and when he refused to repeat the original lies he was sacked. So he used his Congo experiences to write the *Sanders of the River* novels which proved bestsellers and launched his career as an author.

The imagination he used in his fiction could also be useful in reporting real events, as demonstrated by his report of George V's coronation for the *Evening Times*, which he wrote the day before it actually happened. He also wrote about a 'confession' by Crippen (who in fact went to the gallows protesting his innocence of the murder of his wife) for this same paper, which led to it being closed down.

His career as a novelist took off with 46 novels being published in ten years and selling millions. He also wrote plays, having 17 produced in the last six years of his life, including three in the West End at the same time, which earned him £100,000. One of these plays he wrote in four days, and one of his novels over a weekend. On top of this he became a Hollywood screenwriter.

☞ Go up Fleet Street past the Punch Tavern, originally a Victorian gin palace, where employees from the eponymous magazine used to enjoy liquid lunches. Take the second turning on the left, a small passage called St Bride's Avenue. This takes you to the entrance of:

10. ST BRIDE'S CHURCH (St Bride's Av, Fleet St, EC4Y 8AU) This

beautiful church's name refers to a contemporary of St Patrick – St Bride, also known as Bridget of Kildare, who may have been the founder of the first known stone church on this site. Seven St Bride's Churches have followed the original. A small, free museum in the basement explains that Wynkyn de Worde, William Caxton's apprentice, inherited the latter's print business and moved it next door to

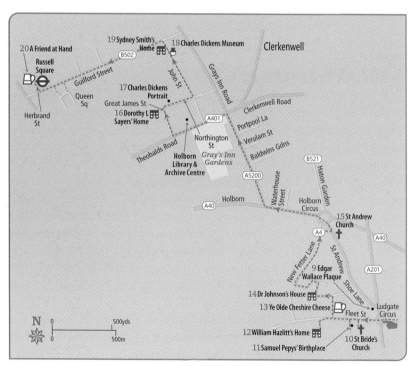

the church. In a late medieval world in which the Church had almost a monopoly on literacy, this made commercial sense. As a plaque upstairs puts it, de Worde was the first printer in Fleet Street. Over the next four centuries, the street became synonymous with the press, journalism and Britain's national newspapers. St Bride's has hosted many baptisms, weddings and memorial services for journalists and newspaper executives. The church pews carry the names of many journalists, and there is a memorial altar for the recently deceased, such as Ann Leslie, George Alagiah and Bill Turnbull. In the basement you can find a memorial stone to tabloid editor and TV personality Derek Jameson, and also the lead plaque from the coffin of 18th-century novelist Samuel Richardson, author of *Pamela* and *Clarissa*.

☞ Return to Fleet Street, turn left, and then first left into Salisbury Court. A few yards on the left is:

11. SAMUEL PEPYS' BIRTHPLACE (Salisbury Court, EC4Y 8AA) A

plaque confirms this is the birthplace of diarist Samuel Pepys, although it wrongly gives the date of his birth as 1632. In fact he was born here when it was a tailor's shop on 23 February 1633. The date of his death is given correctly as 1703.

At the age of 15, Pepys witnessed the beheading of Charles I, and remarked: 'The memory of the wicked shall rot.' He got a job as a government clerk for £50 a year and liked to stroll around London mixing with all classes. For breakfast in a nearby pub called the Harp and Ball, he had a draught of ale and pickled onions, which he often vomited up after heavy drinking the night before. After a short time working in his office, he returned to the tavern at lunch to drink more and sing bawdy songs before visiting prostitutes in St James's Park, and a few more hours in the office.

His wealth increased considerably after he became responsible for ordering supplies of victuals for the navy in 1665, and he benefited from 'rewards' for contracts. He also used money which should have been paid to seamen in the navy to pay the crew of his own private vessel to plunder Dutch ships, and then kept the booty instead of handing a share to the Crown. He was subsequently charged with leaking navy secrets to the French and committed to the Tower in 1679, but the charges were dropped nine months later. Pepys became Secretary of the Navy in 1684, but when it was defeated four years later by William of Orange as part of the latter's invasion, Pepys' position became vulnerable. He was charged with treason and detained, but again was released after a few months.

☞ Continue up Fleet Street and turn left into Bouverie Street. A few yards on the right (just past the corner of Pleydell Street) is:

12. WILLIAM HAZLITT'S HOME (6 Bouverie St, EC4Y 8AX) William Hazlitt (1778–1830), the great essayist, lived here in 1829 as confirmed by a plaque. By then he had been socially ostracised after his exposure as the author of *Liber Amoris* (1823), an anonymous account of his infatuation for his landlady's daughter, a simple girl called Sarah Walker. The revelation that Hazlitt was the author led Robert Louis Stevenson to abandon writing a biography of him. Hazlitt was twice divorced and earned many enemies for his support of the French Revolution, and for his writings in favour of the poor and against those who exploited them. But on his deathbed his last words were supposedly: 'Well, I have had a happy life.'

He also lived in Mitre Court, off Fleet Street, opposite Fetter Lane.

☞ Return to Fleet Street, turn right and a few yards on the left (just past Hind Court) turn left into a narrow passage under an arch, called Wine Office Court. On the right is:

13. YE OLDE CHESHIRE CHEESE (Wine Office Court, 145 Fleet St, EC4A 2BU ⌗ ye-olde-cheshire-cheese.co.uk) This ancient tavern, rebuilt in 1667 after the Great Fire of London, was the local for Samuel Johnson who lived nearby (see below). His chair and an original copy of his dictionary are on display – although there is no recorded evidence that Johnson visited. For example, his biographer James Boswell does not mention the Cheese.) Other literary figures whom the pub claims visited include Alexander Pope, Charles Dickens, Oliver Goldsmith, Voltaire, Mark Twain, Alfred Tennyson, Arthur Conan Doyle, PG Wodehouse and GK Chesterton. Samuel Smith real ales are served, as well as hot food; the pub promotes itself as an 'unashamedly British' chop house, with traditional steak and kidney suet pudding on the menu.

☞ Continue up Wine Office Court and bear left into Gough Square. Turn right then left and in the far left corner is:

14. DR JOHNSON'S HOUSE (17 Gough Square, EC4A 3DE ✆ 020 7353 3745 ⌗ drjohnsonshouse.org ◷ 11.00–17.30 Mon–Sat; Oct–Apr closes 17.00 £) Samuel Johnson (1709–84) lived here in the early 1750s when compiling his famous dictionary (published in 1755). Now the house displays on its entrance one of his most famous quotations: 'When a man is tired of London he is tired of life.' But earlier, in his poem of 1738 called *London*, he expressed his disgust at how the poor were oppressed in the capital, having experienced it himself. Early on he lived on bread and water alone in the Marylebone Fields area where highway robbers operated. He became very shabby, and was later incarcerated in

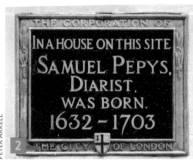

1 On Ludgate House, look for Edgar Wallace's plaque. **2** A plaque marks the site of the house in which Samuel Pepys was born. **3** Charles Dickens' writing desk at the Charles Dickens Museum. **4** The interior of St Bride's Church.

the nearby Fleet Prison for debt. When he had money later in life, he was always very generous to the poor and homeless.

His sense of humour came across when he defined 'lexicographer' in his own dictionary as 'a writer of dictionaries, a harmless drudge'. When his wife died in 1752 he was grief-stricken and observed: 'Marriage has many pains, but celibacy has no pleasures.' He did not remarry, however, having famously commented that this showed 'the triumph of hope over experience'. And he did not use prostitutes, as he disapproved strongly of the trade that dealt 'with women like a dealer in any other commodity... as an ironmonger sells ironmongery'.

In this house are various exhibits relating to the life and times of Dr Johnson. The most significant of the four floors is arguably the attic or 'garret', where the natural light from three sides was a crucial aid to Johnson's writing and editing. His dictionary (which defined 42,773 words in all) was the first to offer multiple entries per word and the first to add citations that illustrated the meaning of a word. The last of those 42,773 words, in case you're wondering, was 'zootomy: the dissection of the bodies of beasts'. Perhaps the most striking artefact here is a copy of a complaint to Johnson from 12 other writers, objecting to the fact that Johnson had written an epitaph for Oliver Goldsmith in Latin rather than English. The letter, on a circular piece of paper, has its authors' signatures around the outside, so that no single author is the main writer; this is the origin of the term 'round robin'.

☞ Turn left out of the house into Pemberton Row and then left into West Harding Street to Fetter Lane, where you turn right. Follow this into New Fetter Lane and up to Holborn Circus. To the right on the corner of St Andrew Street is:

15. ST ANDREW CHURCH (5 St Andrew St, EC4A 3AB
⌀ standrewholborn.org.uk) Bill Sykes, in *Chapter 21* of *Oliver Twist* by Charles Dickens, looks up to the clock tower of this church, notices it is seven o'clock and urges young Oliver: 'You must step out! Come, don't lag behind already, Lazy-legs!' Iris Murdoch (1919–99) in her 1954 novel *Under the Net* also has a character looking at the church tower.

The first written record of the church is from AD951, but Roman pottery, discovered in its crypt, indicates it had been here for much longer. In 1666 it survived the Great Fire of London but was in such a bad state of repair that it was rebuilt by Christopher Wren anyway.

☞ Turn left up Holborn to the Prudential building at Nos 138–142 on the right. Charles Dickens rented rooms through the arch in Waterhouse Square (1833–37), and wrote *Sketches by Boz* and most of *The Pickwick Papers* here.

Continue along Holborn to Grays Inn Road, where you turn right. When you reach the crossroads with the Yorkshire Grey pub on the corner, turn left into Theobalds Road. At No 22, look up for a plaque marking the birthplace of the novelist and memorable Victorian Prime Minister Benjamin Disraeli (1804–81). Just past Holborn Library and Archive Centre, turn right into Great James Street. A little way up the street on the left (just before the Rugby Tavern) by the junction with Northington Street is:

16. DOROTHY L SAYERS' HOME (24 Great James St, WC1N 3ES)
A plaque confirms that detective story writer Dorothy L Sayers (1893–1957) lived here from 1921 to 1929. Her 1930 novel *Strong Poison*, featuring the amateur detective Lord Peter Wimsey, is set in this area. Wimsey appeared in the 1923 novel *Whose Body?* and in 13 other stories. The author became one of the leading crime writers of her day and president of the Detection Club. She later turned to writing plays covering serious historical and theological subjects. An Anglican, she became churchwarden in 1952 at the London parish of St Thomas-cum-St Anne's. Her philosophy was 'The only Christian work is good work, well done.'

☞ Turn into Northington Street and a few yards on the left opposite Cockpit Yard is:

17. CHARLES DICKENS PORTRAIT (16 Northington St, cnr Kirk St, WC1N 2NW) Dickens may well have drunk in the pub on this site when living round the corner in Doughty Street. In his day the pub was called the White Lion; it later became the Dickens Inn, which explains the somewhat frayed portrait near the top of the building. It remained as a pub until at least 1985.

☞ Continue along Northington Street to the Lady Ottoline pub where you turn left into John Street. This leads into Doughty Street. On the right (just past Roger Street) at No 58 is a plaque marking the home of Vera Brittain and Winifred Holtby (page 209). A few doors further along on the same side is:

18. CHARLES DICKENS MUSEUM (48 Doughty St, WC1N 2LX
⊘ dickensmuseum.com ◷ 10.00–17.00 Wed–Sun **££** 🚋; free to Art Pass holders) Charles Dickens (1812–70) lived in this house from 1837 to 1839 when he was writing *Oliver Twist*, which was serialised over two years in a magazine. He also wrote *Nicholas Nickleby* while living here, and completed *The Pickwick Papers*.

As a 15-year-old, Dickens had worked as a clerk for Ellis and Blackmore solicitors at nearby Holborn Court, Gray's Inn. He impressed his employers with his eagerness and intelligence, and entertained his fellow clerks by mimicking 'the low population of the streets of London in all their varieties', as well as popular singers and actors. He stayed there for a year and a half before moving to the firm of Charles Molloy at 8 New Square, Lincoln's Inn. The work here he found dull so he left after a few months. Then he learned shorthand and became a court and parliamentary reporter. This was a great improvement on having to work in a hated blacking (shoe polish) factory for a pittance at the age of 12, pasting labels on pots, while his father was in jail for debt.

He had a pet raven called Grip – which sat on his shoulder as he read to his children at night – and he performed conjuring tricks such as pouring ingredients into a hat and turning them into a plum pudding, and turning bran into a guinea pig. He also liked to roam the 'more dreadful streets of London' at night, including those in Limehouse with its opium dens, and to stare into the dark waters of the Thames.

The museum has over 100,000 items relating to the writer, including original manuscripts, rare editions, personal items and paintings. For Dickens fans, the highlight is probably the chance to get close to the desk at which he completed *The Pickwick Papers* and *Oliver Twist*, wrote the whole of *Nicholas Nickleby* and worked on *Barnaby Rudge*.

☞ A few doors up on the other side is:

19. SYDNEY SMITH'S HOME (14 Doughty St, WC1N 2PL) The author and wit Sydney Smith (1771–1845) lived here, as confirmed by a plaque, from 1803 to 1806. He wished to become a barrister but was pressurised by his father into becoming a clergyman. He became a popular preacher and lecturer as well as a writer. Radical for his times, he supported education for women, the abolition of slavery and Catholic emancipation. In 1831 he became a resident canon at St Paul's Cathedral. Among his aphorisms are:

[About Macaulay] He had occasional flashes of silence that made his conversation perfectly delightful.

You must not think me necessarily foolish because I am facetious, nor will I consider you necessarily wise because you are grave.

Never try to reason the prejudice out of a man. It was not reasoned into him, and cannot be reasoned out.

☞ Continue to the junction with Guilford Street and turn left. Continue along Guilford Street, until you reach a turning on the right, Herbrand Street, where on the right just past the Horse Hospital on the corner of Colonnade is:

20. A FRIEND AT HAND (2–4 Herbrand St, WC1N 1HX ⊘ greeneking.

co.uk) This Greene King pub was first established in 1797 as the Hansom Carriage. The writer Thomas Stearns (TS) Eliot (1888–1965) described the pub in his collection of poems *Old Possum's Book of Practical Cats*, which later inspired Andrew Lloyd Webber's musical *Cats*. Beers include Timothy Taylor's.

☞ After refreshing yourself, turn right out of the pub and walk a few yards to Bernard Street, then turn right to Russell Square tube station just round the corner.

↑ A Friend at Hand was once the haunt of TS Eliot.

24 INSPIRING WOMEN

IF YOU SEEK THEIR MONUMENTS, LOOK AROUND YOU

The epitaph on Christopher Wren's tomb in St Paul's Cathedral translates from Latin as: 'If you seek his monument, look around you.' This walk, starting at Charing Cross station and concluding in Bloomsbury, enables you to admire monuments to inspiring women from the past two millennia: from the Roman occupation of Britain to the present day. Their stories encompass great achievements, and often personal sacrifice, in many walks of life. Meet, among others, Charles II's mistress, a nurse, a heroine of the Crimean War, a campaigner for girls' education, an enslaved West Indian, a spy, a literary society hostess and several scientists and novelists. They all made their mark in what remains overwhelmingly a man's world.

WHERE: London: Charing Cross to Bloomsbury
STATS: 4 miles/1½hrs; easy
START POINT/GETTING THERE: Charing Cross station (Bakerloo/Northern Lines) /// just.grabs.matter ⊖ or 🚆 To Charing Cross. From the railway station, cross the Strand & turn right. From Charing Cross underground station, take the exit for the Strand & turn left along the road.
FINISH: The Lady Ottoline /// maps.cycles.washed
MAP: Any A–Z
TAKING A BREAK: The Nell Gwynne Tavern, The National Portrait Gallery, The British Museum, The Lady Ottoline

↑ Edith Cavell's statue, St Martin's Place. (Jeff Whyte/DT)

☞ Just past the Adelphi on the left is Bull Inn Court and:

1. THE NELL GWYNNE TAVERN (2 Bull Inn Court, WC2R 0NP

⌖ thenellgwynne.com) A pub on this site (the Old Bull Inn) is where diarist
Samuel Pepys met 'the mighty pretty Nell Gwynne' (1650–87) in 1667. She was
involved in a relationship with two poets: the dissolute Charles Sedley and the
foul-mouthed Charles Buckhurst. Nell became the mistress of Charles II (whom
she referred to as her Charles III because of these other two lovers called Charles).

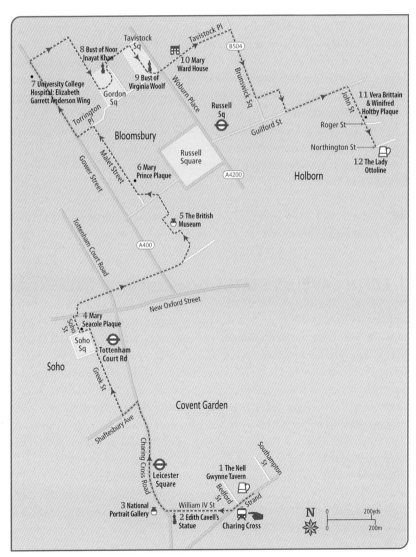

She gave birth to two of his sons. The first, also called Charles, was born in 1670 when she was living in the Cock and Pie pub (where she served the King pigeon pie in bed), on the site of Bush House. The second son, James, was born the following year when the King had moved her into Pall Mall. James died at the age of eight in Paris 'of a sore leg'.

Nell had earlier been pressed into child prostitution in Macklin Street off Drury Lane. When she famously became the mistress of the King at the age of 17, she had no qualms about being a 'kept woman'. When her coachman got in a fight and she asked him why, he said it was because the other man had described her as a 'whore'. When she laughed and said 'but I am a whore', he said he resented being called 'a whore's coachman'. Later, when being booed in her coach by a crowd who mistook her for another of Charles' mistresses, the French Catholic Louise de Kérouaille, Nell stuck her head out of the window and declared: 'Pray, good people, be civil! I am the Protestant whore!' The crowd stopped booing and cheered her heartily.

When Nell died she was buried at nearby St Martin's Church. In her will she gave money to release impoverished debtors from prison.

Nowadays, a regularly rotating selection of real ales is available at the pub and there's a Gin Den for those who prefer mothers' ruin.

☛ Retrace your steps along the Strand and turn right into Agar Street, then immediately left into William IV Street, passing The Chandos pub on the right. Continue into St Martin's Place to find:

2. EDITH CAVELL'S STATUE (St Martin's Place, 29 St Martin's Lane, WC2N 4ER) This British nurse (1865–1915) was executed by a German firing squad in Brussels for helping British soldiers escape to the neutral Netherlands in World War I. She is described on the monument as 'Nurse, Patriot and Martyr'. Yet on the eve of her death she said she did not wish to be considered as a martyr, but just 'a nurse who tried to do her duty'. Neither did she wish to be described as a patriot, stating: 'I realise that patriotism is not enough. I must have no hatred or bitterness towards anyone.' This was originally omitted from the engraving on her monument but is now included. Slogans on the sides praise Devotion, Fortitude, Sacrifice and Humanity, along with 'Faithful until Death' and 'For King and Country'.

Cavell became an assistant nurse at Tooting in 1895 and the following year was accepted for training at London Hospital in Bow Road. She was then night superintendent at St Pancras Infirmary in 1901 and then assistant matron at Shoreditch Infirmary in 1903. In 1907 she was employed as a matron at a training school for nurses in Brussels, and saw it grow from four trainees to 60.

When the Germans occupied Brussels in 1914 they allowed her to continue working in the hospital. When hundreds of British soldiers were left stranded after the defeat in the Battle of Mons just 30 miles away, in September 1914, the resistance movement took two of the wounded to Edith. After treating them she arranged for them to be smuggled over the border into the neutral Netherlands. As part of an escape network, she helped around 200 British, French and Belgian soldiers to escape in this way over the next 11 months. A German police raid led to the arrest of Cavell and 34 others in August 1915. One of the charges was 'conducting soldiers to the enemy' to which she replied at her trial: 'My preoccupation has not been to aid the enemy but to help the men who applied to me to reach the frontier; once across the frontier they were free.' She was sentenced to death and was shot by firing squad at dawn on the day after the sentence was delivered.

☛ Cross the road, turn right into Charing Cross Road and on the left is the entry to:

3. NATIONAL PORTRAIT GALLERY (St Martin's Lane, WC2H 0HE

⌖ npg.org.uk ◷ 10.30–18.00 Mon–Thu & Sun, 10.30–21.00 Fri & Sat) Since opening in 1856 the National Portrait Gallery has aimed to collect and show portraits of 'the most eminent persons in British history'. As society has evolved, so has the collection. Before you go in, pause to notice the 45 portraits of women on the panels of the bronze entrance doors. Tracey Emin designed them for the gallery's reopening in 2023 after a major development project. Emin wanted the figures to represent 'every woman, every age and every culture throughout time'. They are a counterpoint to the carved roundels of men, including artists Hans Holbein the Younger, Sir Anthony van Dyck and Sir Joshua Reynolds, in the façade above the doors.

Emin's self-portrait appears on the gallery's first floor in the Weston Wing as part of a display 'Reframing women and self-portraiture'. The works on show consciously move away from the tradition of female portraits which men create for the male gaze. One of the most striking examples is the portrait of the novelist Zadie Smith, sitting in front of a map of northwest London, where she grew up. The title *Sadie* refers to Smith's original name, which she changed to make herself sound more interesting. The most inspiring work in the display may be the portrait of Malala Yousafzai (b 1997), a girls' education activist from Pakistan who is the youngest ever recipient of the Nobel Peace Prize. Across her face, artist Shirin Neshat has hand-inscribed a poem comparing Yousafzai with Malala of Maiwand, a national heroine of Afghanistan who rallied resistance against British forces in 1880. In the adjacent room 'A Creative Constellation' features contemporary women in the arts, such as Dame Judi Dench and Cate Blanchett, by women photographers.

ANNA WATSON/A

1

RIXIE/DT

2

UWE DEFFNER/A

3

HELEN MATTHEWS

4

1 There are 45 portraits of women on the entrance to the National Portrait Gallery, designed by Tracey Emin. **2** Entrance to the saloon lounge of the Nell Gwynne Tavern. **3** The St Agnes Cup is exhibited in the British Museum. **4** Mary Seacole's plaque in Soho Square.

The gallery has four eating and drinking spaces; we recommend the **Audrey Green café** next to the main ticket hall. You can enjoy a coffee and cake or a sandwich while admiring photography and sculpture depicting performing arts in London.

☛ Continue up Charing Cross Road. Shortly after crossing Shaftesbury Avenue, turn left into Moor Street, then left again into Romilly Street, then right into Greek Street – passing the famous Soho pub The Coach and Horses on the corner. Continue along Greek Street and turn right into Soho Square, following the square around to No 14 and:

4. MARY SEACOLE'S PLAQUE (14 Soho Square, W1D 3QG) Twenty years ago, if you'd asked most people about 'heroines of the Crimean War', they would probably have mentioned Florence Nightingale. But the life of Mary Seacole (1805–81) is now well known, too. She was born in Jamaica to a Scottish soldier and the mixed-race owner of a boarding house for officers and their families. By the 1850s Mary had acquired various skills in nursing, medicine and business; she ran her own boarding house in Jamaica and a hotel for female travellers in Panama, as well as investing in gold-mining speculation in the latter country. But Seacole's fame rests on her deeds in the Crimea, where regiments she had known in Jamaica were fighting alongside the British against the Russians. She offered her services without success to the British government and then to a group of nurses who were working in the Crimea with Nightingale. So, with a relative of her husband, she used her own initiative to set up and run the 'British Hotel' in a small village, providing club facilities, a canteen and medical aid. At one time Seacole supplied the catering for a cricket match between the guards division and other regiments. Though in the end these efforts bankrupted Seacole, sympathetic publicity in the press led to public appeals which reimbursed her. She returned to London and lived at this address while writing her memoirs, *Wonderful Adventures of Mrs Seacole in Many Lands* (1857). A Seacole fund approved by Queen Victoria ensured that, while Seacole's later business ventures met with mixed results and her health deteriorated, she spent her final years in some comfort in London, dying in Paddington. The government of Jamaica posthumously awarded her its Order of Merit in 1991, an online poll in 2004 voted her 'The Greatest Black Briton', and English Heritage unveiled this plaque in 2007.

☛ Turn right into Rathbone Place, then right again into Oxford Street. Cross the road and go into Hanway Street. When you reach Tottenham Court Road, cross it and continue along Great Russell Street, passing Congress House on the right, until you reach:

5. THE BRITISH MUSEUM (Great Russell St, WC1B 3DG
⌂ britishmuseum.org ⊙ 10.00–17.00 Mon–Thu & Sat–Sun, 10.00–20.30 Fri)
This was the world's first free public national museum when it opened in 1759, and the British Museum's statistics can be overwhelming: two million years of human history, eight million artefacts, six million visitors each year. There are far too many woman-focused highlights to list them all; we'll just mention two. Room 40 (the Medieval Room) on the upper floor houses the Royal Gold Cup, which was originally made for the French royal family before becoming the property of several British monarchs and travelling to Spain. It's solid gold with enamel and pearl decorations, including scenes from the life of St Agnes – its alternative name is the St Agnes Cup. The story of St Agnes dates back to the time of the Roman emperor Diocletian (AD284–305). She refused to marry the son of a Roman governor, and was imprisoned in a brothel. A demon, so the story goes, strangled the thwarted son for attempting to rape Agnes, who then restored him to life, upon which he converted to Christianity. The cup depicts these scenes along with the appearance of St Agnes to pilgrims at her tomb with three other female saints. Nearby, in the Roman Britain Gallery (Room 49), look for the Vindolanda tablets which were, at the time of their discovery, the oldest surviving handwritten documents in Britain. They were written on fragments of thin, postcard-sized wooden leaf-tablets with carbon-based ink. The tablets date from the 1st and 2nd centuries BC and provide insight into life in northern England during the Roman occupation. Beneath a copy of a portrait of Claudia Severa (the original is in Naples) is what may be the oldest surviving birthday invitation: 'Claudia Severa to her Lepidina greetings. On 11 September, sister, for the day of celebration of my birthday, I give you a warm invitation to make sure that you come to us, to make the day more enjoyable for me by your arrival… I shall expect you sister. Farewell, sister, my dearest soul, as I hope to prosper, and hail.'

There are numerous **refreshment options**, including cafés in the Great Court; if you want to pause longer, the Great Court Restaurant provides a memorable dining experience.

☛ Exit the museum from the north entrance and turn left into Montague Place. (Or, from the Great Russell Street entrance, turn left along Montague Street and left again into Montague Place.) Turn right into Malet Street. On the right is the University of London's Senate House. High on the wall of the south block, before you get to the main entrance, is the:

6. MARY PRINCE PLAQUE (University of London, Senate House, Malet St, WC1E 7HU) Mary Prince (1788–date unknown) was born into slavery in Bermuda. At the age of 12, her two sisters were sold to different slave traders and,

at 15, she had to move to the Turks and Caicos Islands to work for her new owner in the salt ponds, sometimes for 17 hours a day. Prince came to England with her last owner in 1828, eventually left him and went on to work for Thomas Pringle, secretary of the Anti-Slavery Society. He arranged for an editor to transcribe her life story. *The History of Mary Prince* (1831) was the first account published in Great Britain of an enslaved Black woman's life. It came at a tumultuous time: two years later, an Act of Parliament abolished slavery in the Caribbean and various other British colonies. Prince lived in a house near here at some point during 1829, as the plaque records.

☛ Continue up Malet Street, passing Birkbeck College on the right and RADA (The Royal Academy for Dramatic Art) on the left. Turn left into Torrington Place and then right into Gower Street, passing University College London (UCL) on the right. As part of the University of London, UCL was the first British university to admit women students on fully equal terms to men (in 1878). If you're interested in Egyptology, pause here to visit UCL's Petrie Museum (⌂ ucl.ac.uk/culture ⊙ 13.00–17.00 Tue–Fri, 11.00–17.00 Sat). The founding of this museum and of UCL's Egyptology department became possible thanks to a bequest from writer, traveller and Egyptologist Amelia Edwards (1831–92). Otherwise, continue along Gower Street with University College Hospital on your left. Agatha Christie was a part-time pharmacist here during World War II. Cross the road and turn left into Grafton Way to see the main entrance to:

7. UNIVERSITY COLLEGE HOSPITAL: ELIZABETH GARRETT ANDERSON WING (25 Grafton St, WC1E 6DB) The Elizabeth Garrett Anderson (EGA) Wing of UCH provides comprehensive, high-quality care with the latest technology in the areas of gynaecology, maternity and neonatal care, for women and their babies. It takes its name from the first woman to qualify in Britain as a physician and surgeon. Having privately obtained a certificate in anatomy and physiology, Elizabeth Garrett Anderson (1836–1917) was admitted in 1862 by the Society of Apothecaries who, as a condition of their charter, could not legally exclude her on account of her sex. She was the only woman in the Apothecaries Hall who sat the exam in her year. She studied privately with various professors and, in 1865, obtained a licence from the Society of Apothecaries to practise medicine, the first woman qualified in Britain to do so openly.

As a woman, Anderson could not take up a medical post in any hospital. So in late 1865, she opened her own practice at 20 Upper Berkeley Street. Within a year she also opened St Mary's Dispensary for Women and Children. In the first year, she tended to 3,000 new patients, who made 9,300 outpatient visits to the dispensary. A few years later Anderson was elected to the first London School Board, an office newly opened to women; and was made one of the visiting physicians of the East London Hospital for Children, becoming the first woman in Britain to be appointed to a medical post. But she found the duties of these two positions to be incompatible with her principal work in her private practice and the dispensary, as well as her role as a mother, so she resigned from the posts.

In 1872, the dispensary became the New Hospital for Women and Children, treating women from all over London for gynaecological conditions. In 1874, Anderson co-founded the London School of Medicine for Women and became a lecturer in what was the only teaching hospital in Britain to offer courses for women. She continued to work there for the rest of her career and was dean of the school from 1883 to 1902. This school was later called the Royal Free Hospital of Medicine, and eventually became part of UCL's medical school.

After retirement, Anderson moved back to her childhood home town of Aldeburgh in Suffolk where she was elected mayor, the first female mayor in England – and where her father had been mayor almost 30 years earlier.

☛ Retrace your steps and continue a short distance up Gower Street, then turn right into Gower Place. On the right is UCL's Kathleen Lonsdale Building. Dame Kathleen Lonsdale (1903–71) was a pioneering crystallographer. She was one of the first two women elected as Fellows of the Royal Society, the first female tenured professor at UCL and the first woman president of the British Association for the Advancement of Science. To explain molecular structures to her students, she built models from table-tennis balls. Turn right into Gordon Street and then left into Gordon Square, passing the Institute of Archaeology. On the right is a gate into Gordon Square Gardens. Enter the garden and turn left to find the:

8. BUST OF NOOR INAYAT KHAN Noor Inayat Khan (1914–44), descended from Indian nobility, was a vocal pacifist and supporter of Indian independence, yet felt a strong urge to stand up to the Nazi menace by joining up with the British war effort. This plaque, unveiled by the Princess Royal in 2012, is close to Khan's childhood home in Taviton Street near Gordon Square.

During World War II, Khan worked for the Special Operations Executive (SOE), a secretive organisation tasked with sabotage and espionage in occupied Europe during World War II. Some 13,000 people were employed by the SOE, but Khan showed particular resilience and bravery. With the codename Madeleine, she served as an undercover wireless operator in occupied France – the first woman to do so – and remained in post while most of her fellow operatives were

1 Mary Ward House now functions as a conference and exhibition centre. **2** The Lady Ottoline, Bloomsbury.
3 The Elizabeth Garrett Anderson wing of the University College Hospital. **4** The bust of Virginia Woolf
is situated in Tavistock Square Gardens. **5** Look for the bust of Noor Inayat Khan in Gordon Square Gardens.

hunted down by the Gestapo. After her eventual capture, she refused to hand over sensitive information despite many months of imprisonment, questioning and torture. She was finally taken to Dachau camp and shot on 12 September 1944, aged just 30. Khan was later awarded the George Cross posthumously for exceptional bravery. This bust is the first freestanding memorial to a woman of Asian background in any public space in the UK.

☞ Leave the garden by the gate in the corner nearest the bust and cross into Endsleigh Place. Continue into Tavistock Square and turn right into Tavistock Square Gardens. In the gardens, continue straight, past a tree planted in memory of the lives lost at Hiroshima in 1945 and a statue of Gandhi. In the far right corner you will find a:

9. BUST OF VIRGINIA WOOLF Virginia Woolf (1882–1941) was one of the key figures of the interwar artistic and literary group known as the Bloomsbury Circle. The group became famous not only for their creative output but for their complicated networks of personal relationships. In Dorothy Parker's words, they 'lived in squares, painted in circles and loved in triangles'.

Woolf may have been destined to become a writer from an early age. Her father, Leslie Stephen, who was the first editor of the *Dictionary of National Biography*, encouraged her to read anything in his library, and her home schooling included English classics and Victorian literature. She began writing professionally at the age of 18, while studying classics and history at King's College London. Twelve years later she married Leonard Woolf and they founded the Hogarth Press, which published much of her work. Virginia Woolf is best known for modernist works including the novels *Mrs Dalloway* (1925), *To the Lighthouse* (1927) and *Orlando* (1928) and her essays, such as *A Room of One's Own* (1929). She was a pioneer in the use of stream of consciousness as a narrative device. In a complex personal life, she had various relationships with women and many mental health problems, attempting suicide at least twice before drowning herself in the River Ouse at Lewes in Sussex.

☞ Exit the gardens, turning left into Tavistock Square opposite the Tavistock Hotel, where a blue plaque notes that Virginia and Leonard Woolf lived in a house on the site between 1924 and 1939. Cross into Tavistock Place. On the left is:

10. MARY WARD HOUSE (5–7 Tavistock Pl, WC1H 9SN) This attractive Arts and Crafts Grade I-listed building dates from 1898. It's now a conference and exhibition centre, but its origins are closely connected to the 'settlement

movement', a Victorian and Edwardian reform movement which prefigured the modern welfare state. Its main objective was the establishment of settlement houses in poor urban areas, in which volunteer middle-class workers would share knowledge and culture with their low-income neighbours. One of the driving forces behind this settlement house was Mary Augusta Ward (1851–1920), a novelist and campaigner. The building's facilities developed to include fully equipped classrooms for children with disabilities (one of the first in England to do so), the equivalent of an after-school club, a youth club for teenagers and a centre for pre-natal and ante-natal advice. It was the site of a famous debate on women's suffrage between Millicent Garrett Fawcett and Ward in February 1909, with the vote coming down in favour of women's suffrage. By 1929, Mary Ward House had become a dedicated women's settlement. A legal advice centre opened here during the 1940s to provide both legal assistance and financial advice to low-income individuals.

☛ Continue along Tavistock Place and turn right into Hunter Street. On the left is the Hunter Street Health Centre, formerly part of the Royal Free Hospital School of Medicine. There's a plaque remembering Winifred Cullis (1875–1956), a pioneer of modern physiological research who became, in 1919, the first woman to hold a British university chair in physiology, as Head of Department in the Medical School. Continue into Brunswick Square and left into Guilford Street, then turn right into Doughty Street. On the left at No 58 is the:

11. VERA BRITTAIN & WINIFRED HOLTBY PLAQUE (58 Doughty St, WC1N 2JT) Vera Brittain (1893–1970) was a nurse during World War I and later a writer, feminist, socialist and pacifist. She overcame her father's objections to secure a place at Oxford to read English literature but, as war came, she found her studies increasingly irrelevant. She signed up as a Voluntary Aid Detachment (VAD) nurse and served in London, Malta and near the front line in France – where she nursed German prisoners of war. After the war she returned to Oxford to read history. Brittain's bestselling 1933 memoir *Testament of Youth* recounted her experiences and the beginning of her journey towards pacifism. Winifred Holtby (1898–1935) passed the entrance exam for Somerville College Oxford in 1917 but chose to join the Women's Army Auxiliary Corps instead. After the war she met Vera Brittain at Oxford and the women became lifelong friends, sharing similar political views. Holtby lectured for the League of Nations Union and was active within the Independent Labour Party. She wrote 14 books including six novels, but is best known now for *South Riding* (1936), published posthumously and edited by Brittain.

☞ Continue along Doughty Street to the junction with Northington Street to reach your final stop:

12. THE LADY OTTOLINE (11a Northington St, WC1N 2JF

⌗ theladyottoline.net) You can drink mulled wine (or real ales such as Sharp's Doom Bar, Dark Star and Sambrook's Junction) around a real log fire in this elegantly furnished and decorated pub. On the ground floor there is a picture of Lady Ottoline Morrell (1873–1938) in Bedford Square in 1909. It was at No 44 Bedford Square that she lived and hosted literary parties from 1906 until 1910, when she moved round the corner to No 10 Gower Street.

Born Ottoline Violet Anne Cavendish-Bentinck, she was the niece of the eccentric and reclusive fifth Duke of Portland, and descended from the Hapsburgs. She married the Liberal MP Philip Morrell and had many lovers (including artists Augustus John and Henry Lamb), but was always discreet to avoid embarrassing her husband.

Among those at her literary gatherings were writers such as TS Eliot, Aldous Huxley (who portrayed Lady Ottoline in his novel *Crome Yellow*), DH Lawrence (who based *Lady Chatterley* and a character in *Women in Love* on her) and Walter de la Mare. The Russian ballet dancer Vaslav Nijinsky attended one of her lunches and likened her to a giraffe, adding hastily a 'graceful' not a 'gangling' one. She was six feet tall and accepted the compliment.

But her biggest admirer was the philosopher Bertrand Russell, the third Earl Russell, who danced the hornpipe at one of her parties. They became lovers and he wrote more than a thousand letters to her in less than a year between March 1913 and January 1914. She complained of his bad breath and insisted he shave off his large moustache and cremate it in the fireplace. He said her face was long and thin like a horse and she used too much scent and powder. She did indeed wear flamboyant make-up as well as feathers, huge hats and garish fashions. Lady Ottoline was also frank and outspoken, qualities which Russell admired, and had a robust sense of fun, revelling in the vulgarity of music-hall comedy.

☞ From Northington Street, turn left into Grays Inn Road. From bus stop HD, take the 46 bus to King's Cross (from where the Victoria Line to Oxford Circus then the Bakerloo Line to Charing Cross will return you to the starting point).

→ Karl Marx's memorial tomb. (Anna Moores)

WORKERS OF ALL LANDS

UNITE

KARL MARX

JENNY VON WESTPHALEN,
THE BELOVED WIFE OF
KARL MARX.
BORN 12TH FEBRUARY 1814,
DIED 2ND DECEMBER 1881.

AND KARL MARX,
BORN MAY 5TH 1818, DIED MARCH 14TH 1883.

AND HARRY LONGUET,
THEIR GRANDSON
BORN JULY 4TH 1878, DIED MARCH 20TH 1883.

AND HELENA DEMUTH,
BORN JANUARY 1ST 1823, DIED NOVEMBER 4TH 1890

AND ELEANOR MARX, DAUGHTER OF KARL MARX
BORN JANUARY 16TH 1856, DIED MARCH 31ST 1898.

25 KARL'S TRAIL, ON YOUR MARX

WALK & BUS ROUTE FROM THE HEART OF THE WEST END IN THE FOOTSTEPS OF A REVOLUTIONARY THINKER

Find out in this amble through Soho, Fitzrovia and Bloomsbury – ending in Hampstead and Highgate – where 'the founder of modern communism', Karl Marx (1818–83), fenced with a murderer, smashed street gas lamps on a drunken pub crawl and narrowly avoided arrest, prescribed himself opium for his carbuncles, was summonsed for non-payment of rates and wrestled. By total contrast, you'll see some of the places where he wrote and lectured, and learn about the sad fate of his daughter Eleanor. Also on the route are a couple of significant locations in the history of the African National Congress.

WHERE: London: Leicester Square to Highgate
STATS: 6 miles/2–2½hrs (sections of walking interspersed with 40mins on various buses – worth bearing in mind in order to arrive in Highgate Cemetery before it closes for the day); easy (apart from one short, moderate climb)
START POINT/GETTING THERE: Leicester Square tube station (Northern/Piccadilly Lines) /// finger.vibe.bells ⊖ To Leicester Square; leave station by Exit 2 (Leicester Square & Chinatown) then turn left up Charing Cross Rd
FINISH: Archway tube station (Northern Line) /// drove.elite.from
DROP-OUT POINTS: After 2½ miles & 3 miles (the 1st & 2nd drop-out points are separated by a bus journey), with a 3rd just after 3 miles
MAP: Any A–Z
TAKING A BREAK: The Blue Posts, The Wheatsheaf, The King & Queen, The Rising Sun, Jack Horner, The British Museum, Sir Robert Peel, Whittington Stone

☞ After leaving the station and going up Charing Cross Road, take the first left into Little Newport Street. Go past Leicester Court, where the road becomes Lisle Street ahead, then past Leicester Place, and on the next corner on the left is:

1. GERMAN HOTEL (1 Leicester St, WC2H 7BL) In early 1850 this was the German Hotel (a transit camp for refugees). Marx and his family stayed here after being evicted from 4 Anderson Street, Chelsea. The rent for two small rooms in the German Hotel was high. When they therefore had difficulty paying it, recalled Marx's wife Jenny, 'our host refused to serve us our breakfast and we were forced to look for other lodgings'.

A plaque on the site commemorates composer Johann Strauss (1804–49), 'father of the waltz', who lodged here on his first visit to England in April 1838. At this point the hotel was known as the Hotel du Commerce.

☞ Continue along Lisle Street (through the heart of Chinatown) to the end, then turn right into Wardour Street, then first left into Shaftesbury Avenue, first right into Rupert Street, first left into Archer Street, and on the first corner on the right is:

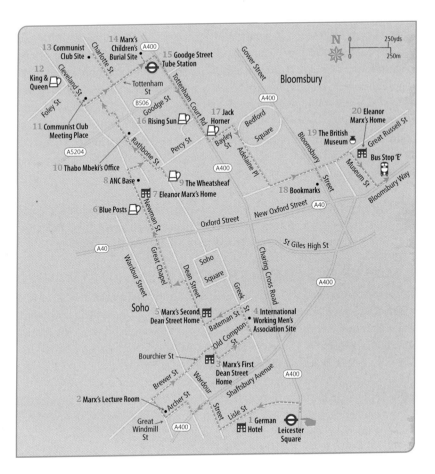

2. MARX'S LECTURE ROOM (20 Great Windmill St, W1D 7LQ)

Marx lectured on political economics here from November 1849 to September 1850 when this was the Red Lion (it is now the Be At One cocktail bar). The course was run by the Deutscher Arbeiterbildungsverein (German Workers' Education Association), of which Marx was a member. His fellow German revolutionary Wilhelm Liebknecht noted at these lectures: 'Marx proceeded methodically. He stated a proposition, the shorter the better, and then demonstrated it in a lengthier explanation, endeavouring with utmost care to avoid all expressions incomprehensible to the labourers. Then he requested his audience to question him. If this was not done he commenced to examine them and he did this with such pedagogic skill that no flaw, no misunderstanding escaped him. He also made use of a blackboard, on which he wrote the formulas – among them those familiar to all of us from the beginning of *Capital*.'

Marx's close comrade, collaborator and benefactor, Friedrich Engels (1820–95), also gave lectures here. One visitor described how they went from the ground floor 'grog shop' up a flight of stairs to a hall-like room which could hold around 200 people at tables with benches. They ate a simple evening meal and 'smoked out of one of the honour pipes lying on all the tables, their jugs of grog before them'. He continued: 'At one end of the hall stood a grand piano, which in unmusical London was the best proof to us that we had found the right room.' They were able to buy a glass of porter and a 'penny packet of tobacco' as well as communist tracts from the association's library.

☞ Turn right into Great Windmill Street, then first right into Brewer Street. When you reach Wardour Street, go ahead through a passageway called Bourchier Street. At the end on the right-hand corner with Dean Street is:

3. MARX'S FIRST DEAN STREET HOME (64 Dean St, W1D 4QQ)
This is where Marx and his family lived from 8 May to 2 December 1850. Referring to this stay, Jenny Marx said: 'We found two rooms in the house of a Jewish lace dealer and spent a miserable summer there with the four children.' The Marxs' son Heinrich Guido (nicknamed 'Fawkesy'), who had been born on 5 November 1849 in Chelsea, died here at less than a year old.

☞ Continue to the right, down Dean Street and almost immediately left into Old Compton Street. Then take the second left into Greek Street. A short distance on the right is the:

4. INTERNATIONAL WORKING MEN'S ASSOCIATION SITE (18 Greek St, W1D 4DS) Here the International Working Men's Association (the First International), of which Marx was a leading member, met from 1864 to 1866. As at the German Hotel, there is a plaque here, but not dedicated to Marx. This one is green, telling us that this is where comedian Peter Cook set up the ironically named Establishment Club which lasted from 1961 to 1964. The site is now home to the Zebrano bar and restaurant.

☞ Continue up Greek Street and turn left into Bateman Street. Continue over Frith Street (with Ronnie Scott's Jazz Club to the left), past the Chinese Mutual Aid Workers' Club on the left (No 12), to Dean Street. Turn right and a few yards on the right (on the corner of Royalty Mews) is:

5. MARX'S SECOND DEAN STREET HOME (28 Dean St, W1D 3RA) A blue plaque at the Quo Vadis restaurant records inaccurately that Marx

lived here from 1851 to 1856 (when his landlord was an Italian cook called John Marengo). In fact he lived here from December 1850. During this time the family lived in great poverty and two more of the children died: first Franziska (who was born here in 1851) in 1852, and then Henry Edgar (known as Moosh or Mouche) in 1855 at the age of eight, from consumption and an inherited disorder.

The overcrowded living conditions in their two rooms here (one being used as a study by Marx) were described by a Prussian police agent who visited Marx to spy on him. The furniture was all broken, he said, and 'the smoke and tobacco fumes make your eyes water so much that for a moment you seem to be groping about in a cavern'. Marx smoked cigars a lot. The agent continued: 'Everything is dirty and covered with dust, so that to sit down becomes a thoroughly dangerous business.' Most of the chairs were broken, except one, which was offered to visitors, but it was also the one on which the children had been 'playing at cooking' and it still had mess on it so 'if you sit down, you risk a pair of trousers'. Marx, he added, led a chaotic existence, often being dirty and drunk, staying up all night and sleeping fully clothed during the day.

Twice in 1853 Marx had to pawn his overcoat while living here. In the 1851 census he is recorded living here as 'Charles Mark, Doctor (Philosophical Author)'.

☛ Continue up Dean Street and turn second left into St Anne's Court, where you can see a plaque outside Clarion House marking the significance of the site for political refugees from France, Switzerland and, latterly, Eastern Europe for more than 200 years.

Retrace your steps to Dean Street, turn left, take the next left into Carlisle Street (with the Nellie Dean pub on the corner), and then right at the end into Great Chapel Street. Follow this to Oxford Street and over it to Newman Street ahead. Follow this to the first corner on the left with Eastcastle Street where you will find the:

6. BLUE POSTS (81 Newman St, W1T 3ET ✆ 020 7637 8958) Marx attended
meetings of the Communist Club at the pub of this name on this site from 1874 to 1877. The pub was rebuilt in 1896. Today the Blue Posts is a free house serving independently brewed cask ales, lagers and ciders and seasonal bar snacks.

☛ Opposite is:

7. ELEANOR MARX'S HOME (13 Newman St, W1T 1PN) Marx's
daughter Eleanor (1855–98) lived at this address in 1883 with Edward Aveling (1849–98) even though he was married to another woman, so defying the conventions of the time. The house was knocked down to make way for a Royal

1 The Wheatsheaf on Rathbone Place is little changed since Marx's day. **2** Newman Passage was possibly Marx's escape route from the police after smashing street lamps on Tottenham Court Road. **3** Marx attended meetings at the Communist Club in the Blue Posts.

Mail sorting office, and it now uses the means of production to make doughnuts, under the name Crosstown. But No 14, the house next door, is still standing and gives you an idea of what Eleanor's home would have looked like.

☞ Continue up Newman Street, to see on the right:

8. ANC BASE (25 Newman St, W1T 1PN) In first-floor offices here, Marxist Ronnie Kasrils, head of intelligence of the banned African National Congress (ANC), in exile from South Africa, trained people to assemble 'letter bombs' to be exploded during the struggle against apartheid in the 1960s. The light explosives were at the bottom of a bucket containing anti-government leaflets which were shot up into the air and spread widely. This attracted huge publicity and assured the Black population that the ANC was still active even though driven underground. Today, the site houses the Nordic Bar, a café-style bar with Scandinavian beers and snacks, TV sport, table football and table tennis.

☞ A couple of doors further on, turn right into Newman Passage (an old cobbled alley through which Marx may have fled from chasing police after smashing street lamps in Tottenham Court Road; page 221) and go through to the corner of Rathbone Street and the Newman Arms (on which George Orwell based the Proles' Pub in his novel *Nineteen Eighty-Four*). At the end of Rathbone Street, a blue plaque marks the spot where a bomb hit a London Auxiliary Fire Station on 17 September 1940, during the Blitz. Harry Erengott (Errington), a fireman who was the son of Jewish immigrants living in Soho, saved two colleagues from the burning building and was awarded the George Cross.

Turn right and walk a few yards into Rathbone Place and the corner of Percy Mews to:

9. THE WHEATSHEAF (25 Rathbone Pl, W1T 1DG ⌂ thewheatsheaffitzrovia.co.uk) This pub dates back to at least 1800 and is much the same as it was in Marx's day, when he attended meetings of the First International in the same street in the 1860s, and once fenced in a salon with a revolutionary who was later hanged for murder.

The latter was Emmanuel Barthelemy, a Frenchman who had fought on the barricades of the Paris Commune in 1848 and been condemned to death but was saved by an amnesty and transported for life instead. One day in December 1854, he set off from the salon in Rathbone Place to assassinate Napoleon III. On the way he decided to collect some unpaid wages for work done for a soda manufacturer at 73 Warren Street, and shot him dead when he refused to pay. For this he was hanged the following month.

According to German revolutionary Wilhelm Liebknecht, who observed Marx and Barthelemy fencing, Marx 'lustily gave battle to the Frenchman… what Marx lacked in science he tried to make up in aggressiveness… unless you were cool he could really startle you'. Barthelemy was critical of Marx because he 'would not conspire and disturb the peace'.

The anarchists set up the International Club in Stephen Mews, behind The Wheatsheaf, in 1883.

Blue plaques on the side of The Wheatsheaf mention that Dylan Thomas and George Orwell both drank here. Many comedians have also performed at the pub. Beers on offer include Abbot Ale and Sharp's Doom Bar, while the food comprises pub standards such as sausages and mash and breaded scampi.

☛ Retrace your steps and continue up Rathbone Street to the Duke of York on the corner of Charlotte Place. To your right is:

10. THABO MBEKI'S OFFICE (49–51 Rathbone St, W1T 1NW) This is another site relating to the African National Congress in exile from South Africa. Thabo Mbeki, a Marxist who later succeeded Nelson Mandela as president of South Africa, worked here from 1967 to 1970.

☛ Go through Charlotte Place to Goodge Street, and continue ahead into Goodge Place opposite (another cobbled passageway). At the other end you will reach Tottenham Street. Turn left and on the next corner is:

11. COMMUNIST CLUB MEETING PLACE (49 Tottenham St, W1T 4RZ) While there is little to see today, the Communist Club met here in the basement spasmodically from 1878 to 1882 and then permanently until 1902. Marx and Lenin both visited. The club had its own choir, billiards table, and food and drink. It was also where William Townshend, a shoemaker who attended meetings of the First International, lived in 1895.

☛ Turn right and a few yards further up Cleveland Street on the left-hand corner with Foley Street is:

12. THE KING & QUEEN (1 Foley St, W1W 6DL ✆ 020 7636 5619) This was the nearest pub to the Communist Club. In 1848 it had been used as a meeting place for the Washington Brigade of the Chartists. It was also a meeting place for the West End branch of the Alliance of Cabinet Makers (who kept a library here). It had 20 flavours of vodka on our visit, including a very palatable Stolichnaya vanilla.

☞ Retrace your steps and turn left into Tottenham Street, then follow it to the crossroads with Charlotte Street. Turn left, and about a dozen doors along on the left (just past Chitty Street on the other side) is the:

13. COMMUNIST CLUB SITE (107 Charlotte St, W1T 4QB) The Communist Club moved to a building on this site in 1903. Lenin was present for the opening of the club, being here for the congress of the Russian Social Democratic Party in the Anglers Club Hall of the English Club, also in Charlotte Street. It was at this meeting that the party split into the Mensheviks and Bolsheviks. Lenin revisited the club in 1911. It was closed by a police raid in 1918. That building no longer exists; today student accommodation occupies the site.

☞ Retrace your steps and turn left along Tottenham Street to Tottenham Court Road, passing a plaque to formerly enslaved abolitionist Olaudah Equiano (1745–97) at No 37 on your right. On the left-hand corner is:

14. MARX'S CHILDREN'S BURIAL SITE (Whitfield Gardens, 79 Tottenham Court Rd, W1T 4TB) Marx buried his eight-year-old son Henry Edgar here in 1855. Marx was so distressed that he had to be restrained from hurling himself into the grave. Two of Marx's other children were already buried there: Heinrich Guido in 1850 and Franziska in 1852, both about a year old. It was then the graveyard of George Whitefield's Tabernacle at 79 Tottenham Court Road (now the American Church). The coffins and remains were all disinterred in 1898 and reinterred in Chingford Mount Cemetery. One gravestone survives, that of John Procter of 94 Tottenham Court Road who died in 1834, aged 74, and his wife Mary who died in 1840, aged 77. On a nearby building is the Fitzrovia Mural, painted in 1980 by Mick Jones and Simon Barber, depicting local life and people with cartoon-style humour.

☞ Turn right into Tottenham Court Road and a few doors down on the same side is:

15. GOODGE STREET TUBE STATION (73 Tottenham Court Rd, W1T 2HG) Marx's daughter Eleanor entertained here when it was the Athenaeum Hall in 1887 and 1890. With her partner Edward Aveling she gave music and poetry recitals. In February 1898 she was lodging at nearby 135 Gower Street to be near Aveling while he was having an operation in University College Hospital. A month later Eleanor died in a house in Sydenham after swallowing prussic acid which Aveling had provided for her. The inquest concluded she had killed herself while

1 Whitfield Gardens was the original resting place of three of Marx's children. The Fitzrovia Mural is painted on the wall of a nearby building. **2** Bookmarks is a Marxist bookshop. **3** The King & Queen on Foley Street was the nearest pub to the Communist Club.

'labouring under mental derangement'. Many suspected Aveling had tricked her into a double suicide pact and then pulled out himself.

☞ Continue down Tottenham Court Road to the corner of Windmill Street on the right, where you will find:

16. THE RISING SUN (46 Tottenham Court Rd, W1T 2ED ✆ greeneking. co.uk) The Rising Sun is one of just six pubs surviving of the 18 that existed during Marx's Tottenham Court Road pub crawl in the 1850s. He was with his German revolutionary friends Wilhelm Liebknecht and Edgar Bauer. In the last pub, well oiled, they encountered a group of 'Odd Fellows' and compared German and English culture with them, predictably ending in a fight. The outnumbered Germans fled, stumbled over some paving stones and, at two o'clock in the morning, used them to smash four or five street gas lamps before a policeman arrived. Marx knew the back alleys well and managed to escape through them (probably Percy Passage and Newman Passage, visited earlier on this walk) to his home in Dean Street.

The Rising Sun is on the corner of Windmill Street where Chartist pork that had been produced on co-operative farms was sold in 1848, and where the Autonomie anarchist club at No 6 was raided in 1892. At another pub 'just off Tottenham Court Road', the last English meeting of the First International took place in September 1871, five years before finally being disbanded in America. Today the pub serves Greene King IPA and London Glory – and pork is still present, as the menu includes honey and mustard sausages.

☞ Continue down Tottenham Court Road, to the corner of Bayley Street, on the left, where you will find the:

17. JACK HORNER (234–236 Tottenham Court Rd, W1T 7QJ ✆ jackhornerpub.co.uk) This Fuller's pub was called The Italian in the 1850s when Marx drank there on his pub crawl (and was renamed the Bedford Head by 1872). A good, if pricey, selection of pies is on the menu.

☞ Turn left into Bayley Street, to Bedford Square, and turn right (past blue plaques to Thomas Wakley (1795–1862), a surgeon and radical MP, and Thomas Hodgkin (1798–1866), an early advocate of preventive medicine. At the end turn left into Great Russell Street, go past the Trades Union Congress headquarters on the right (with a large sculpture of one worker helping another to his feet), to Bloomsbury Street. Turn right and just past the next turning on the right is:

18. BOOKMARKS (1 Bloomsbury St, WC1B 3QE ⊘ bookmarksbookshop. co.uk) We think this socialist bookshop should spell its name 'Bookmarx'.

☛ Return to Great Russell Street and turn right. A few yards further, on the left is:

19. THE BRITISH MUSEUM (Great Russell St, WC1B 3DG ⊘ britishmuseum.org ⊙ 10.00–17.00 Mon–Thu & Sat–Sun, 10.00–20.30 Fri) Marx used the Reading Room here to research many of his great works including *Das Kapital*. He got his reader's ticket in June 1850, and spent the first three months reading back issues of the *Economist*. This was before the new reading room was completed in 1857. In the old reading room he worked on *Address of the Central Committee to the Communist League*, *The Class Struggles in France* and *Eighteenth Brumaire of Louis Bonaparte*. The Keeper of Printed Books was an Italian revolutionary, Antonio Panizzi, who planned the new library, which was built under a glass dome that accommodated thousands of titles.

Marx sat in seat number 07 in the new library and drew on reports of official commissions of enquiry designed to strengthen capitalism by controlling its worst social consequences. Because he suffered from carbuncles he also read medical books and prescribed himself opium, arsenic and creosote.

The Reading Room is still there (the large circular structure in the middle, straight ahead from the main entrance, within the glazed-over Great Court), but has been closed to the public for some years except for special temporary exhibitions.

See also page 204 for more about the museum, and information about **refreshment options**.

☛ As you leave, directly opposite the museum's main entrance/exit is:

20. ELEANOR MARX'S HOME (55 Great Russell St, WC1B 3BA) Marx's daughter lived at this address from 1884 to 1886 with her partner Edward Aveling. To celebrate her 31st birthday in 1886, she staged an amateur performance of Ibsen's *A Doll's House* here. Among the cast with her and Aveling were playwright George Bernard Shaw, and May Morris (daughter of William Morris). The house is now part of Helen Graham House, Nos 52–57.

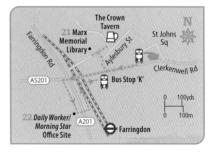

☛ A few yards to the right is the Museum Tavern on the corner of Museum Street, which you go down to the end, then turn left into Bloomsbury Way.

✋ On the same side of the road, next to St George's Church Bloomsbury, is Bus Stop E. Here you can take several buses to Holborn tube station (or Tottenham Court Road in the opposite direction) if you wish to drop out.

☛ To continue, take the 55 bus from Stop E for a ten-minute journey to the St John Street stop (a request stop straight after Hatton Garden). Go back a short distance from the stop and take the first right into Clerkenwell Green. On the opposite side of the green is the:

21. MARX MEMORIAL LIBRARY (37a Clerkenwell Green, EC1R 0DU ✎ marx-memorial-library.org ◷ Reading Room by appt 11.00–14.00 Tue–Thu, tours Mon noon £) Marx's daughter Eleanor spoke here on 'Bloody Sunday' (13 November 1887) and later in support of the dockers' strike on 20 October 1889 and at other rallies. Lenin had an office here in exile from 1902 to 1903 when he edited the Russian Social Democratic newspaper *Iskra*, issues 22 to 38. Guided tours explore the room where Lenin worked and use items from the library's collection to explain events such as the 1871 Paris Commune.

☛ Turn left out of the library and on the next corner is The Crown Tavern. It is worth going upstairs to take a look at the Apollo Room, which was a concert hall in Marx's time.
  Return to Clerkenwell Road.

✋ From here you can get buses to Holborn, Waterloo or Oxford Circus. Or you can go down Turnmill Street, almost opposite, to Farringdon tube station on the right.

☛ To continue the walk turn right, then second left into Farringdon Road, and on the right is the:

22. *DAILY WORKER*/*MORNING STAR* OFFICE SITE (75 Farringdon Rd, EC1M 3HQ) The communist daily newspaper, the *Daily Worker* (renamed the *Morning Star* in 1966), was published here from 1945 until the mid-1980s. As of late 2023, the site was under redevelopment.

You may wish to split the walk into two separate days, in which case continue down Farringdon Road to Farringdon Station to conclude or pause at this point. For the second part of the walk, start from Bus Stop C in Tottenham Court Road; see below.

Return to Clerkenwell Road, turn right and, just past Turnmill Street, on the same side and opposite Clerkenwell Green, you will find Bus Stop K. Take the 55 bus from here for a 15-minute journey to Tottenham Court Road station. Continue ahead a short distance and turn right into Tottenham Court Road.

A short distance on the left is Bus Stop C. From here take the 24 bus for a 21-minute journey to the Queens Crescent stop in Kentish Town. Follow the direction of the bus up Malden Road, and take the third on the left into Grafton Terrace. A short distance on the right is:

23. MARX'S GRAFTON TERRACE HOME (46 Grafton Terrace, NW5 4HY) Marx and his family lived at this address from October 1856 to

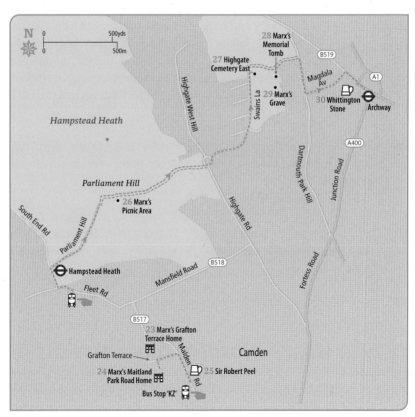

March 1864 (when it was 9 Grafton Terrace, Fitzroy Road, having been built in 1849 beside open fields). While residing here Marx wrote *A Contribution to the Critique of Political Economy* and *Theories of Surplus Value*. And it was also here that his wife Jenny contracted smallpox, from which she never fully recovered.

☞ Just past this house, opposite No 54, is a path to the left behind a block of flats. Turn into this, go down some steps under an arch, and into a crescent to the left. A few yards along this crescent on the left is:

24. MARX'S MAITLAND PARK ROAD HOME (101–108 Maitland Park Rd, NW3 2HE) A plaque on the second floor informs us that Marx lived in this building from 1875 to the end of his life (when it was No 41). Just before this he had lived at nearby 1 Maitland Park Road (when it was called 1 Modena Villas), which has since been demolished and replaced by a block of flats called The Grange. It was in the study there that Marx completed the first volume of *Das Kapital*. For the first time the children had a room each, but the extra space meant extra rent and Marx, who said he was 'as hard up as a church mouse', was summonsed for non-payment. He was nonetheless asked to serve as a constable for the parish for one year in 1868, which he rejected. This was used against him when he applied for British citizenship six years later, and had it refused on the grounds of a police report describing him as a 'notorious German agitator who had not been loyal to his own king and country'.

☞ Return to Grafton Terrace and then to Malden Road and Bus Stop KZ (from which you came). Almost opposite the bus stop is the:

25. SIR ROBERT PEEL (108 Malden Rd, NW5 4DA ⬧ sir-robert-peel. edan.io) This is a friendly community pub with a dartboard and pool table.

☞ From Bus Stop KZ take the 24 bus to Hampstead for a four-minute journey to the last stop (Royal Free Hospital/Hampstead Heath Station). Follow the road ahead to South End Road, past the Garden Gate pub, and right into South Hill Park, past Hampstead Heath railway station. Continue uphill and take the right fork into the road Parliament Hill. Near the top, on the left, a plaque at No 77 notes that George Orwell lived there. This was his home for six months in 1935 while he was writing *Keep the Aspidistra Flying*. Labour leader Michael Foot unveiled the plaque… in 1984.
At the top of Parliament Hill is:

26. MARX'S PICNIC AREA

Marx loved to take his family to picnic on Hampstead Heath on Sundays, even when living in Soho rather than the closer Kentish Town. His friend and fellow German revolutionary, Wilhelm Liebknecht, who often joined them, recalled in *Karl Marx: Biographical Memoirs* (1896): 'A Sunday on Hampstead Heath was the highest pleasure for us. The children spoke of it all week and grown people too anticipated it with joy. The trip itself was a feast. From Dean Street, where Marx lived, it was at least an hour and a quarter, and as a rule, a start was made at 11am... some time was always consumed in getting everything in readiness, the chicken cared for and the basket packed. That basket... it was our commissary department, and when a man has a healthy strong stomach... then the question of provisions plays a very large role. And good Lenchen [the family's housekeeper] knew this and had for often half-starved and, therefore, hungry guests a sympathising heart. A mighty roast veal was the centrepiece hallowed by tradition for the Sunday in Hampstead Heath.'

After their walk to the heath, he continued, 'we would first choose a place where we could spread our tents at the same time having due regard to the possibility of obtaining tea and beer. But after drinking and eating their fill, as Homer has it, the male and female comrades looked for the most comfortable place of repose or seat; and when this had been found he or she – provided they did not prefer a little nap – produced the Sunday papers they had bought on the road, and now began the reading and discussing of politics – while the children, who rapidly found comrades, played hide and seek behind the heather bushes. But this easy life had to be seasoned by a little diversion, and so we ran races, sometimes we also had wrestling matches, or putting the shot (stones) or some other sport.'

They were often joined by Engels who lived in Primrose Hill (page 41).

☞ When you enter the heath, take the path going straight ahead. After a short distance, take the first path to the right which goes up to Kite Hill. At 322 feet above sea level, it has an outstanding view across to south London. Follow the main path down the other side, ignore a path off to the right, and when another path crosses over take the left fork (with ponds down to the left). At the bottom, go left then right at the roundabout into Swain's Lane. Follow Swain's Lane for about 10 minutes with a moderate climb towards the end until you come on the right to:

27. HIGHGATE CEMETERY EAST

(Swain's Lane, N6 6PJ ✧ highgatecemetery.org ⊕ Mar–Oct 09.00–17.00 daily; Nov–Feb 10.00–16.00 daily £; guided tours ££) As you pay the entry fee you will receive a map of

HELEN MATTHEWS

PETER ARKELL

FELA SANU/S

JARNOGZ/DT

1 Marx's Memorial Library in Clerkenwell. **2** 46 Grafton Terrace was the home of Marx in Kentish Town. **3** Hampstead Heath was Marx's favourite picnic spot. **4** Marx used the Reading Room at the British Museum to research many of his great works.

the cemetery showing the locations of Marx's Memorial Tomb (C2) and the original grave where he is actually buried (C3), as well as graves of other Marxists including Yusuf Dadoo (1909–83), the South African communist and anti-apartheid campaigner; the investigative journalist, political campaigner and author Paul Foot (1937–2004); the historian Eric Hobsbawm (1917–2012); and Claudia Jones (1915–64), the Trinidadian communist and founder of the Notting Hill Carnival. If you have no map, follow the path ahead and bear left at the first fork. On the right, where the path bends to the right, is:

28. MARX'S MEMORIAL TOMB Sculpted by Laurence Bradshaw in 1954, this massive bronze bust of Marx on a huge granite plinth is inscribed with his famous appeal from *The Communist Manifesto*: 'Workers of all lands, unite'. At the base is engraved his other famous quotation: 'The philosophers have only interpreted the world in various ways. The point, however, is to change it.' The tomb was unveiled by Harry Pollitt (1890–1960), the general secretary of the Communist Party of Great Britain.

☞ Almost opposite Marx's is the tomb of Herbert Spencer (1820–1903), the philosopher, biologist, sociologist and political theorist who coined the phrase 'survival of the fittest'. Follow the path another 100 steps or so to a single grave to Nora Joyce on the left. Turn right here by Arthur Joseph Lockett's grave. Another 50 or 60 paces on the right (between the graves of Thomas Copp and William Collis) brings you to:

29. MARX'S GRAVE This flat gravestone with no upright headstone is where Marx was buried on 17 March 1883, with about 20 people present. Engels gave the main address. Describing Marx's outstanding achievement, he declared: 'Just as Darwin discovered the law of development or organic nature, so Marx discovered the law of development of human history.'

☞ The cemetery is filled with memorials to stars of the creative arts: writers such as Douglas Adams, George Eliot and Alan Sillitoe, actors from Roger Lloyd Pack to Sir Ralph Richardson, and rock impresario Malcolm McLaren. Once you're ready to move on, to reach the nearest tube station (about a 12-minute walk), return to the entrance, turn right, then immediately right again through Waterlow Park. Keep to the edge of the park on the right with the cemetery fencing, forking right four times, through to Dartmouth Park Hill at the other end. Then turn right downhill, then left into Magdala Avenue. At the junction at the end turn right into Highgate Hill. A short way down on the same side you will find:

GARY PERKIN/DT

30. WHITTINGTON STONE (53 Highgate Hill, N19 5NE ✆ 020 7281 0905) This modern pub has a pool table and dartboard. There is also hot food, a selection of beers including Fuller's London Pride, Sharp's Doom Bar and Wychwood Hobgoblin Ruby, and outside seating.

A stone nearby marks where Dick Whittington, when leaving London, heard the ringing of Bow Bells; he took this as a good sign, and so 'turned again' and returned to the capital and became Lord Mayor. A sculpture of Whittington's cat sits on top of the stone.

👉 A short distance further down is Archway tube station.

↑ Highgate Cemetery East is Marx's final resting place.

26 SAVIOURS, SPITFIRES & SWANS

HEROES & WARRIORS, ANCIENT & MODERN

Maidenhead in Berkshire was a popular Victorian and Edwardian attraction for the great and the good (and the prosperous), with boating parties becoming a common sight on this part of the Thames. Aviator Amy Johnson was based nearby in the early years of World War II, and in the early 20th century a young Stirling Moss, a boy from nearby Bray, began to develop the racing skills that won him worldwide fame. The town's Heritage Centre is an excellent place to find out more about these and other local notables – and you can meet the most extraordinary hero of them all before you even leave the station. Down by the river, unusual examples of human ingenuity await your discovery while, on the other side of the Thames in Buckinghamshire, there's the picturesque neighbouring village of Taplow to explore. The recent opening of the Elizabeth Line has made travel to Maidenhead and Taplow possible using the Freedom Pass.

WHERE: Berkshire/Buckinghamshire: Maidenhead to Taplow
STATS: 5 miles/2hrs; easy
START POINT/GETTING THERE: Maidenhead station /// result.master.twig ⊖ To Maidenhead station (Elizabeth Line, included in the Freedom Pass); head for the railway station's Platform 3
FINISH: Taplow station (Taplow is also on the Elizabeth Line) /// spite.take.refuse
DROP-OUT POINT: After 3 miles
MAP: OS Explorer map 172
TAKING A BREAK: The Boathouse, The Oak & Saw

☞ On Platform 3 you'll find a:

1. SCULPTURE OF SIR NICHOLAS WINTON This artwork by local sculptor Lydia Karpinska, which local MP Theresa May officially unveiled in 2010, celebrates the life of stockbroker and humanitarian Sir Nicholas Winton (1909–2015). His fame derives from his actions in 1938 when he visited Prague (diverting from his original intention to go skiing in Switzerland). There he met many Jewish parents who wanted to get their children to safety, away from the looming threat of the Nazis. Sir Nicholas contacted various embassies to try to make asylum arrangements, but the only positive response came from Britain. With help from other volunteers in Prague, he arranged what became known as the Czech Kindertransport, a series of eight trains that brought children out of Czechoslovakia and through Germany and France to London's Liverpool Street station. Sir Nicholas and his mother greeted the children, most of whom went to live with strangers. In all, 669 children owed their lives to this initiative and estimates suggest that some 6,000 people around the world are descendants of those children. The story became public knowledge 50 years later, when Sir Nicholas' wife discovered a briefcase of

← Taplow Court. (heardinlondon/S)

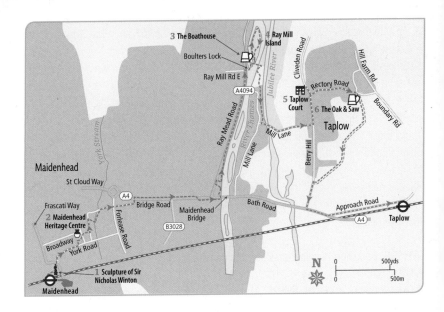

documents and the TV programme *That's Life!* invited him to the BBC studios. The rest of the audience comprised people who owed their lives to him. Sir Nicholas' efforts were the subject of a 2024 film *One Life*, starring Anthony Hopkins.

☞ From the station forecourt, turn left, go over the crossing and turn right into Queen Street. When the road forks, bear right into York Road and, after a short distance, turn left into Grove Road. Across the car park is:

2. MAIDENHEAD HERITAGE CENTRE (18 Park St, Maidenhead SL6 1SL ⚭ maidenheadheritage.org.uk ◷ 10.00–16.00 Tue–Sat £ 🖴) The permanent display on the ground floor of this museum fills you in on the Roman presence in and around Maidenhead and the importance of its location by the river in Saxon times. 'It provided fish and defence' is the concise explanation. Pay a small additional charge to visit the exhibition upstairs about the Air Transport Auxiliary (ATA), a British civilian organisation set up during World War II and based at White Waltham Airfield, two miles from Maidenhead. The ATA ferried new, repaired and damaged military aircraft around – 'anything to anywhere' according to its unofficial slogan, although not to naval aircraft carriers. It also flew service personnel on urgent duty and performed some air ambulance work. Pilots could fly several planes a day, ranging from old biplanes to the latest bombers. Famous ATA recruits included Freddie Laker, destined to shake up consumer aviation years later, and Amy Johnson, the circumstances of whose death when her plane crashed into the Thames in 1941 are still unclear. The

exhibition title *Grandma Flew Spitfires* is in one sense misleading, as most pilots were male. Nonetheless, over 160 women pilots were part of this initiative and theirs is a story well worth remembering. Pauline Gower (1910–47), who set up the women's branch of the ATA, is credited with obtaining its agreement in 1943 to pay women pilots the same as the men. If you're a budding pilot or have one in your family, or just want a taste of what those wartime pilots experienced, you can take your turn for 30 minutes on a Spitfire simulator, complete with replica flight controls and a wide-screen pilot's view of the Isle of Wight, Windsor Castle or 21st-century London. But it isn't cheap (£££; pre-booking required)!

☞ From the Heritage Centre, cross Park Street and walk down the path past the craft beer establishment called A Hoppy Place; a sign outside warns 'SLOW: Drinking in Progress'. At the end turn left into St Ives Road. Immediately after passing Maidenhead Library, turn right through Maudsley Memorial Gardens and cross a bridge over the York Stream. On the other side turn left along the bank of the stream, signposted 'Green Way to Cookham'. When the stream widens, turn right into Bridge Street. Continue as Bridge Street becomes Moorbridge Road. Take the underpass, following signs for 'River Thames'. Emerge from the underpass into Bridge Road. At Nos 79–85 on the left is the Grade II*-listed James Smith almshouse, established in 1661 to house 'eight poor ancient men and their wives, inhabitants of Maidenhead or Cookham, each of them to be 50 years at least.' When you reach Maidenhead Bridge, continue ahead into Bridge Gardens. The bridge, to your right, was built in 1772–77 of brick and Portland stone and is Grade I-listed. The memorial to your left was erected in memory of local benefactor Ada Lewis, and was used as a drinking trough for passing horses. It originally stood outside the Thames Riviera Hotel. Turn left through the gardens, then right to emerge on Ray Mead Road, right and left to return to the riverbank and then continue along Ray Mead Road, passing Riverside Gardens (where there is a café), until you reach Boulters Lock. Turn right over the lock. A plaque on the bridge commemorates the broadcaster Richard Dimbleby who lived on Boulters Island. Follow the road round to the left to:

3. THE BOATHOUSE (Boulters Lock Island, Maidenhead SL6 8PE

⌗ boathouseboulterslock.co.uk) This gastropub is an excellent spot for alfresco dining, but the main point of interest is the artefact by the front door: a green telephone box with a wooden door and a pyramid roof. The Post Office introduced the Kiosk No 1 model, of which this is an example, in 1921 – two years before Frederick Crawley of Newcastle upon Tyne introduced police boxes in Sunderland, and eight years before the first experimental installation of the blue models in

1 Memorial to Ada Lewis, Bridge Gardens in Maidenhead. **2** Boulters Lock. **3** Sir Nicholas Winton sculpture at Maidenhead station. **4** The weir at Ray Mill Island. **5** A green telephone box at The Boathouse – there are fewer than 50 left in Britain. **6** *Maiden with Swans* sculpture, Ray Mill Island.

London. This phone box started its life by the lock in 1926 and remained in operation until 1979; the location was the aesthetic reason for the box being green rather than red. Today there are fewer than 50 green phone boxes in the British Isles.

☞ Continue over a bridge to:

4. RAY MILL ISLAND Ray Mill Island is named after the Ray family who managed a flour mill here. The island was purchased by Maidenhead Borough Council in 1950 and is a public park, with plenty of seating for picnics. Walk past the café and walk up the path along the left side of the island. About halfway along is an aviary and pet enclosure with cockatiels and guinea pigs. At the far end of the island is Boulters Weir, the latest in a series built over the past 600 years. Early weirs had multiple purposes: maintaining a head of water for powering mills, catching fish and creating deeper water for navigation. Today only 50 weirs remain on the Thames, maintaining water levels for navigation and controlling land drainage.

☞ Returning down the other side of the island, you will notice a metallic tree sculpture in a clearing to your right. This is a memorial tree from Berkshire stillbirth and neonatal death charity SANDS, with children's names and dates on each leaf. Close by is the sculpture *Maiden with Swans* by Eunice Goodman.
Turn left over Taplow Bridge to arrive at Taplow Riverside Walk. Follow the path through the park and along the bank of Jubilee River (created as part of a flood-alleviation scheme) until you reach a T-junction by a bridge. To continue the walk, turn left (signposted 'Taplow village').

✋ Alternatively turn right, signposted 'Maidenhead', to return to Maidenhead bridge and retrace your steps to Maidenhead station.

☞ To continue the walk, go over the bridge and up Mill Lane. At the end of the lane turn left into Berry Hill and then continue into Cliveden Road until, on the left, you arrive at:

5. TAPLOW COURT (Cliveden Rd, Taplow SL6 0ER ✆ 01628 773163 ⊘ sgi-uk.org/Local-Community/SGI-Centres/Taplow-Court ⊙ 1st Sun afternoon of the month, May–Sep) Taplow Court is a Jacobean/French Gothic manor house, currently owned by Soka Gakkai International, a lay Buddhist society that is part of a worldwide network of organisations offering educational and cultural activities built around Buddhist principles. In the Iron Age a massive hillfort covered this site; a 7th-century burial mound can still be seen in the garden.

Three local antiquarians excavated it in 1883, discovering a range of items such as a sword, shields, drinking horns and glass beakers. It was the most significant excavated Anglo-Saxon burial site until the discoveries at Sutton Hoo in the 1930s; some of the artefacts remain on display in the British Museum. There has been a manor house on the site since before 1066; the owners have included the monks of Merton Priory and the Earls and Countesses of Orkney. In the mid-19th century the house was given its present appearance by the architect William Burn.

☞ Retrace your steps to the junction with Berry Hill and turn left into Rectory Road, continuing to the centre of Taplow village. Here you can see St Nicholas Church, which dates from 1829, although it was substantially rebuilt in 1911–12. Its predecessor, a Norman church, stood in what are now the grounds of Taplow Court. Opposite the church is:

6. THE OAK & SAW (Rectory Rd, Taplow SL6 0ET ⊘ oakandsaw.co.uk)
Alfresco dining is available in the pub's garden and patio. The Sunday roasts, on which the pub prides itself, use locally sourced meats.

☞ Turn right out of the pub, and then turn right down a public footpath ('Old Friend Lane'). When you reach a T-junction, turn right along the path between two hedges, then through a kissing gate and diagonally across a field to emerge on Berry Hill. Turn left down the hill. At the end of the road turn left along Bath Road, then left again along Approach Road to reach Taplow Station.

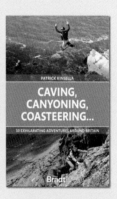

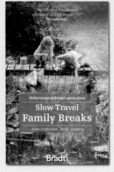

INDEX

Entries in **bold** refer to main entries.

THE BRADT STORY

In the beginning

It all began in 1974 on an Amazon river barge. During an 18-month trip through South America, two adventurous young backpackers – Hilary Bradt and her then husband, George – decided to write about the hiking trails they had discovered through the Andes. *Backpacking Along Ancient Ways in Peru and Bolivia* included the very first descriptions of the Inca Trail. It was the start of a colourful journey to becoming one of the best-loved travel publishers in the world; you can read the full story on our website (**bradtguides. com/ourstory**).

Getting there first

Hilary quickly gained a reputation for being a true travel pioneer, and in the 1980s she started to focus on guides to places overlooked by other publishers. The Bradt Guides list became a roll call of guidebook 'firsts'. We published the first guide to Madagascar, followed by Mauritius, Czechoslovakia and Vietnam. The 1990s saw the beginning of our extensive coverage of Africa: Tanzania, Uganda, South Africa, and Eritrea. Later, post-conflict guides became a feature: Rwanda, Mozambique, Angola, and Sierra Leone, as well as the first standalone guides to the Baltic States following the fall of the Iron Curtain, and the first post-war guides to Bosnia, Kosovo and Albania.

Comprehensive – and with a conscience

Today, we are the world's largest independently owned travel publisher, with more than 200 titles. However, our ethos remains unchanged. Hilary is still keenly involved, and **we still get there first**: two-thirds of Bradt guides have no direct competition.

But we don't just get there first. Our guides are also known for being **more comprehensive** than any other series. We avoid templates and tick-lists. Each guide is a one-of-a-kind expression of an expert author's interests, knowledge and enthusiasm for telling it how it really is.

And a commitment to wildlife, conservation and respect for local communities has always been at the heart of our books. Bradt Guides was **championing sustainable travel** before any other guidebook publisher. We even have a series dedicated to Slow Travel in the UK, award-winning books that explore the country with a passion and depth you'll find nowhere else.

Thank you!

We can only do what we do because of the support of readers like you – people who value less-obvious experiences, less-visited places and a more thoughtful approach to travel. Those who, like us, take travel seriously.

Bradt GUIDES
TRAVEL TAKEN SERIOUSLY